Rendered Safe

Tales of an NYPD Bomb Tech

by JEFF INGBER

Copyrighted Material

Rendered Safe: Tales of an NYPD Bomb Tech

Copyright © 2019 by Jeff Ingber and Donald Sadowy. All Rights Reserved.

No part of this publication may be reproduced, stored in a retrieval system, or transmitted, in any form or by any means—electronic, mechanical, photocopying, recording or otherwise—without prior written permission from the publisher, except for the inclusion of brief quotations in a review.

For information about this title or to order other books and/or electronic media, contact Jeff Ingber at jingber@gmail.com or www.jeffingber.com.

ISBN: 978-0-9854100-1-8 (Hardcover)
978-0-9854100-3-2 (Softcover)
978-0-9854100-9-4 (eBook)

Cover design by Arielle Morris

For Kathy, Donnie, and Kaitlin Sadowy

I don't know if we each have a destiny, or if we're all just floatin' around accidental-like on a breeze. But I think maybe it's both.
—Forrest Gump

CONTENTS

Preface ix
Chapter 1   *Greenpoint* 1
Chapter 2   *Foundation* 17
Chapter 3   *Schatzi* 31
Chapter 4   *The Devil Sent Us Castro* 39
Chapter 5   *Beat Cop* 53
Chapter 6   *Rolling Stone* 71
Chapter 7   *Courage and Suffering* 83
Chapter 8   *False Start* 93
Chapter 9   *Redstone* 101
Chapter 10 *Richie & Tony* 107
Chapter 11 *Challenges* 113
Chapter 12 *The Long Walk* 127
Chapter 13 *Larry Davis* 133
Chapter 14 *The Abortion Bomber* 137

Chapter 15	*Mickey Mouse Stickers*	147
Chapter 16	*Sniper*	151
Chapter 17	*Gorbachev*	155
Chapter 18	*Jaws of Life*	163
Chapter 19	*Prelude*	171
Chapter 20	*February 26, 1993*	181
Chapter 21	*Devastation*	191
Chapter 22	*Futility*	201
Chapter 23	*Chassis Frame*	205
Chapter 24	*Capture*	225
Chapter 25	*Redemption*	235
Chapter 26	*Two Tall Guys*	241
Chapter 27	*TWA Flight 800*	257
Chapter 28	*Letter Bombs*	267
Chapter 29	*Israel*	271
Chapter 30	*Ehud Barak*	281
Chapter 31	*Gaza*	285
Chapter 32	*9/11*	289
Chapter 33	*Buried Alive*	299
Chapter 34	*Recovery*	309
Chapter 35	*Shooter*	315

Contents

Chapter 36	*The Marshal's Office*	319
Chapter 37	*Ghana*	325
Chapter 38	*Reflections*	333
Acknowledgments		339
Bibliography		345
Endnotes		351
About the Author		369
Index		371

PREFACE

APPEARING AS A GROUP OF reverse mountaineers, each of the twelve men and women wore a construction helmet, work boots, and a nonflammable jumpsuit identified by a law enforcement agency logo. They trekked downward in single file through the frigid darkness on a narrow, unstable path slippery from water flowing from burst pipes. Progress was slow, given the urgent need to maintain balance so as not to initiate an avalanche of debris. Periodically, the eerie quiet was interrupted by a falling chunk of material that resounded as if through an amplifier. Their portable box lights, held on straps stretching from shoulder to hip, revealed a kaleidoscope of broken concrete, jagged steel reinforcing bars, and shattered light fixtures. Pulverized vehicles with melted tires were strewn about, many flipped upside down and wiped clean of their paint. Plumes of fire danced around them, the pale blue flames mixing with the bomb residue to create acrid smoke that scorched noses and throats. The sub-basement stank from waste materials cascading down from broken plumbing lines. Enormous red-metal support beams were bowed out and leaning heavily, leaving each person fearing the building would collapse on them.

At one point, the team was stopped by several firemen who pointed toward the outline of a pit the size of a football field. Donald Sadowy of the New York City Bomb Squad guided the assemblage around the edge of the crater to a relatively pristine area on its far side. While the men and women unpacked their equipment in preparation for taking photos, sketches, measurements, and chemical swab samples, Donald peeled off from the group. He stepped onto a massive concrete slab once serving as flooring and now anchored only by rebar, searching for clues to solving what was, at the time, the greatest act of terrorism ever committed on American soil.

CHAPTER 1
Greenpoint

I'm like a wild horse that you'll kill before you'll break it.
—John Anthony Sadowy

IN THE FIRST DECADE of the twentieth century, Pauline Dolinich, traveling with her two older sisters, passed through the Ellis Island inspection station, headed for "Little Poland." All she knew of it was based on a torn, wrinkled photo clutched in her hand, depicting lush farmland and a flowing river. A scene not dissimilar from the Austro-Hungarian village she and her sisters had grown up in. The picture contained no hint of the belching factories, sordid fuel tanks, or massive lumber and shipyards that dominated the streets of Greenpoint and the banks of the squalid Newtown Creek, which separated north Brooklyn from Queens. Once a primeval forest bordered by salt marshes and swamps, by the time of the Great War, Greenpoint's transformation belied its evocative name.

Rendered Safe

Pauline's early years in her adopted country fulfilled its promise. She found reasonably priced lodging with indoor plumbing and built friendships with fellow Eastern European emigrants, who outnumbered the Greenpoint natives. Pauline obtained regular employment with Union Porcelain Works, in a factory the size of a city block that manufactured ceramics and porcelain products. But the highlight of those years was being wooed by John Katulak.

John, five foot five inches and barrel-chested, was born and raised in the Sudetenland, German-speaking sections of northern and western Bohemia and Moravia that after World War I were incorporated within the borders of the newly-created country of Czechoslovakia. He left school early to find work in the Prague shipyards, before emigrating to America. John's entrée into the New World was as an indentured servant working in a Pennsylvania coal mine. He escaped from that grueling, dangerous work well before his three-year term of service ended, making his way to the streets of "Hell's Kitchen," on the West Side of midtown Manhattan.[1] The neighborhood's congested, impoverished, and disease- and crime-riddled tenements made it among the most dangerous areas in the city, if not the nation. A breeding ground for gangs, its many warehouses were ideal locations for illicit distilleries during Prohibition.

After chatting up the locals in any of the multiple languages he spoke, John landed a job in an intimate speakeasy, the Hub Social Club, owned by a gangster

Chapter 1

named Joey Noe. John developed a friendship with the club's German-speaking Jewish bouncer, a local tough named Arthur Simon Flegenheimer, better known as "Dutch" Schultz. Schultz was Noe's childhood chum and the operator of a restaurant-shakedown business of his own. Fast with both his fists and a switchblade, he earned a reputation for brutality.[2] Schultz would eventually become a partner in Noe's Club. Operating in an era marked by a stunning level of municipal and labor-union corruption, Schultz built an extensive bootlegging and extortion business and forced his way to the head of Harlem's numbers racket, which would make him a wealthy young man.

One night at closing time, as the two men were sharing beers, Schultz chided John for having limited ambition and asked what he "really wanted out of life." John replied, "A bar and restaurant in a building where I can raise a family." Dutch drove John over to the East River waterfront in Greenpoint, an area that, in the 19th century, was one of the world's major shipbuilding centers and now was controlled by the International Longshoremen's Association and Albert Anastasia, a founder of the American Mafia and its enforcement arm, Murder Inc. Meandering along the waterfront, they spotted an abandoned four-story brick building with a ground-floor restaurant at 62 Green Street, on a cobblestoned block a stone's throw from a series of active factories.

Rendered Safe

62 Green Street building in 2019

Chapter 1

View in 2019 from 62 Green Street west toward the pier and east side of Manhattan

Schultz, recognizing the location's potential, bankrolled John, a debt that would be erased in October 1935 when Schultz was shot multiple times in the men's' room of the elegant Palace Chop House and Tavern in Newark, New Jersey, by two Mafia Commission hitmen. He died the next day, at the age of thirty-four.[3]

Pauline and John, who in his later years was affectionately referred to as "Nikita Khrushchev" because of his build and bald head, would raise eight children. Their restaurant, known as "John's Bar and Grille," thrived until the late 1960s, becoming a bustling gathering and networking spot for the mobsters and union bosses who ran the Brooklyn waterfront, as well as a favorite drinking venue for the hundreds of longshoremen, sailors, truck drivers, tugboat captains and crew, factory workers, and runners who, on any workday, teemed the area. John was a no-nonsense man with a commanding presence, who communicated largely through body language and facial expressions and was said to be fearless, even when dealing with the most violent of men. He held court daily at the far end of the ornate wood bar by the window, with proximity to him an indication of one's status as a mover and shaker. Ordinary patrons knew not to approach him unless invited, and that the pay phone next to the bar was reserved for bookies, loan sharks, and union bosses.

John's five daughters each worked at the bar and assisted their mother in the kitchen, where they routinely prepared more food than necessary to provide for the neighborhood's neediest. Each of John's three sons served in the armed forces during World War II or the Korean War, and otherwise worked at the bar as a first or second job. The second son, John Jr., after moving to nearby Astoria, Queens with his family, would drive to Greenpoint on Sunday mornings to help his father clean up from Saturday night's business. John Jr.'s son, Arthur, often accompanied his father. "The place smelled of stale beer, with the sawdust on the floor always sticky from spilled drinks. It had tin ceilings and ceiling fans. There was a TV that sat on a wood shelf, which was always on and very popular in a time when a lot of people didn't have one at home. When we arrived, my dad would prop me on a barstool. While he cleaned dishes, Grandpa John would entertain me. My grandpa had no real teeth left,

Chapter 1

so he would call me 'Otto,' which was easy for him to pronounce. He'd feed me peanuts and pour me some beer in a shot glass, and let me play with the jukebox and a candy vending machine."

John's second-youngest daughter was Cecelia Ann, known as "Cissy." An amiable, unassuming girl, Cissy by her teens had developed a penchant for hanging with the local "bad boys," known for their shiny cars, smooth talk, dapper clothes, and fast money. Since childhood, Cissy had been afflicted with grand mal seizures caused by epilepsy. Those episodes often led to a loss of consciousness, severe confusion, and violent muscle contractions.

One evening, while on a date with a man she adored, Cissy suffered a particularly vicious seizure. The man refused to see her anymore. Days later, while waitressing at the bar, Cissy poured her heart out to another man who was a long-time friend and regular patron—John Anthony Sadowy.

Born in a frame tenement house in Greenpoint in 1920, John Anthony, five feet four inches tall with a slim, muscular build, wavy hair, and light-blue eyes, was endowed with a mega-watt smile and the gift of gab. A bright man who spoke five languages, he was a regular at John's Bar and Grille. John Anthony's father was an immigrant who'd returned to his native Poland with a younger sibling, leaving John Anthony in the care of his alcoholic mother. She forced him, upon threat of a brutal beating, to steal money or food from local markets and coal from the docks. John Anthony polished his felonious skills on the Greenpoint streets. By the summer of 1938, John Anthony was an inmate in New York State's infamous Sing Sing maximum security prison.[4] While only a teenager, John Anthony lived among hardened old-timers with violent pasts in an institution well-known for its harsh conditions.

Over the next few years, John Anthony alternated between imprisonment and unrepentant criminality, shunning what he termed "nine-to-five jobs working as a chump for someone else."[5] After spending time in Sing Sing and in the Clinton Correctional Facility in upstate New York near Canada—a locale where it was said the only seasons were winter and July—John Anthony was released in June 1952. Although his parents now were deceased, he returned to Greenpoint, where he found a construction job, resumed committing robberies, and began courting Cissy. In his glow, her light shone again.

The Katulak family held no illusions about John Anthony, who was a decade older than Cissy and clearly troubled. But their worry that Cissy would never enjoy any serious suitor overrode their concerns. The clincher for them was John Anthony's insistence on paying for the wedding. As for Cissy, she clung to her dream of a normal family life and the age-old fallacy of believing she could change her man.

In July 1953, twenty-four-year-old Cissy married John Anthony. Only two months later, with Cissy pregnant, John Anthony and an accomplice were arrested for robbing, at gunpoint, the weekly payroll of Devon

Chapter 1

Industrial, a zipper-manufacturing company in Queens. On April 21, 1954, he was convicted of grand larceny, assault, and robbery in the first degree, and sentenced to fifteen to thirty years imprisonment. When John Anthony returned to Clinton, he was given a cordial reception. "It was like I'd been away on vacation," he recollected.

John Anthony would spend the rest of his life shifting among New York State prisons, with only brief periods of freedom. In September 1971, he was confined to the Attica Correctional Facility, in upstate New York near Buffalo, when a thousand inmates rioted and assumed control of the prison, taking 42 staff hostages. After four days of fruitless negotiation, Governor Nelson Rockefeller ordered state police to retake the prison by force. During the ensuing bloodbath, John Anthony, who had taken shelter on a passageway roof, was blown twenty feet to the ground by a tear-gas canister dropped from a helicopter. He suffered a concussion and went into shock, temporarily paralyzed and initially marked as dead.

John Anthony's residence after Attica was the Green Haven Correctional Facility, in the scenic mid-Hudson Valley near Poughkeepsie. While there, he would become the subject, along with the prison itself, of a book by Susan Sheehan, a noted, Pulitzer Prize-winning writer, entitled, *A Prison and a Prisoner*.[6] John Anthony described himself to Sheehan as a professional criminal, with a specialty in payroll robbery.

On April 25, 1954, four days after John Anthony's conviction for the Devon Industrial robbery, Cissy gave birth to her only child, a brown-haired, blue-eyed son she named Donald John. "My grandparents lived in the railroad apartment above the bar and grille," Donald recalled. "And my mom's apartment was right above them. Living with us was mom's younger sister, my Aunt Margie, who never married."[7]

In his youth, Donald's mother brusquely responded to his inquiries about his father with an insistence he was dead. Donald would first meet his father in September 1966, when John Anthony, after being paroled, returned to Queens and stayed for several days in Cissy's apartment. Cissy, who John Anthony characterized to Sheehan as a "nice, loving, religious woman," hadn't divorced John Anthony. She continued to wear her engagement ring and wedding band, her love for her husband having never been extinguished.

As for Donald, "that first meeting with my father was not emotional for me because he meant nothing to me. It was as if we had let a homeless person sleep on our living room couch for a few days. He showed up, and then he was gone. Afterward, I overheard one of my aunts telling my mother about me, 'You better be careful that he doesn't end up like his father.' And I determined then and there that I would be nothing like my father."

After his brief visit with family, John Anthony resumed his carousing and criminal ways. By February 1968, he'd been convicted of additional felonies and was back in Sing Sing, where he had first been incarcerated thirty years earlier.

Chapter 1

Studies have shown that a boy growing up without a father is more likely to be aggressive, depressed, perform poorly in school, become a substance abuser, and suffer from low self-esteem. Bathed in love and attention from several strong male figures, including his grandfather and his mother's brothers, Donald defied the statistics. "My second home was the bar, and my uncles took it upon themselves to look after me. I learned a lot just by watching how they conducted themselves."

Donald was particularly close to another uncle, Alex Lupack, an Army veteran who regaled Donald with stories of his World War II service interspersed with lessons about camaraderie and patriotism. Alex was married to Cissy's sister Victoria, whose family lived in the apartment above Donald's. "Uncle Alex reminded me of Gary Cooper. He was six feet one, thin, and a kind, thoughtful person who I could talk to about anything. He also was by nature a happy, positive man who would always tell me that every day was a gift." In the warm weather, Alex often could be found on the building's rooftop. "He enjoyed sitting up there at night with artillery binoculars, watching the lit-up Manhattan skyline, which he dubbed his own 'million-dollar view.' He'd drink beers, listen to a ball game, and take care of his pigeons."[8]

Under an umbrella of collective family love, shy and quiet Donald enjoyed a "happy and fairly normal" childhood. "When I first told my wife I never spoke up in school unless I was called on, she laughed and said,

Grandpa John, Mom Cecelia, and Donald on Green Street in Greenpoint in June 1960

'No way!' Then she added, 'You sure made up for it when you grew up.'"

Uninterested in traditional academic studies, and wary of attending the local high school, Eastern District, because of its reputation for violence, Donald enrolled in Automotive High School, located on Bedford Avenue in Greenpoint. "Brooklyn Automotive" was and remains the largest auto trade school in the nation, although it

Chapter 1

Donald, Uncle Alex, and Uncle John in Donald's mother's apartment circa 1978

also offers a standard high school education. Opened in 1937, by the late 1960s the sprawling building, with oversized windows covered by gates and bars and peeling paint throughout, was run-down and neglected.[9]

Automotive High School's motto, carved in stone above the main entrance, reads, "Manhood Service Labor Citizenship," and when Donald attended, it was all male. Many of the students were violent gang members who ruled various sections of the building. Their drug and alcohol use began in the morning. "In those days,"

Rendered Safe

Donald recollected, "Brooklyn Automotive was a really tough place. You couldn't walk in certain hallways or take certain stairways or you'd get the crap beat out of you. The administration had no control and just turned a blind eye. When I first started high school, I even was afraid to use the bathrooms. When I had to go, I hustled across the street to a friendly store owner. Every day I attended that school, I dreaded it. I couldn't wait to graduate." Donald began to carry a tire iron among his school supplies, gaining a degree of respect sufficient to allow him to function more freely.

In spite of its flaws, Automotive High School provided Donald with an understanding of the basics of

Front entrance of Brooklyn Automotive High School

Chapter 1

auto mechanics. Its auto-shop classes covered subjects such as steering-and-suspension, detailing and engine performance, welding, and managing customers. In those pre-computer days, Donald recounted, "auto repair still was a grease-monkey business."

One required class covered how a motor vehicle's powertrain works. "The powertrain," Donald explained, "is how a car transforms fuel into the power that moves it. It includes things like the engine, transmission, drive shafts, differential housing, axles, and the drive wheels. Even with the introduction of computers into cars, a vehicle's powertrain remained basically the same."

That class was a favorite of Donald's. Decades later, the knowledge gained in it would be integral to the defining moment in Donald's professional life.

CHAPTER 2
Foundation

My dad had been a Marine, and I was attracted to men who had a Marine background and qualities. I guess seeing Donald in uniform sparked something in me.
—Kathy Sadowy

ATTENDING BROOKLYN AUTOMOTIVE did not inspire Donald to become an auto mechanic. Nor did he want to labor in a local factory or at the waterfront. "I was looking for a work life that wasn't mundane. And I had a sense of adventure. But I knew I wasn't suited for college, so I struggled with what to do next with my life. I was greatly influenced by my first high school shop teacher, Mr. Ruland, who encouraged me to be a part of something bigger than myself."

Although each of his uncles had served in the U.S. Army, Donald decided to join the Marine Corps. "The Vietnam War draft was going on, and most of my friends talked incessantly about ways to either avoid service or join the easiest military branch. I chose to be part of the military where guys seemed to have the most pride in themselves. Who wanted to be there and would have each other's backs."

Before graduating, Donald, not yet eighteen, asked his mom for her approval. "She was not happy. And my uncles were upset, too." Each uncle tried to talk Donald out of his decision, failing to understand they were instrumental in its making. "I looked up to my uncles and their service. They had made a difference in the world, and I wanted to also."

After his mother hesitated to sign the necessary paperwork, at Donald's request, two Marine recruiters visited his apartment. "My mom and uncles were there. The recruiters told me to wait outside until they were done. They spoke with my family for a half hour and convinced them the Marine Corps would provide me with a great future. My mom reluctantly signed the paperwork." Within a week, Donald, who had never left the confines of New York City, flew to Beaufort, South Carolina. He would not return home for two years.

Following a two-hour bus ride, Donald arrived on Parris Island, surrounded by swamp and marsh, with other recruits late at night. "We stood anxiously on the yellow footprints painted on the pavement in front of the white, spartan wooden receiving barracks that predated World War II. The drill instructor screamed at us at the top of his lungs, 'You have just taken the first step toward becoming a member of the world's finest fighting

Chapter 2

force. You will carry on their proud tradition.'" Donald and the other recruits turned in all their personal possessions and were immediately thrust into a whirlwind of in-processing, buzz haircuts, uniform and gear issue, and medical evaluations.

Ringing in Donald's head was his Uncle Alex's admonition that Marine Corps boot camp would be the hardest thing he'd ever do in his life. "My uncle told me that the drill instructors take you apart and then put you back together to imitate how scary and overwhelming real battle is. And he was so right. The physical demands were great, like all the running with heavy weights. But the real killer was the emotional stress they inflicted. The screaming and hazing. The sleep deprivation. The strict routine demanded for the most basic of things, like speaking, dressing, and personal hygiene. Each mouthful of food you took had to be eaten in a soldierly manner." During Donald's first two nights in Parris Island, after lights out, he buried his head in his pillow and cried himself to sleep. "But I didn't want to come home a failure. I wanted to prove wrong those who I knew thought Marine training would be too hard for me. That helped me to make it through the twelve weeks. By then, I was different. A more disciplined, focused person who believed he could accomplish anything he set his mind to."

After graduating boot camp, Donald was ordered to the Marine detachment in the U.S. Army Training Center at Fort Sill, Oklahoma, 90 miles southwest of Oklahoma City, which had been a frontier cavalry post in the nineteenth century.[10] In the prairie, Donald would train alongside men from various nations, including Germany and South Vietnam. "I got there in late November 1972. What I remember most is the land was flat as a pancake, the rains were torrential, and it already was bone-chilling cold."

Donald and a dozen other Marines, joined by a much larger contingent of Army recruits, were trained in the use of field artillery. "Each shell weighed as much as a Volkswagen. They could travel twenty-five miles or more. When those big guns fired, it was deafening. You could feel the concussive pressure against your body. You had to turn your head because it actually could loosen up the fillings in your mouth." Donald summed up his two greatest lessons while at Fort Sill as "how to put 'steel on target,' and to appreciate moonshine."

Days before Christmas, Donald and three friends drove into nearby Lawton for Sunday church services. They chatted with a member of the church who, after hearing the Marines could not afford the airfare to return home for the holidays, invited all four to his house. "He had a lovely family, and we were made quite welcome. They asked us all sorts of questions. Then, in the middle of the meal, as we were passing around the turkey, the mother of the house mentioned the *Godfather* movie, which she had just seen. Suddenly, she turned to me and said, casually but seriously, 'You said you're from Brooklyn. Are you with the Mafia?' I almost swallowed my fork. My buddies never let me forget that one."

Chapter 2

After two months at Fort Sill, Donald was sent further west, to the Marine Corps Air Ground Combat Center known as "29 Palms." The single largest Marine Corps base, 29 Palms is located in the "middle of nowhere" in the Mojave Desert in Southern California. Now a corporal, Donald lived in a one-story, non-airconditioned cinder-block barracks set on cement slabs, with metal tin roofs and spartan open squad bays. "We had these eight-foot high fans that sounded like B-52 bombers warming up on the tarmac. All they really did was recirculate the hot air." On the many days when the temperature rose above 115 degrees Fahrenheit, "black flag" conditions would be declared, and all outdoor physical activity ceased.[11]

At 29 Palms, Donald had ample opportunity to shoot rifles, shotguns, pistols, and machine guns. "That base was all about live-fire training," Donald recalled. "I thought I was a good shot coming out of boot camp, but 29 Palms really honed my marksmen skills. But, otherwise, you were in a year-round dreary, sandy, dusty environment, with scorpions and snakes galore and not much to do but watch movies, swim in the huge outdoor pool, and drink beer."

After eighteen months, bored and impatient to explore the world, Donald volunteered to join the Third Marine Division, first formed during World War II, that operated in Asia. "My commanding officer, the battery gunnery sergeant, thought I had lost my mind. But I needed to get out of the desert." Before being shipped out to Okinawa, Donald returned home on leave for two weeks. He spent most of his time hanging out with old friends. One was Donna Orminski. "Donald was my first boyfriend," Donna reminisced, "although it was never more than innocent puppy love between us. I was one of the few people who knew that Donald's father was in prison, and his mother had little time to spend with him. Given his home situation, it's pretty remarkable that Donald managed to stay out of trouble. Instead of repeating history, he went the complete opposite way."

Donald asked Donna about Kathy Ann Burkart, a girl from the neighborhood who was her long-time best friend. Kathy had moved two years earlier with her family to Queens Village, a residential middle-class neighborhood in eastern Queens. Donald had always liked Kathy. "I knew her from when she was twelve and I was thirteen, when Donna introduced us to each other. She was a blonde, thin, shy, and very thoughtful and caring girl. We ran in the same circles but never dated."

Donna's and Kathy's families both belonged to the Church of the Ascension on Kent Street, a small Episcopal congregation dating back to the 1850s, housed in a 19th-century stone A-frame building. "Father Bill Davidson," Donna explained, "who headed the church, was a wonderful man. He installed a stereo system and TV in the basement and opened it for use by local kids as a gathering place, not wanting us to be hanging out on the streets." One Saturday, Donna had asked Donald to join her at a church dance that offered dinner. Donald initially was uncomfortable. "I was raised as a strict

Chapter 2

Roman Catholic. In those days, it wasn't usual for kids of different religions to mix socially. But Donna insisted." Kathy also attended. "The first time I saw Donald, he was wearing combat boots and an Army field jacket. To everyone, including me, he seemed nutty. It was during the time of Vietnam War protests, and that kind of getup wasn't popular."

After her conversation with Donald, Donna called Kathy and urged her to reconnect with him. "I always thought of Donna and Donald as a couple," Kathy reminisced, "and I told Donna I didn't want one of her hand-me-downs. But she persisted. 'He's a great guy,' she kept saying."

Kathy and Donald arranged a dinner date at a steak restaurant in Forest Hills. Donald wore his Marine uniform. The two were together much of the next three days. "Donald and I talked about everything and realized we had a lot in common, including our values." By the end of the third day, having revealed their souls to each other, the two were smitten. And Donald was overwhelmed with a sense of urgency. "Being home on leave from the military, time got compressed and more precious." Donald impulsively proposed, and Kathy accepted. "Agreeing to marry someone three days after your first date with him is kind of crazy," she reflected. "But something in me was certain it was right."[12]

Donald and Kathy kept their engagement secret. After Donald left for Okinawa, the two wrote to each other regularly, even though the letters took two weeks to arrive.

Serving with the Third Marine Division, Donald traveled throughout the Pacific. One stop was Japan's Mount Fuji, where he endured a month of cold-weather training on a mountainside of lifeless volcanic rock.[13] "Camp Fuji was tough. We lived in Quonset huts that were rotting and falling apart. They leaked when it rained, and there never seemed to be any hot water. We looked like homeless people." Donald and his fellow Marines learned to acclimate to the altitude and difficult terrain, live in deep snow and move through it, and shoot weapons while dealing with the frigid temperatures. "In that cold, which sapped your strength, everything took a longer time, even simple things like lacing your boots. Maybe the hardest part was just staying dry."

Donald's transport ship was stationed in the South China Sea during the end of April 1975, when Saigon fell to the North Vietnamese and Viet Cong armies. He followed the developing story on the Armed Forces Network. "Unlike today, when you can get all the news you want instantaneously, we had access to one radio and one TV channel. You saw and heard what they wanted you to see and hear. People at home knew a lot more than we did."

Donald and his shipmates had trained for amphibious landings on the Navy's landing ship tanks, known as "LSTs," which have an oversized door that drops down to serve as a ramp for unloading vehicles, a special flat keel allowing the ship to be beached and stay upright, and twin propellers and rudders that protect from grounding. They were told they might become part of an

Chapter 2

assault force tasked to retake Vietnam. "I knew LSTs had been crucial to the Normandy invasion, and I imagined I'd be participating in a D-Day-like attack against the North Vietnamese. We packed up our civilian gear, put it in foot lockers, and went on standby. Each day was an emotional rollercoaster."

Weeks later, as the prospect of invading Vietnam faded, tensions on the ship escalated again when military conflict arose between Cambodia and the United States in what became known as the "Mayaguez incident".[14] "Our staff sergeant," Donald recalled, "had us muster up on deck. Armorers, the guys who repaired and maintained our weapons, came around with wooden crates. They had each of us take out all the ammo and hand grenades we could carry. We were scared, not knowing what was going on, except that it was serious. Fortunately, I never had to fire any shots in anger."

On his next leave home, in October 1975, Donald and Kathy married in City Hall. "We didn't tell anyone," Kathy recounted, "not even my parents or sister or brother. Or Donald's mom. Only Donald's Uncle Alex, who stood for us, knew. But the news gradually leaked out."

After thirteen months in the Pacific, Donald rotated back to the States. "My three buddies and I caught a transport out of Kadena Air Base in Okinawa to the Marine Corps air station in Iwakuni, Japan, near Hiroshima, to Wake Island for refueling, and then on to Hawaii. The whole time, I never got off the plane and wasn't able to get comfortable."

Stuck with a long layover in Honolulu, the four Marines stowed their bags in lockers and strolled to an airport restaurant for steak and beers to celebrate being back in the USA. "It was lunchtime, but the restaurant was fairly empty. We stood in our summer tropical uniforms, waiting to be seated. Two waitresses kept walking by but refused to acknowledge us. After fifteen minutes, we decided to seat ourselves. The waitresses finally came over, gave us dirty looks, blurted out, 'We don't serve people like you,' and stormed away. Then the manager, a stout guy with a gut, hustled over and repeated that we wouldn't be served. Our mood shifted from shock to anger. We were gonna kick the shit out of this guy and break up the place."

Two older men sitting nearby rushed over and persuaded the Marines to let them talk to the manager privately. "Those guys were ex-military and tough looking. I don't know what they said, but we got served our steak and beers. And those two, once they found out we had just arrived back in the States, insisted on picking up our tab."

The pervasive anti-military sentiment of the time reared its head again when Donald parted ways with his friends, retrieved his seabag, and made a stop in a men's room. "While I was standing at the urinal, three guys came over and called me a 'baby killer' and other names. I snapped, grabbed the closest one by the throat, punched him, and shoved his head down a commode, which I kept flushing. Realizing I might hurt him bad, I

Chapter 2

stopped and threw him on the floor, where he lay crying with snot running down his nose. The other two ran out."

Donald's final year in the Marines was spent at the sprawling Camp Lejeune Marine Corps base on the North Carolina coast. "The barracks were Colonial-style buildings that I thought were luxurious because they had air conditioning, and the ceiling didn't leak when it rained. We trained constantly in the woodland, which had beautiful grasses and trees, away from the oceanfront and beaches. It seemed like an unending camping trip. One day, I was caught in a torrential downpour and took cover under a Charlie Brown palm tree, with four leaves. I lay there, using my helmet for a pillow, thinking 'Why am I doing this?'"

As Donald neared his end date as a Marine, several noncommissioned officers who acted as career planners encouraged him to re-enlist. While he was considering that, Donald unexpectedly was promoted to sergeant and assigned his own living quarters, which was unusual. "I was thrilled. I was tired of living like an animal, and now I had clean sheets, a warm bed, and hot showers. But I knew it was a ploy to keep me in the Marines. So, at the end, I said to the recruiters 'Thanks, but no thanks.' I'd had enough."[15]

Donald would characterize his four and a half years in the Marine Corps as having taught him "not only soldiering and survival skills but, also, self-motivation and self-confidence. I learned how to think, speak, and observe. How to be responsible for myself, yet also be a team player. It was the foundation for everything else I did in my life."

Arriving home for good in August 1976, Donald took the written test to join the New York Police Department. As an applicant with two-years-plus of active service in the U.S. military, Donald was exempt from the college-credit requirement. "My new dream was to become a cop." But it was a time of municipal cutbacks and fiscal hardship for the City, and no new police recruits were being taken on. Instead, Donald found work at Delta Welding, a boiler repair shop owned by Donna Orminski's father. "That work was physically harder," he admitted, "than much of my Marine duty."

The following August, on a beautiful day, Donald hopped on the subway to Midtown East to take a test to become a customs border patrol agent. Afterward, he embarked on a power stroll that took him past the United Nations complex, on First Avenue in the mid-40s. "I looked and walked like a Marine. Tight haircut. Perfect posture. No waist. Thirty-six-inch step. Highly shined shoes. Some U.N. security guys were hanging outside. They yelled out to me to come chat with them. Told me they were looking for good people. The starting pay was a lot better than for a border patrol agent. In an instant, I decided to junk that idea." Donald initiated an interview and background-check process that lasted for months, and culminated in his being offered a position with the U.N. security staff.

Chapter 2

During the summer of 1977, as often seems the case, the world was chaotic. Zulfikar Ali Bhutto, the first elected Prime Minister of Pakistan, and his government were overthrown in a military coup.[16] Somalia invaded Ethiopia over a land dispute. Libya and Egypt fought a five-day border war. Each of these crises was formally brought to the Security Council for discussion by the U.N. Secretary-General, Kurt Waldheim, one of the most famous and influential men in the world. Donald would come to know him well.

CHAPTER 3
Schatzi

My boss screamed, 'They love him more than they love each other. We have to find him, or we'll both be fired!'
—Donald Sadowy

ON OCTOBER 2, 1977, shortly after Donald began working at the U.N., he and Kathy again wed, this time in the petite English-style St. Thomas Episcopal Church in Bellerose Village before friends and family. "I was in school," Kathy recounted, "and also had three jobs, assisting an oral surgeon in Greenpoint near the Oak Street apartment we lived in, working at Dunkin Donuts on weekends, and tutoring. We had to use gift money to help pay for our wedding expenses. We didn't take a honeymoon because we were broke."

One of the wedding guests was Donald's father. "After I got out of the Marines and came home," Donald remembered, "I felt the need to speak with my dad. I found out he was staying in a detention center in Long Island City, being prepared for release from prison, and decided to visit." Donald asked Kathy to accompany him. "Donald and I spoke with his father for quite a while. He came across as very likable and chivalrous. Overly so. He had me feeling badly for him after telling us he was dying from a brain tumor he'd gotten from the Attica riot. But Donald told me that probably wasn't true, which it turned out not to be."

For Donald, the meeting was yet another disappointment. "He was unrepentant about his life and his abandonment of me. That might have been a defense mechanism, but it was hurtful nonetheless. I maintained a slight relationship with him afterward, helping out with groceries and the like at times, but I was ashamed of being his son. And, sure enough, it wasn't long before he committed another bank robbery and got put away again."

On Donald's first day of work at the U.N., which was a Sunday, he was assigned to guard the Secretary-General's official residence, a redbrick Georgian double-wide townhouse at 3 Sutton Place between 57th and 58th Streets overlooking the East River. The stately building, with a private back garden, had been constructed in the 1920s by the famed financier J.P. Morgan for use by his daughter, Anne, when she stayed in New York.[17] It was donated to the U.N. in 1971, and Waldheim was the first Secretary-General to live there.

Donald's assignment was solo and expected to be easy, as the Waldheims were out of town that weekend at their summer house in Ridgefield, Connecticut, where

Chapter 3

they indulged their passion for riding horses. Donald's commanding officer, John Fallon, guided him through the five-story building and demonstrated how to use the alarm system. After telling Donald "no one is in the house, and no one is expected," Fallon announced he was returning to U.N. headquarters. Donald followed his boss out of the house and to his car. It being a beautiful day, Donald left the front doors open to air the place out.

When Donald returned to the townhouse, he settled into a small security office by the front entrance, set the alarm, made himself a cup of tea, and sat reading the newspaper. "The place was quiet like a church on Monday. But after a few minutes, I heard the floorboard creak slightly several times, as if someone was coming down the stairs. I hustled over to the grand, winding wood stairway with beautiful moldings to find this grungy dog waddling down. He couldn't have been more than two feet long, with stringy hair like dreadlocks. And I thought, 'Shit, when I left the doors open, he must have run inside."

Fearing the dog would poop somewhere in the house, or do other damage, Donald raced after him through the entire house. "Up the stairs and down the stairs. From the wine cellar to the top floor. Finally, I gave up, shut off the alarm, and opened the front and patio doors. Didn't hear a sound after that, so I assumed he'd run out."

Later in the afternoon, Fallon returned. "He asked me how the day had gone, and I proudly told him I took care of the one problem, getting rid of some mangy mutt that had wandered into the house. Fallon's face turned white, and he grabbed me by my jacket lapels. 'Are you out of your mind!' he screamed. 'That was Schatzi, the Waldheims' dog.'" The two men embarked on an exhaustive room-by-room search that ended when Donald, lying on his stomach, found Schatzi hiding under a bed, quivering. "I got reamed out for days by my boss. As for Schatzi, sadly, he soon met his end when he got run over accidentally by one of Waldheim's chauffeurs."

As was traditional for many New York City kids, when Donald would trick-or-treat on Halloween, he'd carry a charity box for the U.N. Children's Fund. But Donald's self-described naïve, black-and-white view of the U.N. changed upon hearing stories of rampant corruption deeply imbedded within the organization. "One example were guys who bragged about conniving to get an assignment to Namibia [which was a U.N. protectorate transitioning to independence from South Africa]. There, they'd buy bags full of uncut, blood diamonds, stuff them in a diplomatic pouch, and mail them to themselves in New York. They'd pick them up when they got home, head over to the Diamond District, and resell the stones at a huge profit." Donald also heard the abundant rumors of thefts by senior U.N. officials of cargo loads of medicine, food, and other relief supplies meant for people in war-ravaged regions, to be sold on the black market or to warlords.

Soon, Donald witnessed fraudulent practices firsthand. Foreign U.N. workers are exempt from U.S. taxation.

Chapter 3

Americans, however, are required to pay Federal income and Social Security taxes, although they are reimbursed by the U.N. "We'd submit our tax forms to the United Nations," Donald explained, "and get a check which we were supposed to send on to the IRS. Many Americans inflated their tax liability and kept the difference, or pocketed the entire U.N. check. The practice was so wide-spread that I felt pressured to join in, but I refused to. When an audit finally came, I watched as many guys were hit with tens of thousands of dollars in back taxes they couldn't pay."

Overlooking the East River, the buildings that comprise U.N. headquarters are in a neighborhood that, in 1948, when construction began, was an unsightly mess of slaughterhouses, light industry, and railroad barges. The U.N. complex spans several blocks, and its levels include three below ground, containing shops, security offices, warehouses, parking, a petrol station, and machine rooms. During Donald's first year at the U.N., he often was assigned to the midnight to eight a.m. shift. "We had to patrol the long corridors, which required a lot of walking, pushing buttons at each floor end to show we'd made the security sweep. It was real tedious work. As few—if any—people were around, many security guys drank on the job."

To alleviate the burden, Donald brought in a fiberglass skateboard. "I got good at using it. That worked out well until one night when I was flying through a floor, and I nearly crashed into my boss, who was backing out of an office. I startled him so that he dropped his set of master keys, and his hat fell off. The only thing I could think to say was 'Hello, Sarge.' I kept zipping down the hall as I heard him yelling my name. I got to the end, picked up the board, and went to next floor. I knew I'd be in for it."

Donald was summoned to the office of Harold Trimble, the global head of U.N. security. Trimble, who everyone called 'the Colonel,' was a World War II and Korean War veteran who had retired from the Royal Canadian Army Service Corps. He had military-style cropped hair, a florid face, and a waxed handlebar mustache twisted upward akin to Hercule Poirot's. "The Colonel wore a suit and tie like a commanding officer would wear a uniform, and spoke quite distinctly. Impressive in a mild-mannered way."

Donald stood at attention, hat under arm. "Trimble's office was huge. His back was to me as he gazed out a window with a grand view of Manhattan. He turned, and there was a report in his hand. He told me I'd been written up for various violations by my sergeant, who had recommended that my employment be terminated. But I wasn't nervous because, as the Colonel was telling me this, he was trying to not laugh out loud. I assured him I would never ride a skateboard again. 'Let's consider the matter ended,' he said. Then, as he was famous for, he dismissed me with the words, 'Carry on smartly!'"

*

In September 2007, forty years after he began working at the U.N., and in conjunction with that year's opening

Chapter 3

session of the General Assembly, Donald returned to the U.N. for a reunion with former colleagues. "I'm standing and talking to a young man who had just started on the security staff. I asked what they have him doing and he says he patrols the corridors on the midnight to eight a.m. shift. I mentioned I know how physically demanding that job is, and he instantly launched into a story about some guy years ago who had used a skateboard to get up and down the corridors. As he tells me about this 'legend,' who got caught and almost lost his job over it, I glance around to see my buddies watching us and laughing. I realized they had set this up, making sure the kid had no idea who I was."

CHAPTER 4
The Devil Sent Us Castro

We were Waldheim's first line of defense. Not only every visitor but, also, every phone call, first went through us.
—Nick Panzarino

BY HIS SECOND YEAR of U.N. service, in spite of the Schatzi and skateboard incidents, Donald had impressed his seniors enough that he was asked to join the bodyguard detail for the Secretary-General and his family. Waldheim had decided to bolster his security after the March 1978 kidnapping in Rome of a friend, Aldo Moro, a former prime minister of Italy who was president of its Christian Democracy party. The kidnapping had been carried out by a group of left-wing Red Brigades members who killed Moro's five bodyguards. Waldheim, along with Pope Paul VI and others, sought to find a peaceful resolution with the terrorists, to no avail. Two months later, Moro's bullet-riddled body was found in the trunk of a car, after he had been submitted to a political trial by a "people's court." Those at the U.N. who knew Waldheim would report that as the one time Waldheim appeared emotional.

One afternoon, Donald was driven to 3 Sutton Place for an interview. "I was nervous because Waldheim had a reputation for being haughty and dismissive." Donald was escorted into the oak-paneled library. "A maid came over pulling a pushcart with a polished silver tray of coffee and desserts. And then Mrs. Waldheim entered and asked me to sit beside her. I soon realized she would be the decision-maker, not the Secretary-General. Mrs. Waldheim ran the show for her husband, including planning dinners, trips, and holiday gatherings, and handling staff matters."

Kurt Waldheim's wife, known as "Sissy," was Elisabeth Ritschel, a fellow Austrian he'd wed during the war. They had three grown children—two daughters, Liselotte (who would work at the U.N.) and Christa, and a son, Gerhard. Donald was impressed by Mrs. Waldheim. "She was over six feet tall, old-school European, and had a commanding presence. Always looked perfect. Textbook posture. Every hair in place. A woman of great formality in her manner, body movements, and speech. She acted like royalty, but I never felt she deliberately tried to talk down to me. She just was who she was."

For most of the half-hour interview, Donald spoke about his military experience and training. Mrs. Waldheim's final question to him was, "Would you ever hesitate to protect my family by any means necessary?"

Chapter 4

After Donald assured her that he would have no such reluctance, she nodded her approval and said, "You may leave now."

Years later, Donald reflected on his interview with Sissy Waldheim after reading that she had been an ardent Nazi Party member who as a teenager had renounced her Roman Catholic faith and joined the League of German Maidens, the young women's equivalent of the Hitler Youth. "I remembered that Mrs. Waldheim's first words to me were, 'Where are your people from?' I wondered what she really thought of my mongrel background."

Donald would serve in Waldheim's security detail for close to two years. "Waldheim always was very serious and business-like. It was difficult to read his mood. He worked hard, often getting to his office by eight and staying until midnight. But he was at all times polite and treated me well."

Donald was struck by the physical stamina of Waldheim, who was in his early sixties. "On nice days, Waldheim would skip the car and walk the mile to the 'Glass House,' our name for the Secretariat building, where his office was. [The 39-story Secretariat building was the first skyscraper in New York City to use a glass-curtain wall as its outer covering.] He was a power walker with a long stride, and he kept up a good pace. I'm only five eight, so his steps seemed twice mine. I had to jog to stay with him. When we finally arrived at the building, I'd be sweating and breathing hard. It was my cardio for the day." After Waldheim ended his U.N. career and returned to Austria, he was hit and mildly injured by a passing tram. "That didn't surprise me," Donald observed. "He wasn't one to look both ways."

Also serving in Waldheim's security detail was Nick Panzarino, a tall, thin, thick-mustached Air Force veteran who had been prevented from joining the New York Police Department by the City's fiscal crisis. He and Donald would stand guard in Waldheim's office suite, which contained a conference room spacious enough for meetings with his top assistants, a private dining room in which he held working luncheons for ambassadors, visiting diplomats, and other guests, a bedroom he rarely used, and a bathroom. "I was told," Donald remembered, "President Kennedy once asked to take a bath there, but when he ran the tap water in the tub, it came out brown with rust. After that, somebody was assigned to run the water every day in case another head of state decided he wanted a bath."

Donald and Nick Panzarino often were stationed at Waldheim's residence as part of his 24/7 security. "Nick and I," Donald recalled, "were extremely dedicated to protecting the Secretary-General and his family. Our thought was that someone looking to do violence might get past one of us, but no one was getting past both of us." Each man developed a fondness for Waldheim, with Panzarino describing how "typically when Waldheim came home, he would stroll into our side office and sit for a few minutes and chat. Even ask us questions about our families. At Christmas-time, he and his wife would

Chapter 4

Donald guarding the Secretary-General's residence at 3 Sutton Place

throw a cocktail party for the staff and give each of us presents for our kids."

Donald's new responsibilities brought him into close physical contact with a who's who of global heads of state and celebrities. "People like Mohammed Ali, Jacques Cousteau, Jackie Onassis, the Shah of Iran [whose sister lived in Sutton Place], and Boris Yeltsin. Waldheim enjoyed hosting dinners for them in his residence, followed by drinks upstairs in the library. I felt like a fly on the wall to history. I was exposed to so much I had to sign a document pledging to not reveal anything I heard or saw."

One of the many dignitaries whom Donald provided protection was Yasser Arafat, the Egyptian-born head of the Palestine Liberation Organization for decades. "Arafat always carried a pistol, even when he was at the U.N., which ordinarily was not allowed. That's because he was always in fear of being assassinated. That fear was significant enough that body doubles were used when Arafat was being transported around town."[18]

One of the U.N. events that Donald attended was a UNICEF benefit music concert held in January 1979 in the General Assembly Hall, which has a seating capacity of 1,800. The show, videotaped and broadcast the following day on NBC around the world, was intended to raise money for world hunger programs and to mark the beginning of the International Year of the Child. Its moderator was the English media personality David Frost, who'd originated the idea, with comedians Gilda Radner and Henry Winkler also introducing the performers. "I got to hear and see up close some of the biggest names in pop music at the time, like the Bee Gees, Olivia Newton-John, and Rod Stewart. Henry Fonda showed up to read from Anne Frank's diary. At the end, Waldheim

Chapter 4

accepted a parchment on which all the artists had signed over their royalty rights."

Donald's favorite visiting dignitary was Pope John Paul II, to whose security detail he was assigned when the Pope made his first visit to the United States in October 1979 and addressed the General Assembly. "It was as if I was standing next to God," Donald would tell family and friends. As a thank you, Donald and each of the other U.N. security guards received rosary beads and an elegant box covered in crushed blue velvet, inside of which was a bronze medallion with the pope's image on one side and his seal on the other. That gift started Donald on a lifelong hobby of collecting challenge coins from around the world.

Fidel Castro appeared at the U.N. during the same month of the Pope's visit. "The old-timers always talked about Castro's first visit to the U.N. in 1960, when he spoke for almost five hours, the longest speech in U.N. history. That visit was legendary because Castro's entourage, afraid of being poisoned by U.S. officials, killed, plucked, and cooked chickens in their rooms at the Shelburne Hotel and extinguished cigars on expensive carpets. After the hotel threw them out, local civil rights leaders arranged for the group to stay at the Hotel Theresa in Harlem. Castro set up headquarters there, waving from the balcony to thousands of supporters and hanging a Cuban flag."

On October 11, 1979, Castro arrived at JFK Airport at 1 a.m. He then headed to Manhattan in a motorcade of close to fifty vehicles, which included Secret Service and State Department officials, Cuban security officers, and dozens of NYPD officers. Before Castro arrived at the Cuban mission at 38th Street and Lexington Avenue, around which the NYPD had created a four-block frozen zone, a helicopter with a searchlight checked rooftops in the area and a Bomb Squad dog walked down the avenue sniffing garbage piles.

Donald was in the room when Castro met with Waldheim the following day. "Castro was massive, with hands huge like baseball gloves. Although he was tall—even taller than Waldheim—Castro wore three-inch heels on polished black combat boots and a stovepipe military hat to elevate him further. He even trimmed his beard in a tapered way so it wasn't rounded but elongated." After the conference with Waldheim, Castro spoke before the General Assembly. "I was surprised when he ended after forty minutes. He called Americans 'imperialists' and demanded $300 billion for poor nations. We had a running joke that the devil sent us Castro, and God sent us the Pope." From Fidel Castro's bodyguard detail, composed of dozens of armed men, Donald received a bottle of rum and a box of Cohibas. "I didn't smoke cigars, but my father-in-law and uncles did. It sure made them happy."

One morning, before one of numerous Security Council meetings on the conflict in the Middle East, Donald was asked by his supervisor to report to the Delegates Lounge on the second floor of the General

Chapter 4

Assembly building. "It's a football-field-sized open room with 30-foot-high windows overlooking Japanese cherry trees, rose gardens, and the East River, filled with artwork, tapestries like one of the Great Wall of China, cushy leather chairs and couches, coffee tables, and unlimited refreshments. Only diplomats and their assistants were allowed in. They'd go there to relax and chat. You'd hear every language imaginable."

Donald was instructed to "keep the peace," make sure no unauthorized persons entered, and confiscate any cameras. As Donald stood observing, various representatives from Arab nations entered. "They stretched, took off their jackets, loosened their ties, got coffee and one of the international newspapers, and sat reading leisurely, as people today would do in Starbucks. In came Moshe Dayan, the Israeli Foreign Minister, followed by two guys who looked like they could kill you with their pinky and would be happy to do so. I thought, 'Holy shit!' But Dayan and the Arab diplomats started chatting as if they were long-lost brothers. They openly and politely shared the antagonistic positions they soon would present to the Security Council. I was shocked, being a babe in the woods and not yet understanding that hypocrisy and theatrics were an essential part of the U.N. game."

Donald accompanied Waldheim to many U.N. ceremonies. "When a new member joined, they'd make a big deal about raising its flag on 'flag row' in front of the General Assembly building. One event that particularly

47

struck me was when Vietnam was formally admitted. Speaking in fluent French, Waldheim lauded that country's admission. Given that the war had ended only a few years ago, it gave me the creeps."

*

In late 1977, new Israeli Prime Minister Menachem Begin met with Kurt Waldheim at the United Nations. "Waldheim towered over Begin," Donald recalled, "and made a constant effort to lean forward to make himself not as tall. At one point, Waldheim escorted Begin to the Meditation Room, a small, dimly lit room shaped like a trapezoid with benches, no windows, an abstract mural, and a stone altar in its center.[19] It's meant for use by all faiths for silent prayer and meditation. I was standing next to Begin when a brief memorial ceremony was conducted. Begin, together with Waldheim, placed a wreath on a stand commemorating Count Folke Bernadotte, the first United Nations Secretary-General, who was assassinated in Jerusalem in 1948 by a paramilitary Zionist group. Talk about irony, and politics making for strange bedfellows. Here was Begin, who headed another Zionist group that after the war bombed the King David Hotel in Jerusalem, and Waldheim, who served in the Nazi Army, acting like the closest of buddies."[20]

Along with the rest of the world, Donald would learn only years after he left U.N. service a more complete history of the early life of his former boss. Kurt Waldheim was born in 1918 outside Vienna, Austria. In 1938, while

Chapter 4

a law student, he joined the National Socialist student union and the *Sturmabteilung*, the Nazi Party's original paramilitary, also known as the "Brownshirts." When World War II began in September 1939, he was drafted into the *Wehrmacht* (the German armed forces). In late 1941, while participating in the invasion of Russia, for which service he would receive the "Iron Cross," he was wounded and hospitalized in Vienna. During his decade as Secretary-General, Waldheim's official U.N. biography obfuscated his activities during the remainder of the war. Describing that period in his life, Waldheim offered only that, while recuperating in Vienna, he completed his legal studies, receiving a doctorate in 1944, and entered the Austrian Foreign Ministry. Waldheim worked for the Ministry until he was appointed as Austria's representative to the U.N. in 1964. In 1971, he ran unsuccessfully in the Austrian presidential election. Despite his defeat, Waldheim was elected as Secretary-General of the U.N. the following year.

Only in 1986, after Waldheim announced his candidacy for the presidency of Austria, came the revelation that, in March 1942, he had been posted to the German high command in Yugoslavia. Waldheim spent much of the war as an intelligence and administrative officer attached to units involved in ruthless attempts to stamp out partisan resistance through "cleansing operations" that took the lives of hundreds of thousands of Serbs, Jews, and communist Croatians via massacres and large-scale deportations. General Alexander Loehr, under whom

Waldheim served, was hanged in 1947 by a Yugoslav tribunal for war crimes. Waldheim himself was the recipient of a high award by the virulently anti-Semitic Nazi puppet regime in Croatia.

Regarding the deportation of tens of thousands of Jewish men, women, and children to concentration camps, Waldheim later admitted he had known of them but added, "I did not know there were these gas chambers. I did not know what was being done to the Jews." The U.N. War Crimes Commission found these claims to be "incredible." In 1948, a report prepared by the Commission found there was sufficient evidence to prosecute Waldheim for murder and "putting hostages to death." That conclusion was kept secret.[21] When Waldheim died in 2007 at 88, *The New York Times* obituary described his having lied about membership in Nazi organizations and putting his "signature on documents linked to massacres and deportations."[22]

The U.N.'s structure limits the power and autonomy of the Secretary-General, who is beholden to the near 200 member states and their competing agendas and views. Nonetheless, the position of Secretary-General is a highly visible and prominent one. In November 1975, the General Assembly adopted the infamous Resolution 3379, which stated that "Zionism is a form of racism and racial discrimination." (That resolution was revoked by the General Assembly in 1991.) Waldheim went on record opposing the resolution, but did not actively work to stop it. Wags joked that if "Alzheimer's Disease" means forgetting

Chapter 4

who you are, "Waldheim's Disease" means forgetting you were a Nazi.

The U.N.'s failure to aggressively and meaningfully address terrorism may be said to have begun under Waldheim's watch in September 1972 after eleven Israeli athletes were murdered by the Black September, a Palestinian terrorist group, during the Munich Olympics. The General Assembly dithered on adopting measures designed to prevent such violence and focused instead on discussion of "the root causes of terrorism." To this day, the U.N. has not been able to agree on a definition of "terrorism," because such a concept would remove the political distinction many make between the actions of "freedom fighters" and terrorists. The organization's failures in this vital arena, a part of the world's often benign attitude, would come home to roost in its home city two decades later, with Donald in the thick of the battle.[23]

CHAPTER 5
Beat Cop

I told Donald not to talk for the next two hours. Not one word, except for police business. Two hours later, he asks, 'Can I talk now?' I yell back at him, 'No!'

—Larry Riccio

ONE DAY IN 1980, Donald escorted Henry Kissinger to Waldheim's study, where the Secretary-General was having his portrait painted. "The artist took a break, and Waldheim and Kissinger settled in over coffee and cookies, chatting rapid-fire in German. Before their conversation ended, they switched to English, and Waldheim confided in Kissinger he wanted to go back to Austria and run for President. And that's exactly what he did."

In the summer of that year, three years after taking the test to become an NYPD officer, Donald heard from the Department, which, because of the easing of the City's fiscal crisis, had resumed hiring. Donald considered leaving the U.N. "Everyone thought I was nuts. I had a secure job. I was in like Flynn, as the saying went."

Donald struggled with his decision, having to convince his mind of what his heart already knew. New York City was a sewer of crime, mob activity, street gangs, and drug lords, and cops were being killed at an alarming rate.[24] Finally, Donald gave notice he was resigning. "I thought to first speak with Waldheim, but I was too uncomfortable to do that." Instead, Donald followed the chain of command to obtain permission to meet with Trimble. Donald once again found himself standing at attention in Trimble's office until the Colonel smiled and said, "Stand easy, and have a seat."

Donald handed over his letter of resignation, but Trimble wouldn't accept it. "He urged me to stay, giving me a bunch of reasons. He asked me to at least wait a bit and think it over. I said I couldn't delay any further and that I had a burning desire to be a policeman. Being on the U.N. security force for the rest of my work life would be too limiting a career. He understood, wished me luck, and told me, if it didn't work out, he'd hire me back. I left his office and immediately went to clean out my locker."

In October 1980, Donald joined the 23,000-member NYPD, down from more than 30,000 in 1974. As with all cops, his service began with a six-month training program at the Police Academy, located in a drab building between Second and Third Avenues on East 20th

Chapter 5

Street in the swank Gramercy Park neighborhood.[25] The physical aspects of the program, including live-fire exercises, boxing matches, and conquering an obstacle course through running, climbing, and crawling at a fast pace, weren't difficult for Donald. And, given his military service, Donald already had an instinct for police work that normally took years to develop. "What I realized was that younger recruits were somewhat handicapped because the Academy relied more on lectures than on situational engagements. Some of them had never fired a gun before."

The arena Donald struggled with was academics. "We literally had dozens of pounds of books and a minimum of two hours of reading after classes. I found the hardest part to be understanding the penal law. What applies and what doesn't in each situation? What specific activity is required to charge a perpetrator? I ended up going for tutoring."

A noted guest lecturer at the Academy was Detective Edward Zigo, famous for having played an instrumental role in tracking down and arresting David Berkowitz in 1977 for the "Son of Sam" serial murders that had terrorized New York.[26] "Ed was a great guy," Donald recollected. "He was a detective's detective, looked up to by every cop. And he was quite a character, as were most of the detectives. His job was 24/7 for him. His mantra was never to leave a stone unturned or give up. His lectures about how to approach an investigation always were packed, with all of us hanging on every word."

After graduation from the Academy, Donald's first job was with a neighborhood stabilization unit attached to the 76th Precinct, known as "Brooklyn South." Neighborhood Stabilization Unit (NSU), which performed community policing, were largely staffed by rookies. A six-month assignment to an NSU was designed to ease Academy grads into police work by providing field training under the guidance of veterans.

One of Donald's trainers was Detective Jimmy Russo. "Russo," Donald explained, "was a master hostage negotiator known to be able to walk into any dangerous crowd and calm things down." Donald witnessed Russo's skills firsthand one Sunday evening after receiving a report that groups of men from the Satmar and Betz Hasidic sects, carrying rocks, bottles, and sticks, were facing off on a Williamsburg street, preparing to fight.[27] "Although it was out of our Precinct, Jimmy and I were the first policemen to arrive on the scene. We pulled our car up slowly. I was nervous, knowing that these guys could be quite violent.[28] The situation seemed like a powder keg. Jimmy told me to leave my nightstick in the car, not to put my hands anywhere near my gun or holster, and to follow his lead. We walked through a crowd in which everyone was wearing black coats, fedoras and fur caps, excusing ourselves constantly. Meanwhile, more people with angry expressions kept joining. When we got to the middle, where the leader of each sect stood, Jimmy put his arms out gently and asked politely if he could address them. He lowered his voice, forcing them to lean forward to

Chapter 5

hear him. Whatever he said, it was quite funny, because the two men started laughing hysterically. Then Jimmy started laughing. After some more conversation, he got the two men to order their people to back off. The crowd began dispersing just as literally dozens of police cars were arriving with sirens on and lights flashing."

One day, Donald and another rookie were assigned to a seasoned sergeant for live instruction on how to make a stop for a traffic violation. "Beforehand, the sergeant gave us the standard directions on what to do after we pulled a car over, like calling the stop in to the dispatcher, putting your hat on, getting out of your car slowly, keeping your eyes on the driver, asking for driver's license, registration, and insurance card, and explaining why you'd stopped them." But there was another piece of advice that stuck with Donald throughout his NYPD career. "He told us we have a basic choice in how we approach police work. We can enforce the law to its letter. Bang people with summonses left and right. Lock them up for small misdemeanors. Which will make the community hate you and all other cops. Or we can enforce the spirit of the law. Give the driver a chance to tell his story. First observe and evaluate, because people communicate more nonverbally than verbally. If he has a reasonable explanation, maybe give him the benefit of the doubt. You don't always have to write the summons. You have a lot of power and leeway as an officer."

On that day, the two rookie officers and the sergeant manned a police car on Ocean Parkway in Brighton

Rendered Safe

Beach, waiting to spot a traffic violator. "It was a beautiful morning," Donald recalled. "The neighborhood was predominantly Jewish, with lots of Orthodox women out pushing baby strollers. Suddenly, right in front of us, a dark Oldsmobile rolls through a stop sign onto the Parkway. The sergeant nods and says, 'Have at it.'"

Donald turned on the overhead lights, tapped his siren, and drove behind the Oldsmobile, which immediately pulled over. "We call in the stop, put our hats on, and walk toward the car. Halfway there, the driver door opens quickly and an old gentleman in a black suit and fedora jumps out. He yells, 'Officers, I'm the local rabbi. I'm on my way to see a very sick person.' I tell him to get back in his car, but instead he comes up to me. In the meantime, a crowd has gathered. The rabbi throws his arms up and shouts, 'Thank God you stopped me! I could have hit someone and killed him!' Then he leans close, puts his arms on my shoulders, and whispers, 'Give me a stern warning, but don't write the ticket.' I lost it, laughing so hard I was crying. The rabbi strode back to his car as the crowd applauded, and drove off. The sergeant, despite all his talk about enforcing the spirit of the law, was real pissed at me."

After months of duty in the NSU, Donald was deemed ready to "fly solo." His first day on the new job began with roll call. "I'm standing there, among older officers, in my brand-new uniform. My shoes are so new the leather squeaks when I walk. They're spit-shined so good that you need sunglasses when the light hits them. The sergeant,

Chapter 5

carrying a clipboard with all our names, is inspecting us. He gets to me, stops, and stares at my name tag. Then he scowls, and with a thick Irish brogue snarls, 'What the hell kind of name is Sadowy?' Before I can think of an answer, he steps back, puts on an evil grin, and says in a loud voice, 'Oh, Lord—we have us a Communist.' This brought on hysterical laughter from the other cops, who were expecting the newbie to be tormented."

As was the standard plight of rookies, Donald was assigned to foot patrol, with the seasoned officers taking the radio-car slots. Donald's beat was in the heart of Brighton Beach, known as "Little Odessa" owing to its large Russian émigré community. "On my first day on patrol, I'm happily walking my beat, smiling, tipping my hat at people, and waving to shop owners. Although I didn't get much response, because the Russians didn't trust cops, and I was the new kid on the block. But that was okay."

In preparation for foot patrol, and on the advice of a veteran cop, instead of using the nightstick the Department provided, Donald had bought one made of cocobolo [dense hardwood from Central America].[29] "It felt like a piece of iron. I'm showing off by twirling the stick backwards in front of a coffee shop whose name was written only in Cyrillic. Within seconds, I clocked myself right behind the ear. I fell sideways onto a plate glass window, which fortunately didn't break, before knocking over a corrugated garbage can and landing on my butt. My hat flew off my head, and my summons book shot out of my back pocket. I saw stars."

Two middle-aged Russian women, as wide as they were tall, came running over. "They helped me up and led me into their little shop, which had old furniture, balalaikas on the wall, fans hanging from a tin ceiling, wire tables and chairs, and a huge samovar on the wood counter. As I sat, other people picked up my nightstick, hat, and summons book. The women served me hot tea with honey in a fancy glass that sat on a beautiful silver holder, and offered me stuffed cabbage and pastries. After that day, everyone seemed to know who I was and would smile and wave at me. I asked Uncle Alex, who spoke fluent Russian, to teach me greetings, which I practiced." Also helping Donald's acceptance into the community was that "we were given no quotas for issuing summonses or tickets. We had a lot of discretion."

Months later, it was time for Donald and his fellow NSU colleagues to be assigned to a permanent post. "We stood in line, and the sergeant read out the precinct each guy would be going to. As expected, they all were in Brooklyn, as it was standard for your assignment out of the NSU to be in a precinct in the same borough. Most were what we called 'A-houses,' which were the areas with the highest levels of crime and danger. But when the sergeant came up to me, he yelled out, '17th Precinct.' That precinct covered midtown east in Manhattan and might have been the most prestigious one in the whole city. I said to the sergeant, 'This must be a typo.' He sneered at me and barked, 'Pack your gear, and report at 0700

Chapter 5

tomorrow!'" Donald surmised he had been transferred to that precinct because of his U.N. experience.

Much of Donald's time during his stint at the 17th Precinct was spent on routine foot patrol. One of the first Precinct officers Donald met was Greg Solis, also on his first permanent assignment. "One night," Solis recounted, "Donald and I were summoned to a fancy restaurant on the East Side because of a bomb threat. It was a common event in those days. Could happen simply because a diner didn't like his bill. We walk in, and an attractive young waitress comes over to us and asks, 'What's going on?' Without skipping a beat, Donald answers, 'I'm here to rescue you.' As if he was Luke Skywalker. Well, her eyes lit up. She gave Donald a big grin, took him by the hand, and led him into the kitchen. They were there for a while, with her stuffing him with food."

As a rookie, Donald often was tasked with manning a stationary post, known as a "fixer," which was a temporary booth situated outside a foreign embassy or other diplomatic mission. "In those days, fixers didn't have heat, air conditioning, or electricity. Nor were they leak-proof. And our uniforms weren't user-friendly. Standing for long hours on bad-weather days, you froze, sweated profusely, or stood in a puddle of water that made your feet feel like sponges."[30]

One night during which a monsoon rain joined forces with a fierce wind, Donald and another newbie drew the assignment of guarding the Turkish mission, across from the U.N. complex. (John Caliendo, who'd taught Donald the ropes when Donald joined U.N. security, later would quip, "Donald left the U.N. and ended up right across the street from it.") "We stood there drenched and shivering. A radio car pulled up, and the driver, taking pity on us, asked if he could bring us coffee. I said 'Sure, thanks.' The other guy said, 'Hey, could you get me a Twinkie and a Coke?' I got hot coffee. He got the nickname, 'Twinkie and a Coke.'"

During his first year in the 17th Precinct, Donald was taken under the wing of two senior patrol officers—Larry Riccio, whose broad, mustached, intense presence was labeled by Donald as "making him seem big-bear like"—and Jeff Matlin, who was a lookalike for a young Tom Selleck. "Jeff Matlin," Donald recalled, "particularly liked to make arrests. He was what we described as a 'collar man.'"

Matlin and Riccio taught Donald basic street tactics such as how to speak to people, to recognize who doesn't belong on the street, to quickly evaluate whether someone was a physical threat, to take charge of a tense situation and calm it, and to safely handle domestic disputes, violent homeless people, and armed criminals. "After some time," Donald explained, "I could look across the street at someone and know that he was 'dirty.' I also learned never to let my guard down and to always be assessing my surroundings. I got attacked a few times by guys who were well dressed, looked normal, and seemed to be interested only in asking me for directions. But they were

Chapter 5

psychos who wanted to fight a cop. Once, a nice-looking middle-aged woman suddenly jumped on my back and started grabbing my hair and clawing at my face."

When Donald and Larry Riccio were paired together, Donald often took on the "good cop" role. "In a situation involving a person who was highly agitated or distressed, Larry usually would let me take the lead. I'd be businesslike but adopt a soft and polite manner and try to maintain nonaggressive body language. I'd ask the person to settle down and tell him that I wanted to hear what he had to say. But if he wouldn't calm down after a couple of minutes, Larry would step forward like a grizzly bear and read the guy the riot act, telling him he was about to be handcuffed and arrested. That usually worked to change behavior. We labeled that as giving someone a 'two-minute warning.'

Donald learned to be as tough as the circumstances required. "No one I ever locked up during my career ever said, 'Okay officer, I'll go quietly. I got bit, sucker punched, kicked in the balls, spit on in the face, and knocked to the ground. A few times, while making a violent arrest, I got hurt enough to have to go to the hospital. But I also put some perps in the hospital. It went with the territory. I tried to never let it become personal, because then you risk losing your humanity and becoming a bitter person who paints people negatively with a broad brush."

Along with Matlin, Riccio grew fond of Donald. "He knew and respected the pecking order and how to approach seniors. He was always looking to learn, and he absorbed what he learned."

Senior cops enjoyed Donald's quirkiness. As told by Riccio, "He went through phases, the first being a crazy Russian immigrant. Donald would come into the precinct house in dingy clothes wearing a sable hat. He'd run up to one of us, drop to his knees, and in a heavy Russian accent beg for political asylum. He wouldn't stop until you burst out laughing." Other routines followed, including "Indiana Jones," with Donald wearing an outback fedora, bomber jacket, and khakis, and "Jack Lord," (of *Hawaii Five-O* TV fame) with Donald over-combing his hair and sporting a shoulder holster.

Irreverent humor among cops is the norm, and therapeutic. On one of Donald's birthdays, Riccio and Matlin gifted him two T-shirts. One read, "Help Me, I Can't Stop Talking," while the other announced "I'm Talking And I Can't Shut Up!" "I'd ride with him in the patrol car," Riccio remembered, "and he'd be telling me this long, never-ending story. Went on a loop from A to Z and back to A again. I'd sit there praying for a 911 call to come in so I could interrupt him."

One cold February night, Donald was riding with Riccio on the midnight-to-8 a.m. shift. "I always was at the wheel," Riccio explained, "because Donald drove like Mr. Magoo." (Mr. Magoo was a cartoon character, popular in the 1960s and 1970s, who constantly ended up in comical situations because of his extreme nearsightedness.) Donald was asleep in the passenger seat as

Chapter 5

the car approached a midtown bronze statue of a commuter. "I drive up, jam on the brakes, point frantically out the window at the statue, and yell, 'Donald, he's got a gun!' Donald wakes up startled and tries to draw his revolver from his swivel holster while opening the door. As he's struggling, I'm straining not to laugh. It took him a precious few seconds to figure out the guy wasn't real. Later, I bought him a poster of that statue."

Another time, the two were called to an apartment of an elderly woman who had died. "We come in," Riccio recalled, "and see she's sitting upright on a sofa in front of a TV that's on. It's as if she's still watching. I leave to report the death from my patrol-car radio. When I get back, Donald is sitting on the sofa next to the woman, with his head on her shoulder and sound asleep, as if he was her son. If I hadn't woken him, he would have slept like that until the morgue wagon arrived. I just wish we'd had cell phones with cameras back then."

One night, they received a call that the "Subway Slasher" had appeared on the platform at the East 51st and Lexington Avenue station. Because of gridlock on the street, Donald and Larry exited their car and ran for blocks, arriving at the scene at the same time as another officer, Curtis Whitehead. "The perp," Donald recounted, "a short, slight, black male, who had killed before, this time had wounded three people with a super sharp meat cleaver. There was pandemonium on the subway platform, but the three of us were able to surround him. It was a really tense situation. You could see his flared nostrils and menacing expression and body posture. His grip on his cleaver was tight. We all were within his kill zone, being only about fifteen feet from him, and he refused to drop his weapon.[31] It was one of the few times in my career that I thought I might have to kill someone, until Larry growled that if he didn't lay down the cleaver, he'd be shot dead. The perp stared into Larry's stone-cold eyes for a moment and then dropped the cleaver. I was feeling really good about the collar until the Duty Captain showed up and gave us all a command discipline for not having our hats on!"

NYPD officers (from left) Jeff Matlin, Larry Riccio, Donald, and Chuck Flynn on the night Donald was inducted into the NYPD Honor Legion

Chapter 5

NYPD Officers Curtis Whitehead, Larry Riccio, and Donald arrest the "Subway Slasher" in the summer of 1981

The U.N. complex dominates much of the 17th Precinct. "One time," Riccio recounted, "we were driving by the U.N. and Donald recognized a security guard he knew. 'Jaya,' he screams out. The guy acknowledges him, and the two start jabbering away in some foreign language. I had no idea if Donald really knew what he was saying. Happened all the time."

For the NYPD, dealing with the diplomatic community itself was not inherently unsafe but often was a headache. United Nations' property is deemed international territory belonging to the member states, to be administered by the U.N. NYPD officers cannot take action on U.N.

67

grounds unless invited in. The tension between the NYPD and U.N. security was heightened by the U.N. being an inward-looking institution with little active outreach to city government. On several occasions, Donald was asked to help negotiate an argument between U.N. and NYPD officers. Jeff Matlin was impressed that, "If there was a bomb scare at the U.N., their security force normally wouldn't let us in to investigate. But when Donald was with us, they'd wave us in happily. Even offer us coffee."

Much NYPD-U.N. conflict centered on parking tickets and driving violations accumulated by foreign diplomats, who used immunity to skirt fines and arrest. Determining the protections afforded by diplomatic privilege and immunity involves understanding an intricate status-based system. For example, ambassadors, envoys, and charges d'affaires, and their immediate family members enjoy complete personal inviolability, which means they may not be handcuffed, arrested, or detained, and neither their property, including vehicles, nor residences may be entered or searched. Diplomatic agents also receive complete immunity from the criminal jurisdiction of the host country's courts and, thus, cannot be prosecuted no matter how serious the offense unless their immunity is waived by their government.

But these considerations do not exempt diplomatic officers from the obligation to conform to national and local laws and regulations. While police officers are obliged, under international custom and treaty law, to recognize the immunity of an envoy, they need not

Chapter 5

ignore or condone the commission of crimes, and they are allowed to stop a mission member or dependent and issue a traffic citation for a moving violation. Because of his years with the U.N., Donald understood these legal intricacies. He also knew the identification required of a diplomat when pulled over for a traffic violation, including an ID card issued by the U.S. State Department or U.S. mission to the U.N., passport or visa, and driver's license.

One day, Donald and Riccio were in their patrol car when a Cadillac with the U.S. Department of State's distinctive diplomatic license plate pulled up next to them. Donald recognized the driver as a Third World country staff member who was a chauffeur for a diplomat. "He gave me a fuck-you grin and proceeded to run a couple of red lights. Larry shrugged, but I was livid, so we chased him down just before he got onto the FDR Drive. I asked to see all the required credentials, including his driver's license, registration, U.N. ID, mission ID, and his *laissez-passer* [travel document issued by the United Nations]. His grin turned into a look of alarm. I wrote him up for a half-dozen moving violations, taking a really long time to do so. That required him to go down to Motor Vehicles to keep his driver's license. I did this day after day, all around the U.N. Gradually, the word spread throughout the diplomatic community, and a lot of the bullshit stopped."

CHAPTER 6
Rolling Stone

We'd charge into a building like the cavalry, and they'd run like cockroaches.

—Donald Sadowy

FOR DONALD, LACK OF ability to be proactive, to expand his responsibilities, and to use his analytical skills led to restlessness. After two years in the 17th Precinct, he applied to join the NYPD's Street Crime Unit, a plainclothes anti-crime group tasked with the apprehension of armed felons. Its motto was, "We Own the Night." Working high-crime neighborhoods, the SCU officers often disguised themselves as potential mugging and robbery victims.[32]

"Getting an appointment to see the captain of the SCU," Donald explained, "was like trying to meet the Wizard of Oz. I finally succeeded. He was a crotchety guy who reviewed my monthly reports, saw I had a small number of arrests, and told me I didn't have enough activity. My delegate from the Patrolman's Benevolent Association, the rank-and-file union, who was with me, interceded, telling him I was on a fixed post most of the time with not a lot of opportunity to make arrests. But the captain just dismissed me."

Donald next applied to the NYPD's Emergency Service Unit. The ESU is one of a number of units within the Special Operations Division, which included the harbor patrol, aviation unit, mounted squadrons, and the Strategic Response Group, which responds to citywide mobilizations and civil disorders. ESU maintains what is known as the "House of Props," including heavy rescue trucks, generator trucks, motorized inflatable boats, jet skis, and forcible-entry equipment such as hydraulic rams. Often labeled as "the 911 for cops," the Unit responds to major, high-risk incidents such as dealing with lethal weapons or emotionally disturbed persons, jumpers from bridges and buildings, and air and sea rescues, and performs tactical and technical rescue duties for other departments such as the Hostage Negotiation Unit.[33] The ESU aids the Bomb Squad on suspicious-package calls, including evacuating the immediate area, setting up a command post from where Bomb Squad officers can enter the "hot zone" quickly and safely, and assisting those officers into and out of their bomb suits. The ESU also maintains a canine unit that helps with searches for perpetrators and missing persons.

Donald heard of the ESU's great reputation in the Department. "The ESU guys are supermen. They learn

Chapter 6

how to climb ropes, jump out of helicopters, and scuba dive to rescue people, tranquilize dogs and other animals, qualify to use all types of special weapons, act as snipers, provide emergency medical treatment, pick locks, lift subway cars, and dozens of other skills. I wanted the assignment so badly that in my interview with a panel of ESU bosses, I stammered and stuttered, and my mind went blank. Even though they were very nice, I psyched myself out."

Ever the rolling stone, Donald persisted in finding more stimulating employment, gaining an interview with the Tactical Police Force unit, an elite mobile unit used to respond to riots or protests and to augment precincts during flare-ups in the crime rate.[34] They were considered the shock troops of the NYPD. "Those were the big, burly guys," Donald described, "who would flood an area on the verge of riot or overwhelming criminal activity and kick ass and take names. But my luck ran out, or so I thought, because right after I applied, Ben Ward, who had become the first black police commissioner, disbanded the unit for being anti-minority."[35]

Opportunity arose when leading members of the Manhattan business community, fed up with conditions in the Lower East Side, met with Mayor Ed Koch and Commissioner Ward to urge them to clean up the district. "In the early 1980s," Donald explained, "the Lower East Side and Alphabet City, next to it, were the most dangerous neighborhoods in the city. Their housing projects were filled with heroin addicts, drug dealers, and drunks.

73

Rendered Safe

People would openly line up on sidewalks and outside buildings to buy drugs. Any green space was overrun with garbage. Rats roamed freely. Robberies would happen in broad daylight in a crowd. Even a Mulberry Street mafia capo was robbed at gunpoint. The only reasons to go there were Yonah Schimmel's Knish Bakery and Katz's Deli, but you were taking a risk doing so."

Koch was persuaded, and in January 1984, the NYPD launched Operation Pressure Point, a major offensive to eradicate the open-air drug markets on the Lower East Side and "retake the streets." The vicinity was saturated with uniformed officers assigned to patrol, in marked and unmarked police vehicles, and in multiple-passenger police vans. This coverage was supplemented by mounted patrols and drug-sniffing dogs. Other agencies, such as the Housing Police and the Drug Enforcement Administration's Joint Narcotics Task Force, also participated in the undertaking.

Ward reluctantly reached out to former TPF unit staff to bolster the existing Manhattan South Task Force. "They had saved a lot of the applications for the TPF, including mine, and I was asked if I still was interested. The next day, I reported for duty with the task force. It took months, but we finally cleaned up the area and took it back from the bad guys. We used helicopters, spotters on roofs, and paddy wagons. We cuffed everyone we could grab and searched for drugs and weapons. We made so many arrests they had to set up a special booking station

Chapter 6

in the 7th Precinct for several months. Nobody acted with malice, and we made sure to do everything by the book, but Al Sharpton and the ACLU still accused us of brutality." The TPF did take its lumps. "Several cops were seriously hurt. Some shot, some stabbed. One kid was hit with a cinderblock thrown from the top of an abandoned building near the Williamsburg Bridge."

By the end of the year, more than 11,000 arrests had been made in the target area, property valued at more than $3,000,000 was seized, and 45,000 summonses were issued. Lower East Side residents reported feeling more secure and less fearful, attendance at religious services increased, drug overdoses at a local medical center decreased, mothers brought their children back onto the streets, and the level of overall serious crime dropped dramatically.

Once the Lower East Side was cleaned up, Donald was forced to seek out another job. "On some of our TPF assignments, we had been joined by older guys from the Bomb Squad, who trained us on all types of booby traps and improvised explosives. They carried themselves differently. They looked like military men in civilian clothes. On a break, I talked to one of them and told him I was interested in being on the Squad. He looked at my baby face, laughed, and said, 'They won't take you. You don't have enough time on the job. Don't embarrass yourself.'"

Donald applied anyway. "On one of my off days, I showed up at the Bomb Squad headquarters on the second floor of the 6th Precinct building on West 10th Street in Greenwich Village. It was a suite of shabby rooms behind a plain beige steel door, with ceiling tiles hanging out, paint peeling, and old military furniture that looked pre-World War II.[36] I told a couple of guys, who turned out to be ex-Marines, I was there to speak about joining the Squad. After some strange looks, they invited me into a back room. We talked for quite a while over coffee, which they boasted was the best in the city although I wouldn't know because I drink tea. They liked my Marine background, but it seemed I'd hit a dead end until a week later, when I got called back to interview with Charles Wells."

Members of the Manhattan South Task Force in 1984. From left, Teddy Sampson, Larry O'Leary, Sammy Bomilie, Brian Kennedy, Tommy Lowe, Kevin Jones, Donald, Sergeant Leonard, Kevin Doherty, Sergeant Abrams, Mike Guedes, Ed Fallon, Lee Reeves.

Chapter 6

Entrance to the NYPD Bomb Squad offices

Board with photo and name of every NYPD Bomb Squad member since 1903

Rendered Safe

Board with photo and name of each of the six Bomb Squad members killed in the line of duty

Wells, born in the Bronx and raised in Staten Island, at the time was a sergeant in the Squad and a participant

Chapter 6

in the unit's recruitment process. He had served for thirteen months in the late 1960s in Vietnam as a Marine Corps engineer, demolition specialist, and mine sweeper. During those months, Wells also acted as a "tunnel rat," one of the men who, when an enemy tunnel was discovered, would crawl in to surveil and potentially plant explosives to destroy it. (Entering those tunnels was extraordinarily perilous, as North Vietnamese and Viet Cong soldiers, booby traps, venomous snakes and insects, and poison gas potentially lay in wait.) During his service on the Squad from 1972 to 1985, Wells personally disarmed more than 100 bombs. "Wells was quiet and low key," Donald recalled, "but I knew he was a living legend among the NYPD rank-and-file. He reviewed my background, and I could tell he liked my Marine service. Charlie told me the Bomb Squad was shorthanded and encouraged me to formally apply."

Only one slot was available, and Donald was up against two more-experienced policemen. "I got lucky," Donald admitted. "One of them passed the physical test but failed the psychological one. The other passed both tests but changed his mind about joining the Bomb Squad when his wife objected. Kathy was not too pleased, either. We talked about it for a long time. I told her about the Squad's reputation for safety and having far fewer fatalities than street cops. And I explained I'd rather deal with inanimate objects than unpredictable people. I finally won her over."

Kathy's remembrance is different. "Donald came home to our house in Queens Village, which we had just bought, and asked, 'What do you think about me joining the Bomb Squad?' I said, 'Are you crazy? Absolutely not!' He stared at me and said, 'Too late. I'm in.'"

One day, at morning roll call, Donald's boss, an Ernest Borgnine double of Russian origin, instructed Donald to remove his collar brass. "He tells me that, as of noon, I don't work for him anymore. I thought it was a practical joke, and remained standing waiting for orders, expecting to be assigned to cover a demonstration at Dag Hammarskjold Plaza scheduled for that day. So, he tells me to go to a pay phone and call the Wheel [the duty desk]. I did, and was ordered to report the next day to the Medical Unit at the Police Academy for an assessment of Bomb Squad fitness."

The Academy's Medical Unit was a dreary place whose walls were coated by chipped olive-green paint and floors covered with battleship-gray, heavy metal desks from the World War II era. "There were no windows, and the lights came down from the ceiling like pendants, which cast an eerie glow. It was a scene out of a 1930s black-and-white horror movie." Donald was run through a physical evaluation. "Afterward, I was seated on a stool next to two serious-looking, elderly shrinks behind desks who were holding clipboards. They asked me my name. I gave it and then, trying to lighten the mood, twitched my head, assumed my best Peter Sellers impression, and said, 'You're expecting maybe Inspector Dreyfus?' They each responded with a deadpan stare, and I thought, 'Holy shit, I've blown it again.' But I saw

Chapter 6

one of them write on his clipboard, 'Sense of humor.' I relaxed and sat calmly as they took me through a series of pictures I had to interpret, followed by questions that seemed to go on forever."

In February 1985, Donald officially became a member of the NYPD Bomb Squad. "I was overwhelmed with that achievement. Me, a grandson of immigrants who grew up poor, shy, and frightened of everything, was now a New York City bomb technician. I could have won gold at the Olympics and not have been prouder." In the fullest chapter of his professional life, Donald would spend a decade and a half with the Bomb Squad, years that would place him in the eye of the storm.

CHAPTER 7
Courage and Suffering

On New Year's Eve 1982, I was manning a fixed post in front of the U.S. mission on First Avenue and 45th Street. That night was brutally cold. As I stood with the wind cutting through me like a knife, I heard the bombs go off in the distance.

—Donald Sadowy

TODAY, NEARLY EVERY moderately sized city hosts a Hazardous Devices Team. The NYPD Bomb Squad, the country's first, originated at the turn of the 20th century. It was a time when the nation was terrorized by *La Mano Nera* ("the Black Hand"), an Italian-American crime syndicate engaged in various forms of extortion, using murder, kidnapping, and other means. A forerunner of the Mafia, the Black Hand arose in Italian neighborhoods in New York City and spread to various segments of society throughout the nation, threatening thousands. Its blackmail typically would begin with the delivery of a letter containing sketches in black ink of a hand, skull, and crossbones. A "tribute" would be demanded, under threat of mutilation or death. If the letter's ultimatum wasn't met, the next delivery might be a bomb thrown into the target's house or business. No one was exempt, even the famous, such as the tenor Enrico Caruso, who paid protection money.

In September 1904, NYPD Commissioner William McAdoo asked Officer Giuseppe (Joseph) Petrosino, who headed the Department's Homicide Division, to form and lead a separate team to address the problem. Petrosino was a stout, powerfully built man born in Padula, a village in southern Italy. Known as the "Italian Sherlock Holmes," he was the first Italian police detective in the nation. By 1908, Petrosino's team, initially composed of only five officers and dubbed the "Italian Squad," had apprehended several members of the Black Hand, including its chief bomb-maker. Petrosino continued his assignment with intensity and success until March 1909, when his inquiry into the criminal background of New York mobsters led him on an undercover mission to Palermo, Sicily, where he was shot to death in Piazza Marina, the town square.

Five years after Petrosino's death, a formal NYPD Bomb Squad was established in place of the Italian Squad. In March 1915, a 25-year-old Squad detective, Emilio Polignani, went undercover to infiltrate Italian-American anarchist circles and thwart an attack on St. Patrick's Cathedral. When the U.S. entered WWI in April 1917,

Chapter 7

the Squad assisted the War Department in countering German espionage efforts. After the war, the Squad's focus shifted to addressing labor unrest, radicals, and racketeers.

Of course, not all attacks were prevented. On September 16, 1920, shortly before noon, a single-top, horse-drawn wagon containing one hundred pounds of dynamite with five hundred pounds of cast-iron slugs exploded on Wall Street across from the Morgan & Co. building, which housed the world's most important banking firm. Dozens were killed and more than a hundred wounded, a horrific crime (and the deadliest terrorist attack in American history until the 1995 Oklahoma City bombing) whose perpetrators were never brought to justice.

While most law-enforcement jobs are inherently dangerous, bomb-technician work carries unique risk. The Squad's guidelines for bomb disposal, which became the national standard, warn, "The history of bomb disposal is scarred by injury and death." Each member of the Bomb Squad must have complete trust and confidence in his fellow bomb technicians.

On July 4, 1940, during the first New York City World's Fair in Flushing Meadow, an electrician working in the British Pavilion heard a ticking sound coming from a stray canvas bag and alerted police. The bag was carried to a service road at the perimeter of the Fairgrounds, where detectives from the Bomb Squad cut a strip off the bag and peered inside to spot numerous sticks of dynamite. Seconds later, the device exploded, releasing a pulverizing amount of heat and gas. Given that it was July 4, those who heard the explosion assumed it arose from fireworks. Two of the detectives, John Lynch and Ferdinand Socha, were killed instantly, the first Squad officers to die in service since Petrosino, and a third seriously injured. That murderous act was never solved, nor the motives behind it conclusively determined, although there was speculation it had been planted by the Irish Republican Army. The tragedy led to deployment of the Squad's first bomb-disposal truck, designed by the Squad commander, James Pyke, the separation of the Bomb Squad from the Forgery Unit, which had been an odd combination, and the establishment of a formal training requirement for all Squad members.

Later the same year, an ex-Marine and electrician named George Metesky, later known as the "Mad Bomber," began planting dozens of pipe bombs in phone booths, lockers, lavatories, and under seats in public spaces such as Grand Central Station, Macy's, the Port Authority Bus Terminal, Radio City Hall, and the Paramount Theater, causing numerous injuries and terrorizing city residents. The decade-and-a-half manhunt for the Mad Bomber, who took time off during World War II because he believed setting off bombs during the war wasn't patriotic, eventually was spearheaded by a newly formed Bomb Investigation Unit that would swell to 76 members and work exclusively on the Mad Bomber case. In January 1957, police arrested Metesky at his home in Waterbury, Connecticut, with his capture

Chapter 7

having been aided by the open correspondence Metesky established with the *New York Journal-American*.[37]

A new Bomb Investigation Unit technique was the construction of a psychiatric criminal profile of a suspect's physical, personality, and character traits. That method was widespread in crime literature, with the most famous example being Sherlock Holmes, who had the habit of profiling each person he met, even with the scantest of clues. But this practice hadn't before been rigorously put into play in the United States, and many Bomb Squad detectives, used to working cases based on hard forensic evidence and logic, were particularly skeptical of the approach.

In 1960, a man dubbed the "Sunday Bomber" struck New York City public spaces multiple times, killing one and injuring dozens more before disappearing, never to be positively identified. Later in that decade, and more so in the 1970s, New York City became a battleground for various militant groups purportedly advocating racial justice, national independence, ethnic pride, or revolution, including the Black Liberation Army, Fuerzas Armadas de Liberación Nacional (aka, "FALN," a Puerto Rican nationalist group), Fighters for a Free Croatia, Omega 7, and Weather Underground. There was a significant increase in explosive events, with bombs at times being detonated throughout the city seemingly as fast as bomb technicians could be dispatched to deal with them.

Yet the Bomb Squad maintained a notable safety record until September 11, 1976, exactly twenty-five years before 9/11. On that day, a bomb seated in a metal pot was left in a 25-cent luggage-locker at Grand Central Terminal by two Croatian nationalists before they hijacked a TWA jet after takeoff from LaGuardia Airport.[38] Four Squad officers removed the device and brought it to the Squad's detonation facility at Rodman's Neck, a desolate peninsula of land in the Bronx near Orchard Beach and City Island that juts out into Long Island Sound. Crouching behind a wall of sandbags, one of the officers attempted to defuse the bomb using an experimental device designed to cut wires remotely. When that failed, they left their protective cover and approached the device. Suddenly, the bomb's safety mechanism shorted out and it exploded, killing Brian Murray, a married 27-year-old with two young sons. The other three officers were wounded with one, Sergeant Terence McTigue, being disfigured and partially blinded.

Murray, recruited into the Squad in September 1972, had been trained as a bomb technician in the Air Force and worked with munitions during his service in the Vietnam War. "It was a natural segue for Brian," recalled his wife, Kathleen. "Bomb Squad work was something Brian knew he was qualified for and something very few others could do. It was a skill set that elevated his position from his first assignment, directing traffic."[39]

One noteworthy change made as the result of Brian Murray's death involved the official status of Squad officers. "At the time," Kathleen Murray explained, "the Bomb Squad was outside the purview of the Detective Division.

Chapter 7

Brian was never promoted to detective, although he clearly performed as one. This oversight did much to bring down morale in the Squad. After Brian's death, promotion to detective was given to all Squad members. It took the life of an officer to light a fire under the city administration."

By the early 1980s, the level of radical activity in the city had lessened, with two notable exceptions.[40] One occurred on the morning of March 17, 1981, when two Bomb Squad detectives—Kenneth Dudonis and James O'Connor—responded to a report of a suspicious ticking package in a cardboard box lying in front of the Bleecker Street headquarters of the Youth International Party (aka, the "Yippies"), a radical, countercultural group known for its theatrical pranks such as throwing fistfuls of real and fake dollars from the balcony of the New York Stock Exchange's visitors' gallery down to the traders below. While the detectives were examining the package, which contained a pipe bomb filled with sodium chlorate and sugar, it exploded, seriously burning the detectives' faces and arms and putting them out of active duty. After that incident, the Squad members were provided with flame-resistant jumpsuits made of Kevlar with ceramic inserts and lined with a fire-resistant material. "You'd put them on starting with the thick army-green pants," Donald explained. "Shoes next, then the bulky green jackets, which extended from the back of your head to your thighs. Only your hands were exposed."

On New Year's Eve 1982, an evening during which the core of the NYPD was patrolling in and around Times

Square, four powerful explosives planted by the FALN detonated in lower Manhattan and Brooklyn at separate law-enforcement targets during a span of ninety minutes.

A thirty-three-year-old uniformed NYPD officer named Rocco Pascarella was first to be injured. While conducting a security sweep of the rectangular police headquarters building at One Police Plaza on Park Row, near City Hall and the Brooklyn Bridge, Pascarella noticed among the trash littering the ground a soiled paper bag filled with newspaper and a Kentucky Fried Chicken container. (A saying in the Bomb Squad is that half the job is "figuring out what's inside the container.") As Pascarella moved closer to investigate, his foot accidentally brushed against the box, triggering detonation of a bomb because it was "hang fire," with its timer having run down to zero but momentarily jammed so any vibration or movement could complete the circuit and set it off.

Pascarella was found dragging himself on his elbows among shards of glass by two Squad detectives—Anthony Senft, thirty-six and a ten-year veteran, and Richard Pastorella, forty-two and a fifteen-year member of the police force, and their German shepherd, Hi-Hat, trained in explosives detection. Pascarella was placed on a gurney by medics, who were frantically trying to prevent him from hemorrhaging and bleeding out. In spite of his pain and shock, the courageous Pascarella insisted he not be taken to the ambulance until he could tell the Bomb Squad detectives what had happened to him.

Chapter 7

An hour later, while lifting the blanket that had been placed on a suspicious package partially wrapped in newspaper lying against a building column in St. Andrew's Plaza, which houses the Manhattan federal courts and the offices of the U.S. Attorney, Senft and Pastorella each was blown fifteen feet into the air when the bomb inside exploded. Pastorella later testified before a Senate Committee investigating the clemencies granted by Bill Clinton to a dozen FALN members that "I lost all of the fingers on my right hand, the sight of both eyes, and seventy percent of my hearing. I had to endure thirteen major reconstructive surgery operations on my face and my hand. I have twenty-two titanium screws holding my face together. I have shrapnel from that device embedded in my stomach, my shoulders, and my head."

Senft's injuries also were horrific. "On that day, I received a lifelong sentence without the opportunity for parole. My sentence includes five reconstructive operations on my face, the loss of all my sight in my right eye, sixty percent hearing loss in both ears, a broken nose, a fractured hip, and severe vertigo. My eardrums burst, and I had to keep putting cotton and Vaseline in my ears to allow water to go down. And I also had a brain injury that was like getting a hundred concussions at one time."

As a result of the New Year's Eve tragedy, and after Mayor Koch became visibly distraught after visiting the three officers in Bellevue Hospital, the city administration provided the Squad with substantially more money for training and modernized equipment. One enhancement was fitting each bomb helmet with a blower assembly that would pump in air so the face mask would defog. The Squad also replaced their bomb-disposal trucks, which dated back to the 1940s and held IEDs [improvised explosive devices] within a wire meshing,[41] with ones that featured a diving bell-style thick steel drum. Resembling a small cement mixer, the containment chamber was made to buckle out during an explosion and confine it, with vents allowing pressure to escape while containing shrapnel.

The 1976, 1981, and 1982 incidents collectively put half the Squad members on the sidelines, and rendered many in the NYPD unwilling to volunteer to join the Bomb Squad, leading to it being shorthanded. As is often the case, from the suffering of a few, unique opportunity was provided to others.

CHAPTER 8
False Start

What happens in the office is bullshit. What happens on the street is real. The most important thing is signing out and going home in one piece.

—George Murphy, NYPD Bomb Squad

BY 1984, THE BOMB SQUAD was part of the Detective Bureau's Forensic Investigative Division, which contains a police lab, latent-print section, firearms-analysis section, and crime-scene unit. For Donald, being a Squad member made an immediate impact. "Instead of a uniform, I wore a suit and tie with a pin on my lapel that was half light blue and half white with a bomb pointed down and a lightning bolt, which was our logo at the time. And all of a sudden, I was required to be present at many prominent public events."

Donald found the Squad, which at the time was down to sixteen members split into teams of two or three, to be surprisingly cliquish. "Half the guys were Vietnam vets. Some of those were Bronze Star and Purple Heart winners. Others had been Marine Corps combat engineers. The other half had come from the Emergency Services Unit. Those 'E-men' didn't want me on the Squad, believing I hadn't put in enough time in the NYPD. They made me feel like the odd man out. For the most part, we wore street clothes rather than our dress uniforms. One of the E-men openly criticized my attire and told me to get a new wardrobe. 'Don't embarrass yourself or us,' he growled. So, I took out my credit card, went to Macy's, and bought a bunch of new suits and outfits."

While Donald waited to receive formal explosive-devices training, he was assigned to a team headed by two experienced detectives. "Those detectives made clear they didn't want me. On the first day, neither even showed me how to sign in. Even little things like my drinking tea instead of coffee would have them rolling their eyes. I'd come to work feeling crappy and thinking, 'What did I get myself into?' One of them told me to my face he didn't want to train me, but he had no choice."

Donald found support among fellow military vets. One was George Murphy, a senior bomb tech and the first person to welcome Donald. "George was a fearless, knowledgeable, skilled tech. He'd been an Army pathfinder in Vietnam. One of those guys dropped into place to set up and operate pickup zones and helicopter landing-and-evacuation sites. Incredibly dangerous work, and he was wounded several times."[42] One day, George

Chapter 8

pulled Donald aside. "'Ignore those assholes,' he told me. 'Focus on learning.'"

Also supportive and inclusive was Charlie Wells. During Donald's first year on the Squad, Wells invited Donald to join him and a half-dozen others at a meeting of the FBI's Marine Corp Association. The widely attended event was held each year on or near November 10, the date in 1775 on which the Marines Corps was established by decree of the Second Continental Congress. Ex-Marine Squad members who worked closely with the FBI became regular participants. That year, the reunion was held at Camp Smith, a military installation operated by the New York Army National Guard in Cortlandt Manor near Peekskill, 30 miles north of New York City. One of those who frequently attended was baseball great Ted Williams, an ex-Marine pilot who served in both World War II and the Korean War. Williams particularly enjoyed hanging out with the Bomb Squad members, so much so that each year they would bring him a Squad hat and include him in their group picture.

Soon after Wells, Donald, and the other Squad members arrived at Camp Smith, they spotted Williams. "I said to the guys," Wells remembered, "'let's go over and say hi to Ted.' Donald immediately turns to me and says, 'Ted who?' 'Ted Williams,' I reply. And Donald goes, 'Who's Ted Williams?'" Well, we began busting his balls and never let up, accusing him of being a Russian spy who didn't grow up in the U.S. Of course, his nickname became 'Ted.'"

Rendered Safe

Three months later, Wells was on night duty when a bomb exploded at the office of the Patrolman's Benevolent Association in lower Manhattan, planted by a group calling itself the "Red Guerrilla Defense" in protest of the union's support of officers indicted in the deaths of African-Americans. Wells called Donald's house to ask him to join the investigation. Kathy answered the phone. "I'm doing a thousand things at once," Wells recounted, "and when she picked up, I forget to identify myself. I just blurted out, 'Can I speak to Ted?' She goes, 'There's nobody here named Ted.' Then I hear Donald yelling in the background, 'No, wait, that's me.' I can only imagine what Kathy thought."

As a new member of the Squad, Donald's responsibilities centered on caring for its canines, which were

Donald and Ted Williams at Camp Smith in 1984

Chapter 8

From left, William H. Webster (FBI Director), Paul X. Kelley (Commandant of the Marine Corps), and Donald at Camp Smith circa 1986

kept in Rodman's Neck. The location of a Navy base post during World War II, Rodman's Neck since 1959 has housed NYPD helicopters and boats, a firing range with more than 150 shooting lanes, and a firearms training and tactics facility. The Bomb Squad has its own fenced-in compound within the Rodman's Neck complex containing administrative and classroom buildings, iron vaults to store explosives and IED evidence, and kennels, as well as a detonation section known as "The Pit."[43]

Methods used by the Bomb Squad to detect, handle, and render safe explosive devices have evolved over the decades. Examples of older approaches were suspending the device in a vat of motor oil to clog the moving parts of the timing mechanism and the use of gripping mechanisms attached to long poles. In the 1930s, X-rays began being used to examine suspicious packages.

Bomb-sniffing dogs were introduced in 1971. A dog is an ideal explosive detector. Its nose extends from the nostrils to the back of its throat, giving it an olfactory area and receptor cells many times greater than a human's. Also, compared to a human, much more of its brain is assigned to smell-related operations, and its breathing and sniffing functions aren't mixed. Rather, when air enters a dog's nose, it splits into two separate paths—one for breathing and one for smelling. And when it exhales, the air exits through a series of slits on the sides of its nose, meaning that exhaled air doesn't disturb the dog's ability to analyze incoming odors. "Strictly speaking," Donald clarified, "the dog doesn't smell the bomb. It's trained to smell certain vapors, such as dynamite, black and smokeless powder, or TNT, and then sit down and not touch the item."

Labrador Retrievers are often the dog of choice for bomb techs, not because that breed is superior at sniffing but because of their trainability and work ethic. "Newbies like me," Donald recalled, "often had to go through the 'dog shit' program. [The dogs were referred to as "shit machines."] It's a lot more than just putting a dog on a leash. I'd inspect and walk the Labs, clean and hose down their kennels, feed them, and sweep up their poop. As a handler, you have to watch and understand each dog

Chapter 8

and its behavior. How he's doing, and how he's gonna try to fool you to get what he wants. It often was tedious work, but I came to love and respect those dogs. A few were legends, and all were pretty smart and knew the routine. When to work, play, poop, or nap. They taught me the ropes. And, on some days, they seemed like my only friends."

CHAPTER 9
Redstone

A saying in the Bomb Squad was that you're a "grunt" until you come back from Redstone.

—Donald Sadowy

IN THE NEVER-ENDING chess match between bomb-maker/planter and bomb tech, training for the latter is critical. After several months on the Squad, a slot opened up for Donald at the Hazardous Devices School in the Redstone Arsenal in Huntsville, in northern Alabama near the Tennessee border. During World War II, Redstone had been a chemical weapons manufacturing complex. Post-war, it became home to former Nazi German rocket scientists who were brought to the U.S. One was Wernher von Braun, considered the "father of American rocket technology and space science." (Von Braun also was the "father" of the infamous V-2 rocket program that killed thousands of military and civilian personnel during the last year of WWII and, thus, a highly controversial historical figure.) His Redstone design group, which developed the first large American ballistic missile, would be merged in the late 1950s into the newly created National Aeronautics Space Administration.

By 1971, Redstone was a focal point for IED training and certification, which teaches identification of explosive devices and neutralization strategies.[44] A sprawling 455-acre campus run jointly by the FBI and the U.S. Army, it now contains classrooms, explosive ranges, and mock villages complete with a train station, apartment complexes, a movie theater, and a strip mall. Among its many resources are teams of chemists who study the residue of an explosion to determine its source.

The four-week training program was a combination of rigorous lab, classroom, and field programs that Donald would repeat every three years for recertification. "We lived and trained in Quonset huts that dated back to the 1950s, with only fans to cool you off. Once at Redstone, I realized I knew so little about my chosen field of work. The instructors were great and taught us bomb-making literally from scratch. The physics and chemistry of it. How electricity works. All the ways of building, defusing, and disposing of explosives and triggering devices. How to properly use X-ray gear, including figuring out how to best set the pulses based on the depth of the container. The different ways in which a bomb might be disguised or detonated. I was overwhelmed at first. Yet I loved every day. The worst

Chapter 9

part was putting on heavy protective suits and walking around under the hot Alabama sun."

As Donald recalled, "Redstone didn't tolerate any cowboys, like guys who would say, 'Heck, I'll just cut that wire.' The instructors wanted us cutting a wire only when you know where that wire comes from and leads to. To gather information quickly such as how the package was found and called in. To use other bomb techs at the scene as an extra set of eyes and as a second opinion. And to think steps ahead. For example, to understand a small bomb may be openly planted to draw attention away from a bigger bomb nearby."

Donald especially valued the field training, where simulated threats taken from real-life circumstances would be presented. "They'd put you in a bomb suit with a partner, send you into a building where there was an IED, and drill us on how to best handle the problem. Disable the IED in place? Remove it? Which method? The worst thing was when a buzzer went off or a light flashed, meaning the IED had exploded. Also, the instructors routinely introduced problems. The portable X-ray machine broke. Your dog got sick. You lost your hand-entry kit. The IED is being held by a suicide bomber in a public space. There's a hostage. Other police- and fire-department personnel are on the scene, and you need to coordinate with them. All of this would get your adrenaline up right at the time when you needed to calm down, use a logic tree, and maybe think out of the box.

Later, back in the classroom, the team members would stand up and review what they did and why. Better to make your mistakes in school."

All of the nation's non-military bomb techs go through this program. "After Redstone, I could call fellow bomb techs from around the country who'd trained with me, and they'd tell me whatever I wanted to know about an IED situation that happened in their area."

Redstone also welcomed bomb techs from friendly countries, and Donald trained with Australians, Brits, Canadians, Germans, Israelis, New Zealanders, and others, all united by a common passion. "We talked together about anything new that had developed around the world. Techs would present on emerging methods of subterfuge, different types of explosives and deployment, and which bad guys were active where." While shooting the breeze, the techs would share practical tips, such as what tools they kept in their hand-entry kits, which were personalized to individual preferences. Donald's kit, which was the size of a shaving kit, evolved to contain medical scalpels with different blades, plastic knitting needles, tongue depressors, wire cutters, a Sheetrock knife, a K-bar knife, and other tools. For Donald, "the kit was more important than a firearm."

Donald was particularly impressed by the British and Israeli bomb techs' ability to deal with IED situations of all types. "Only the Brits [because of the violence in Northern Ireland at the time] and Israelis matched the NYPD Bomb Squad in level of activity. A British bomb tech was colloquially known as a "Felix," in reference to the cat with nine lives. Redstone was based on the Felix School in England. Some Felixes were reluctant to cooperate with the NYPD because there were so many Irish Catholics on the force. The Israelis were more forthcoming. Plus, there was this emotional component to their work that was hard to describe, but evident. It wasn't just about public safety. It was about survival."

CHAPTER 10
Richie & Tony

Richie's maimed hands felt my face. It rocked me to my core.

—Donald Sadowy

AFTER DONALD RETURNED from Redstone, he received a negative evaluation from his sergeant, who recommended Donald be removed from the Squad. "It might have been the kiss of death for me," Donald explained, "but Charlie Wells and another sergeant, Joe Ahearn, who also always looked out for me, interceded with the Commander, Lieutenant Bill McCarthy. McCarthy assigned me to another team for reevaluation. With the second team, led by Jack Kelly, Detective First Grade and the most senior man on the Squad, I did well. Kelly never seemed to smile, although he had a dry sense of humor. They gave him the nickname 'Chuckles.' He had a big sweet tooth, so the guys would tape empty candy wrappers to his locker door."

Rendered Safe

Also on Donald's new team was Detective Pete Dalton, who had joined the Squad two years prior. Dalton, born and raised in Flushing, Queens, had police work in his DNA. "My grandfather, an uncle, and others in my extended family had been in law enforcement. It was a family tradition. I saw that Donald was a very energetic guy, and I told him to calm down and keep his mouth shut and eyes open. Analyze before taking any action. Never guess. Donald was a good guy who had gotten a bad rap." Donald credits Kelly and Dalton with teaching him "how to diagnose and disarm bombs and hoax devices, investigate and determine facts, write up reports, put a case together, and testify in court. And, even more importantly, they taught me the inner workings of the Detective Bureau and how to survive, including dealing with all the egos."

Donald's circle of friends grew. One was Dan McNally, who had been an Engineer Platoon Leader in the Army National Guard before joining the NYPD and later transferring into the Bomb Squad. "Donald always was trying to make the Squad a little nicer. He would often volunteer to cook, and I'd consider myself lucky to be on duty when he did."

Donald's Redstone experience had him chomping at the bit to handle IED calls. But he remained an apprentice. "In the Squad, they won't let you suit up or handle devices on your own for at least eighteen months to two years, until they feel you're up to the task. As the saying goes, 'You know just enough to hurt yourself.' During

Chapter 10

that time, your head is spinning from all there is to learn, including who is who in the Squad. I was taught how to gas up the response vehicles, check the equipment on them, maintain the robots and bomb suits, set the X-ray pulse level based on the type of density of the container material, develop and interpret the resulting film, including understanding what are the power sources, switches, detonators, and explosives, handle all the paperwork, and dress and undress the person who is putting on the bomb suit. Mostly, you stand back, observe, and try to keep out of people's way."

Donald learned constantly during the probationary period. "When the team would be called to a possible IED, together we'd visually examine and X-ray the device, and then analyze the situation until we invariably came up with the right solution. Everyone had input. For example, one vital tip I received was, if circumstances allowed, you should let the IED 'cook' for an hour because, in those pre-wireless technology days, most homemade explosives used a 60-minutes kitchen timer."

One afternoon on the Upper West Side, Donald was on a job with two other Squad members—Don Hurley and John Santos. "There was a suspicious package on the steps of a brownstone," Hurley recalled, "which turned out to be nothing. John was suited up and examining the package while Donald and I watched nearby. We thought we'd cleared the building but, all of a sudden, a little, frail lady who looked like she was in her nineties, wearing pajamas and a robe, meanders down the steps and stands next to John. Donald and I started running toward her screaming, 'Get back!' We didn't realize that she was stone-deaf. And John couldn't hear us because he was wearing a bomb helmet. Finally, he looks up and sees the woman. The sight of her startled this big, burly Squad guy as she calmly asked him, 'What are you doing, Sonny?' I picked her up as gently as I could and ran down the block to hand her off to waiting EMTs."

As his apprenticeship period was ending, Donald sought to probe a couple of the veteran Bomb Squad detectives about certain IED-handling techniques. "Both were old enough to be my father. Each one took offense. 'Who are you to be quizzing me?' they told me."

Charlie Wells picked up on the conflict, and he and Donald broke bread one afternoon. "I told Charlie that I wasn't asking questions out of morbid curiosity. I felt

Elderly woman being rushed away from a potential IED

Chapter 10

at times we did our jobs on auto-pilot, in the sense that we never came together as a Squad to discuss lessons learned. What went wrong at times and why officers might have been injured or killed. Charlie, who had been a close friend of Brian Murray, was receptive. One day soon after, a detective asked me to follow him into a back room and offered me a chair at a table. Sitting across from me were two men who were larger-than-life figures—Richard Pastorella and Anthony Senft. The detective left the room and quietly closed the door."

After they were seriously wounded on New Year's Eve of 1982, Senft and Pastorella had been placed on administrative leave, never to return to active duty. But they remained respected members of the Bomb Squad. Donald observed between the two men a closeness "that's hard to put into words. Two brave men who became partners for life. After Richie returned home from his long hospital stay, he received a phone call from President Reagan, who told him, 'God still has a purpose for you.' That spurred him and Tony to form a policemen's support group sanctioned and supported by the NYPD, which has prevented many cops from committing suicide."

Pastorella broke the tense silence by gently placing his hands on Donald's face, to read his expression. "Then Richie grasped my hand and whispered to me, 'I want you to feel and see the missing fingers.' He pulled off his sunglasses and said, 'Look in my face. See how my eyes were blown out of their sockets. How my face is rebuilt. I never want that to happen to anyone else.' I sat there

111

quietly as Richie and Tony went over what had occurred in great detail, including what could have been done differently. When they were done, Richie grabbed Tony's forearm, and Tony helped him out. As they exited, I could see through the open door that everyone in the Squad room had stood. I stayed by myself in the back room for a long time, too overwhelmed to move."

CHAPTER 11
Challenges

The worst fireworks situation I ever encountered was when a mentally imbalanced couple stood together, and one placed an M-80 in his mouth and lit it. Tore huge holes through them. Those 'suicide by firework' incidents were more common than you'd think.

—Donald Sadowy

AS DO FIREMEN, Bomb Squad members spend much time sitting around and waiting. In Donald's era, that was done mostly in the "Cave," a room located next to the main office that doubled as a galley and a lounge, with two sets of bunk beds stacked foot to foot and a refrigerator and other kitchen appliances built into a wall. "In the Cave, we did a lot of talking about IED situations that we'd experienced or that might come up. In that way, the older guys passed on their knowledge and savvy."

Action was initiated by a transmission coming in over the SOD's citywide radio. "At all times," Donald explained, "a Squad member would sit in the office monitoring that frequency. You'd get good at tuning things out on the radio until you heard certain words like 'explosion.' Unfortunately, a lot of the calls were false alarms or even crank ones. They became the bane of our existence."

As Donald recounted, "When a request for the Squad arrived, the Sergeant would yell, 'Who's up?' If it was my team, we'd each grab our personal black rectangular nylon bag with our name on a leather nameplate. One guy would take the keys, another a radio, and a third a dog, which was coaxed into a crate padded by a thick rubber cushion. Once the dog and all of us were in the truck, we'd hit the siren, put the overhead lights on, and drive to the location. After letting the dog stretch its legs and pee, the officer would give the dog a command, either verbal or by hand, and remove the leash from its collar. The dog would sniff around but not touch the item. If it recognized the smell of explosives, it would step back, turn toward handler, and sit. If the dog didn't detect any explosives, it would turn around, remain standing, and wait for the command to come forward."

There are many ways to transform otherwise harmless chemicals and matter into deadly explosive force. The most common IED during Donald's time on the Squad was a pipe bomb, often planted by drug dealers to kill rivals or destroy their drug labs. Its component materials are inexpensive, and the device is relatively simple to assemble because it requires only the metal or PVC pipe itself, an explosive filler such as dynamite, and a fuse or

Chapter 11

timing device (historically, a wrist watch, alarm clock, or kitchen timer, but now more likely a cell phone or motion sensor). Sometimes, they are attached to a tank of propane gas to enhance destructiveness.

Rendering safe various types of grenades also was a common occurrence. "We would frequently get called to a house where hand grenades had been discovered stored in an attic or basement," Donald recalled. "That usually happened after a World War II or Korean vet had passed away. Which is why we had reference books on military ordnance, including foreign ordnance, going back to the 1800s."

A famous Bomb Squad story involved Detective Denis Mulcahy, who'd grown up in the rolling hills of Ireland's County Cork and emigrated to the U.S. in 1962 at the age of seventeen. Mulcahy joined the National Guard and was sent to Fort Dix, in New Jersey, and then on to Fort Knox in Kentucky, where he received demolitions training. When he left the Army and joined the NYPD, his IED background led him to be invited to join the Bomb Squad. One day, Mulcahy and his Squad partner, Brian Murphy, were examining a Brooklyn tile store through whose front plate glass window a grenade had been thrown. "It had the earmarkings," Mulcahy recounted, "of organized crime, although we couldn't prove that." The grenade had lodged under a table. Mulcahy crawled next to it and noticed the safety pin and ring were gone and that the striker was in a cocked position, kept from hitting the primer only by a piece of corrosion on the

115

metal housing. Mulcahy placed his thumb with the nail facing up over the primer. The striker came down sharply but struck against his thumb nail. Mulcahy gently wrapped his fingers around the grenade and calmly called for Murphy, who secured back the cock striker, unscrewed the housing of the grenade, and separated the explosive from the firing system, allowing Mulcahy to remove his thumb.

In the dance of death between IED and potential victims, remote techniques slowed the music to a more favorable pace. When Donald became a bomb tech, navigated robots were becoming more available to detect and diffuse devices. Robots for bomb handling and disposal originated in 1972, when a British Army Lieutenant-Colonel, Peter Miller, pursued the idea of using the chassis of an electrically powered wheelbarrow equipped with a special hook to tow cars and other suspect devices so they could be safely detonated. When the prototype, "Wheelbarrow Mark 1," proved difficult to maneuver, scientists were brought in to improve the control and tracking systems. Originally manipulated by a series of ropes, each robot soon was fitted with a telecommunications cable used to transmit commands to its electrical systems (later to be controlled by a remote navigation system). Cameras were placed on the robot's outer casing, with front and side views transmitted to the operators' monitors. Also, a "pigstick"—the Army's term for a strong waterjet—was added. This allowed for the disabling of bombs on the spot by firing a high-pressure

Chapter 11

stream of water at wires on the device, disrupting the triggering circuit.

"For many decades," Donald explained, "the standard way of defusing an explosive device was hand entry. Two guys who weren't even wearing bomb suits would put a dog on the device, and then each would get down on one knee and kiss his rosary beads. One guy would hold the device steady while the other would cut it with special tools. It was similar to performing surgery—no guessing, and no room for slip-ups. And, obviously, not all that safe, so robots were a godsend. But they weren't usable in some situations, like when the IED was located in a tight space."

The year Donald joined the Bomb Squad, it had at its disposal two Canadian-made robots. "Sadly, we got them due to the blood spilt by Richie and Tony, and Mayor Koch's determination not to let that happen again. They were primitive machines, with four motorcycle chains, two on each side, six wheels, two arms, two car batteries, and a bunch of relay switches that, when it rained, usually would short out. The motor for the claw that would grab items was the same as for the Volkswagen Beetle windshield wiper. Each was hooked up to a hundred-foot cable that always seemed to malfunction. Those robots looked to me like two kid cars. Years later, the robot they showed in the opening scene in the movie *The Hurt Locker* reminded me of what the Squad had then."

Donald and his team responded to a variety of IED situations, most of them initiated by amateurs. "Unfortunately, it doesn't take much knowledge or money to craft a crude IED. When I started, the know-how was out there in books and VCR tapes or through word of mouth. You could go into a hardware store or supermarket and, with some basic knowledge of chemistry, buy the right products. Then you put them in a confined container that could be anything—the more familiar and mundane, the better—hook up a fuse system, and you have an IED. There were a lot of bad guys willing to do that."

Mark Torre, the current, long-standing head of the Bomb Squad, agrees, adding, "It's easy to make an IED, but it's also easy to screw up, particularly if you use just a recipe found on the internet. Or get too fancy with your triggers. Accidentally connect the trigger to a power source, and you're done. The best deterrent is publicizing those times when a guy blew himself up."

Handling potential IEDs was only part of the Squad's duties. Dealing with hazardous chemicals was another. One Friday afternoon, Donald and Tom Connelly, another former Marine, were summoned to a public high school. "Over the years, chemistry teachers had improperly sealed and stored picric acid. [Picric acid, an explosive, was used in chemistry lab testing.] Now it had become deteriorated and unstable. But instead of calling a chemical-removal company, the principal, not wanting to answer to the Board of Ed on the high cost of removal, called 911. Not the first time I had encountered this. I told him that, if it had not been for my boss, I would have put him in handcuffs and done a perp walk out of the building in front of the media."

Chapter 11

Donald and Detective Donald Hurley demonstrating to NYPD officers the proper use of one of the first Bomb Squad robots

Donald and Squad Officer Tom Connelly removing picric acid from a public high school

Rendered Safe

The calendar dictated much of the Squad's work. "In June and July," Donald explained, "we'd be swamped with dealing with fireworks, all of which were illegal for use in New York. Organized-crime gangs would purchase truckloads of fireworks in other states, truck them into the city, store them in warehouses and garages in different boroughs, and sell them on the street. Any fireworks seized by NYPD or the Feds would be taken to Rodman's Neck to be disposed of through controlled burns."

In the summer of 1989, police in upstate New York seized 28 twenty-foot tractor trailers filled with fireworks. The trailers were driven to Rodman's Neck, where Donald was tasked with disposing of their contents. Assisting him was Richie Hackford, who had recently joined the Squad. Richie was, in many ways, stereotypical. "My grandfather emigrated from Ireland at the turn of the century. At that time, few guys wanted to be a cop. He basically got the job right off the boat, because he could read and write English. My dad was a cop and a World War II vet. And my uncle and several cousins were cops. I knew the psyche of cops, and I loved it. Like the fact everyone observes everyone else. If you come to work wearing one brown sock and one black sock, or if your tie doesn't match your suit, you can expect to be ribbed all day. After I retired from the NYPD, there were two things I missed. One was being able to drive like a maniac with the lights and siren on, and the other was all the ball-busting."

Richie took an unusual path to the Bomb Squad. When he was seventeen, he dropped out of Hillcrest High

Chapter 11

School in Jamaica, Queens and enlisted in the Navy. Among his assignments were crane operator and weapons handler, loading intercontinental ballistic missiles and nuclear torpedoes as part of a submarine force. After leaving the Navy, he worked as an emergency-medical-services technician before joining the NYPD.

As made clear by Mark Torre, "to be accepted into the Bomb Squad, you have to have something to offer besides your good looks. It could range from electrical or mechanical training, experience in operating heavy equipment, explosives background, or investigative or writing skills." Richie's "something" was his expertise since his teenage years in scuba diving, which was his entrée into the ESU. While an ESU member, Richie began training Bomb Squad officers to become certified divers, which led to an offer to join the Squad.

Richie and Donald became close. "Donald impressed me from the start because he was an extremely motivated person. He lived and breathed the job, and you could depend on him. And he always looked to be helpful. Donald wasn't the most senior guy on the Squad but, because safety counts over rank, he was a top dog."

By each August, the Squad would turn its focus to the September opening of the U.N. General Assembly, when numerous heads of state and other foreign notables and their delegations and families would arrive. "We would coordinate and hold planning meetings with the foreign mission staff and several agencies on security," Donald recounted, "including Port Authority of New York and

New Jersey[45] and U.N. headquarters reps. If the arriving person was a head of state, the U.S. Secret Service would take the lead. Otherwise, the lead was the protective liaison section of the State Department. Together, the agencies would develop a top-secret itinerary and arrange for a 24/7 security team. The Squad deployed dedicated search-and-response teams, some located on the U.N. grounds but tucked away from view. One of our jobs was to search each of the vehicles that would take the visitors from the airport to their Manhattan hotel and on to the U.N."

One of those who routinely worked with the Bomb Squad on dignitary protection was Dan Smolanick of the NYPD Intelligence Division, who was the Department's liaison to the U.N. "We relied heavily on the Bomb Squad," Smolanick noted, "to do sweeps with their dogs to make sure sites were clean. When the U.N. General Assembly was in session, at five in the morning, before anyone arrived, we would have the Squad come in with their dogs and sweep the hall, including the holding rooms, approaches and departures, the back part where the speakers gathered, and the dining-room area if there were luncheons or dinners scheduled. We got to know Donald that way. Donald, who became the Squad's liaison to the Intelligence Division, was pleasant, plainspoken, and would drill home basic, useful advice like 'Stay alert, stay alive.'"

Smolanick and his partner, Steve Chiarini, asked Donald to participate in the periodic four-day

Chapter 11

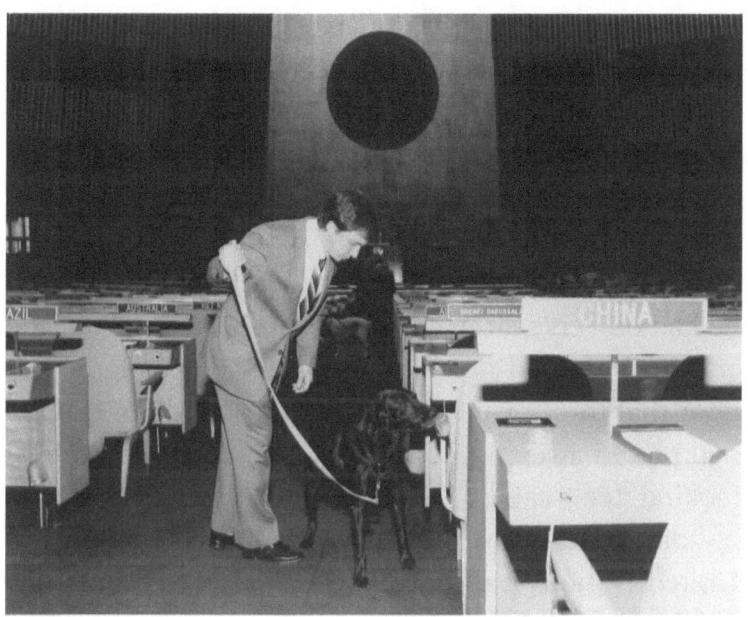

Sweeping the General Assembly Hall with "BB" in October 1985 during the 40th anniversary celebration of the U.N.

dignitary-protection-training course they organized for NYPD officers and detectives. "We would give Donald a two-hour slot during one day of each session," Chiarini explained. "He was fantastic. He'd come in with various types of homemade IEDs. One was contained in an old wooden case meant to carry vintage wines. Another was a cigar box that a bomb-maker had planted dynamite in, using a pocket watch as the timer and an improvised blasting cap fit into a cigar tube. (A blasting cap, or detonator, is a small explosive device used to detonate a larger, more powerful one such as TNT or dynamite.) Donald would demonstrate how they were constructed and how they worked. Explain things like types of explosives, pressure releases, and electrical and mechanical timers. He'd stay until every question was answered. One thing he drilled into us was that you don't know what a bomb looks like because anything could be a bomb. A radio. A doll. A bicycle tire. A traffic cone. It could even be inserted into an animal. One time we went outside, and he had officers search a car. They inspected the outside and then entered it. There was a shoebox lying on the floor that they tossed aside. But that was where Donald had placed a replica of an IED, to show that harmless-looking items can be the deadliest."

Smolanick also appreciated Donald's knowledge of United Nations internal politics. One day, Smolanick received a call from U.N. security reporting that an unclaimed attaché case had been found sitting in a corner of the U.N. library. He ordered U.N. security to clear the library, and notified the Secret Service, which brought their own bomb-sniffing German shepherd. "The dog sniffed the attaché case," Smolanick recalled, "and sat, indicating there was something suspicious in it. I wanted further confirmation, so I brought in the NYPD Bomb Squad. Donald arrived and suggested we not second-guess their dog. So, instead of using his dog, he suited up and did a hand-entry exam of the case, discovering there was nothing in it but papers. He explained that non-Bomb Squad dogs are cross-trained to detect both IEDs and drugs, and guessed that the attaché case, which turned out to be owned by an African diplomat, had

Chapter 11

been used to bring in narcotics. While there was nothing we could do about that, Donald helped prevent us from both pissing off the Secret Service and creating a diplomatic brouhaha."

Each November, the Squad's attention would be redirected to the well-attended public events taking place during the holiday season, such as the Rockefeller Center tree lighting and the New Year's Eve celebration in Times Square. "The planning for those events seemed endless," Donald remembered. "December was a particularly intense time for the Squad. After that, for the first few months of the year, we'd catch a break and be able to work on routine things like vehicle and equipment maintenance and sending guys for training."

*

Central to the experience of being a Bomb Squad member was making the "long walk" from the safe area to the potential IED. Don would take on that duty innumerable times.

CHAPTER 12
The Long Walk

Getting suited up was kind of like knights getting their heavy armor put on them by others in medieval times.
—Donald Sadowy

WHEN BRIAN MURRAY was killed by an IED in 1976, he wasn't wearing a bomb suit. "We did have protective suits at the time," Charlie Wells explained. "They were known as 'supporter suits.' They had heavy headpieces that lay flat up against your face, with slits for seeing out. But testing showed that, if an IED went off, wearing the headpiece might lead to having your head ripped off. So, no one wore them except when TV cameras showed up after the bomb had been defused."

After Murray's death, Charlie Wells noted that "the Squad was given the same suits the London bomb techs were using in Northern Ireland.[46] Those suits were the best ones available. But they didn't provide full protection if you were standing near the bomb when it went off. Even if the suit stopped the shrapnel, the positive and negative pressure waves caused by the blast could crush your organs inside."[47]

Bomb suits, intricate contraptions laden with Velcro, Kevlar, and steel plates, also led to other problems. Donald Hurley was one of the ex-Marines who served in the Bomb Squad during the early 1980s. "I got hurt once when I took a package out of a building while wearing the suit. It was a cold day, and the face shield fogged up. I fell down the stairs and ruptured two discs on my back." Richie Hackford explained that in those years, "there was no protection for the back of your legs. So, when you left the package, you had to walk backwards, which was tricky."

Nonetheless, bomb suits provided some degree of safety. Donald's first long walk was to investigate a suspicious paper bag lying by the side entrance of a hotel, near large plate glass windows. "We were on a four-to-twelve tour in midtown Manhattan," Donald recalled. "Major hotel unions had been on strike for a while, and other unions were in solidarity with them. In those types of situations, things tended to get ugly."

When the Bomb Squad techs arrived on the scene, they asked the usual questions. Who was first on the scene? What time was that? What makes the bag suspicious? Who might have planted it? Then, with an ambulance and containment truck nearby and an outer perimeter set up, ESU members helped Donald into the bomb suit. "The suit weighed about 65 pounds," Donald explained.

Chapter 12

"Once you were in it, your body core temperature went up. You became top heavy because of the helmet, jacket, and ballistic plates. Your vision and depth perception were affected because the inch-and-a-half face plate is set at an angle and curved to deflect a bomb blast. Maybe most important was that you had to learn to slow down your breathing, or else you might hyper-ventilate and not be able to think clearly. My Marine Corps background, where they drilled into us the importance of focusing solely on the task at hand and 'improvising, adapting, and overcoming,' helped me to do that reflexively."

As explained by Richie Hackford, "A bomb tech is told that when you take that long walk, you need to have nerves of steel. And you can't worry about getting hurt. After you get done, then you can freak out a bit about what you just did." Donald kept that admonition in his head as he walked to the bag. "I didn't have a death wish. None of us did. So, I was scared. But I trusted my training and my teammates' skill and experience. I knew that Jack Kelly and Pete Dalton wouldn't have let me take the walk if they didn't feel I could handle the situation."

Donald quickly set up his portable X-ray machine. "Obviously, you wanted to be near the IED for as short a period of time as possible. You never knew what could trigger an explosion, even something like static electricity. I did peek into the bag and was able to see that it was a pipe bomb. There's a lot that you try to determine in those few seconds, even before you have an X-ray to study, to get the odds as much in your favor as possible. For example, what's the power source? Is the timer electrical or mechanical? Is there a proximity sensor with a time delay? Is there a remote trigger? How much powder is in it? There are so many ways for a device to function, so the information you want to know is endless."

Donald shot the X-ray, created a cassette of the resulting image, and brought it back to Pete Dalton in the safe area, who developed the X-ray on site and determined it was live. "The X-ray," Don explained, "is what's really going to tell you what's there and how it's put together. Although X-ray interpretation is surprisingly subjective, particularly if the outer package is complicated. To be good at it, you've got to be doing it for years." After a discussion, Donald and Pete used a robot to pick up the device and bring it to the containment vessel for transport to the Rodman's Neck range.

As Donald drove home that night, he replayed the experience in his head. "I felt good about defeating the IED and the guys who'd planted it. And it was nice to get congratulations from Jack and Pete, although they made sure to remind me that it had been a relatively easy situation and not to feel that I knew it all. Or to get a swelled head. That last point was reinforced when I got home, and Kathy, after having a difficult day at home, handed me a bag of trash to throw out and then, as soon as I walked into the house, asked me to help her get the kids to bed."

Donald would take dozens of long walks over the course of his career. "I never stopped being fearful. But

Chapter 12

that never caused me to freeze up or fail to take the proper action. Which is what I'm most proud of."

*

Soon after completing his first long walk, Donald was promoted to Detective Third Grade, the first level up from Officer, trading in his patrolman's silver shield for the multi-colored Squad one.[48] "That promotion," Donald explained, "which came about eighteen months after I joined the Squad, indicated that my team leader and sergeant felt confident I was now able to handle a case from start to finish. Meaning that I could suit up, do the long walk, render the device safe, mark, bag, and tag evidence, work with the guys in the lab, refer the case to the Arson and Explosion Squad [the Bomb Squad's sister unit, which performs "shoe-leather" detective work] or elsewhere, and then prepare a case for court. I had finally ended my apprenticeship."

CHAPTER 13
Larry Davis

As he was led out of the building in handcuffs, people leaned out of their windows, clapped, and screamed "Lar-ry! Lar-ry!".

—Don Sadowy

LARRY DAVIS WAS BORN IN May 1966 in a Bronx housing project as the youngest of fifteen siblings. During his teenage years, he built a lengthy record of arrests and convictions for various violent felonies. By the fall of 1986, he was a suspect in the investigation of seven murders, including the execution-style killing of four men in a Bronx drug-den apartment whom Davis considered his competition.

Acting on a tip, on the evening of November 19, 1986, a team of officers and detectives from the Bronx 41st Precinct and the ESU gathered outside a six-story Fulton Avenue building in the Morrisania section of the Bronx, where two of Davis's sisters lived in adjoining ground-floor apartments. Wearing bulletproof vests, a dozen of them entered the building planning to apprehend Davis. Armed with a 16-gauge sawn-off shotgun and a .45-caliber semi-automatic pistol, Davis fought back. During the shootout, Davis took full advantage of his knowledge of the layout of the darkened apartments and the presence of children and other bystanders to shoot six officers (wounding four of them seriously) and then escape out a back window. It was the largest number of officers to be wounded in one incident in NYPD history.

With the help of family contacts and friends, Davis eluded capture for the next seventeen days despite a massive manhunt that attracted nationwide attention. On the afternoon of December 5, police received a tip that Davis had been seen entering the Bronx housing project that another of his sisters lived in. ESU officers surrounded the 14-story building, had it evacuated, closed off local streets, and posted sharpshooters on nearby rooftops. Not finding Davis in his sister's apartment, they began a systematic search of the building. As the pursuit moved higher, Davis forced his way into a family's 14th-floor apartment. When a neighbor and her son arrived, Davis held both families at gunpoint.

Police set up a command post in a nearby apartment. By 1:30 a.m., the Hostage Negotiation Unit had established telephone contact with Davis. At one point, Davis threatened to kill hostages with a hand grenade. This prompted ESU to request Bomb Squad support. John Santos and Donald answered the call. "The apartment

Chapter 13

Davis was holed up in," Donald recalled, "was at the end of a hallway, facing down the corridor. From a tactical point of view, it provided a kill zone for Davis. So, the officers at the scene had to position themselves inside the doorways left and right. They wore heavy bulletproof vests, and we gave them the leggings from several bomb suits for further protection in case Davis tossed the grenade at them."

To assure Davis that he would not be harmed, police showed him the press credentials of three reporters in a nearby apartment, and allowed him to speak to his girlfriend. At about 7 a.m., Davis surrendered. "Police Commissioner Ben Ward had shown up by then," Donald recounted, "out of concern that the ESU guys would kill Davis. Which they wouldn't have done because they're professionals. As Davis slowly walked out with his hands behind his head, he started to cry. One of the ESU officers, who had been there all night, yelled out to him, 'Act like a man!' Ward, who was standing at the end of the hall, heard this and became livid. He ordered that officer transferred out of ESU, which was done the next day."

Donald watched as Davis exited the building. "Once he saw the media throng and all the sympathetic bystanders, his servile attitude changed completely. He yelled out to them [in a preview of what his legal defense would be] that 'cops gave me the drugs and guns. I was just trying to defend myself.'"

Donald and John Santos then entered the apartment. "First, John stopped and spoke softly to a woman who had been taken hostage along with her baby, assuring her that there was no more danger. After we escorted them to waiting EMTs, we searched the apartment. I discovered the hand grenade, which was hidden inside a couch facing the front door, which Davis had been sitting on for hours. John recovered Davis's .45-caliber pistol, which had been placed underneath the skirt of the couch so that Davis easily could grab it."

During his racially charged trial, Davis's attorneys, well-known civil-rights activists William Kunstler and Lynne Stewart, asserted that he had been framed. Despite the testimony of more than 50 prosecution witnesses plus fingerprints and ballistic evidence, Davis was acquitted of attempted-murder and aggravated-assault charges stemming from the shootout with police.[49] He was, however, found guilty of six counts of weapons possession and sentenced to 5–15 years' imprisonment. Davis later was found guilty of murdering a drug dealer and sentenced to serve an additional 25 years. In February 2008, Davis was stabbed to death at the Shawangunk Correctional Facility, a maximum-security state prison in Ulster County, in a fight with another inmate.

*

As the 1980s progressed, Donald's expertise in dealing with difficult IED situations grew exponentially. Those skills would be tested by a case that proved to be the greatest challenge to the Bomb Squad since the Mad Bomber.

CHAPTER 14
The Abortion Bomber

I come home from defending my country and get called a 'baby-killer,' while others were murdering the unborn with impunity.

—Dennis Malvasi

DENNIS JOHN MALVASI WAS born in the slums of East New York, Brooklyn, in January 1950, the seventh child of a woman who first gave birth at the age of fifteen and eventually had twelve children by at least three different men. For most of his childhood, he'd lived in the St. Joseph Home, a Catholic orphanage in Peekskill, New York. At seventeen, Malvasi walked into the Times Square Armed Forces Recruitment Office and enlisted in the U.S. Marines. Advised that because of his age, he would need parental consent, he paid a passerby $20 to sign as his mother. "At that moment," Malvasi recounted, "I felt really alive, really wanted."

Rendered Safe

Malvasi served two tours of duty in Vietnam, including seeing combat during the Tet Offensive in 1968. Working as a field radio operator linking air support and evacuation aid, he came under heavy fire on numerous occasions. After being honorably discharged in May 1970, Malvasi returned to New York City, drifting among odd jobs. One was working for the Grucci Brothers setting up fireworks displays, which led him to obtain a pyrotechnic license. One day, on a whim, Malvasi answered an ad for an Avenue A theater company and became an actor overnight, appearing in a number of productions.

Malvasi's life changed direction in September 1972, when he was arrested after both stabbing and being stabbed by a man during a traffic altercation. He pleaded guilty to second-degree assault and was sentenced to five years' probation. The following year, while residing in a tough Lower East Side neighborhood, Malvasi was jumped by three men on his way home from a rehearsal and knifed. Malvasi began packing a gun for protection, and, in November 1975, he was arrested on a subway platform for carrying an unlicensed .25-caliber semi-automatic pistol. Convicted on a reduced charge of attempted criminal possession of a weapon, his second felony, Malvasi was imprisoned in the Great Meadow Correctional Facility in upstate New York for two years.

Upon his release, Malvasi returned to acting, this time in the Troupe Theater, a seedy off-off Broadway playhouse on West 39th Street. A religious Catholic, Malvasi also became involved with Our Lady of the

Chapter 14

Roses, an extremist Christian fundamentalist group led by Veronica Lueken, a Long Island housewife who claimed the Virgin Mary and Jesus Christ spoke through her. Lueken's adherents believed "armed struggle" was necessary to remove the sinfulness of modern life and bring peace to the world. In the group's view, the foulest of sacrileges was abortion.

In December 1985, a tube packed with explosive powder burst into flames inside a vacant men's room at the Manhattan Women's Medical Center on East 23rd Street. It was the first attack on an abortion clinic in New York City history and the beginning of Malvasi's terror campaign. The following October, one early morning, a pipe bomb containing a half-stick of dynamite blew a hole through the wall of the Eastern Women's Center on 30th Street. Flying glass injured two nearby pedestrians.

Two weeks later, after an early-morning phone call to police, an IED composed of three sticks of dynamite attached to a travel alarm clock, Du Pont blasting cap, and nine-volt battery was discovered underneath a couch cushion in the Queens Women's Medical Center.[50] Denis Mulcahy arrived with his Squad partner, Chris Brower. Donning a bomb suit, he peered at the device through his protective visor. Mulcahy observed that the face of the clock, which was ticking, had been taped over. "So," Mulcahy explained, "you really didn't know what kind of time you had on your hands. It was a simple device, but it could have done a lot of damage. Since the space was too tight to use a robot, I decided to render it safe then and there by disconnecting the battery, which was the power source. We subsequently realized upon testing that the bomb had been set to go off the night before, but the tape holding down the connecting wire to the blasting cap bubbled up a slight bit, leading to the clock hand passing the detonator without striking it. I later learned Malvasi was very bothered that his device hadn't worked."

For diffusing that bomb, Mulcahy received the NYPD's Medal of Valor. "That," Richie Hackford explained, "and many other accomplishments was why Mulcahy was known as the 'godfather' of the Bomb Squad. When he said something, you listened."[51]

The Bomb Squad members took note that Malvasi's devices were both well-made and varied in their design, which was unusual. As Donald noted, "Malvasi wasn't an amateur lighting gasoline with a match. And, at least initially, he didn't seem to want anyone to get hurt. The call to Glenn alerting us about the bomb at the Queens Women's Medical Center was made by Malvasi because he didn't want it to go off when people were in the office." Glenn was Squad Detective Glenn Welch, by whom Malvasi's initial calls were answered. Malvasi developed a bond with the soft-spoken ex-Marine. "After a while, when Malvasi called, often just to chat, he would insist on talking to Glenn. No one else. Glenn would try to keep him on the phone so the call could be traced. But Malvasi always called from a public pay phone and never stayed on the line too long."

Chapter 14

In the early evening of December 16, 1986, Malvasi met a real estate broker in front of a building at Second Avenue and 23rd Street, ostensibly to discuss renting space there. Once inside, Malvasi pulled a gun on the broker and handcuffed him to a stairway railing. Malvasi proceeded to break into the offices of Planned Parenthood. There, he upped the ante on his bombing game by planting both an incendiary device (smokeless powder in a cigar tube) designed to start a fire and an IED composed of fifteen sticks of dynamite. Each was set to go off soon after he left the premises.

The powder set the carpet aflame. But the main bomb, which, had it detonated, would have collapsed the front of the building and killed or severely wounded the broker, was a "hang fire." The smoke activated the sprinkler system alarm, alerting firemen who then discovered the remains of the incendiary device. They called in ESU officers, who, in turn, summoned the Bomb Squad. Squad detective Steve Dodge and his colleagues searched the entire building. In the patient waiting room, where several cops were conversing, they discovered the unexploded bomb. Concerned that the fire's heat might ignite it, the Squad officers disarmed the IED by gingerly snipping the wires leading from the timer to the blasting cap. They then noticed, nestled within the sticks of dynamite, a sacramental medal containing symbols and text related to the life of Saint Benedict of Nursia. One of the oldest and most honored medals used by Roman Catholics, it is referred to as the "devil-chasing medal." It became

141

popular after its formal approval by Pope Benedict XIV in the 18th century to ward off spiritual and physical dangers, especially those related to evil and temptation.

The investigation of the Abortion Bomber became a national news story. It was led by agents from the NYPD Arson and Explosion Squad and the Bureau of Alcohol, Tobacco, Firearms, and Explosives, known as the "ATF," a law-enforcement agency within the Treasury Department at the time, whose responsibilities included the investigation and prevention of federal offenses involving the unlawful use, manufacture, and possession of explosives. Through both a fingerprint on one of the sticks of dynamite that matched a print on a pyrotechnic license granted by the New York Fire Department and a sketch of the suspect provided by the broker, Malvasi was identified as the bomber. By then, he had gone into hiding and, with the help of the anti-abortion network, remained out of law enforcement's grasp despite more than 300 federal agents and NYPD detectives and their support staff working around the clock to locate him. "Part of why Malvasi was so hard to catch," Donald explained, "was that he was a master of disguise. He could stroll into a clinic dressed as a woman, wearing a wig and makeup, and no one would think him odd. So, even if there were several U.S. Marshals standing about providing protection, it wouldn't prevent his planting a bomb."

Closely following the Abortion Bombing saga was John Miller, a local WNBC news reporter who decades later would become the NYPD's Deputy Commissioner

Chapter 14

of Intelligence & Counterterrorism. It was Miller who in February 1987, on the nightly news, broke the story that law-enforcement authorities had determined Malvasi to be the Abortion Bomber. That same night, while driving home, Miller received a call on his two-way radio from Maria Uliano, who worked the station's night desk. "Maria told me she had just received a call from a woman who had dated Malvasi. The woman insisted Malvasi was a nice, religious guy who wouldn't hurt a fly. Maria asked if she knew Malvasi's phone number, and the woman gave Maria the last number she had. Maria looked it up in our Cole's cross-reference directory and determined it was for an 'Ed Nowicki,' with a location on West 26th Street."

Miller drove to the address. "It was a giant warehouse in a mixed residential and commercial neighborhood that took up the entire block between 25th and 26th Streets and 11th and 12th Avenues. I went in through a side door. There was a security desk but no guard anywhere. I scanned the directory on the wall. There was a 'Vietnam Veterans Art Project' listed as being on the 20th floor. I got into the elevator, but it only went up to the eighteenth floor. When the elevator door opened, I was staring at a pitch-black floor. I began thinking that I was an idiot for going further, because the phone call to Maria could have been made simply to lure me here. But I took out my flashlight and walked up the stairs two flights. I pushed open the door to what I thought was the twentieth floor, and, there before me was the lit-up

143

skyline of Manhattan. I now understood that the twentieth floor was the roof. I went forward and saw there was a small utility building on the roof next to a water tower. The door to it was locked. I shone my flashlight through the window and could see wires, cans, tubes, and the like. I realized this was the hideout where Malvasi put together his bombs."

Before leaving the roof, Miller searched an open trash can at the top of the stairs and found a credit card bill with Ed Nowicki's name and a parking violation for a car that had been parked on Tenth Avenue and 22nd Street. The next day, which was a Friday, Miller walked that block and noticed a Catholic Church. "Remembering the discovery of the Saint Benedict medal, I knocked on the door. A man wearing a brown leather jacket and cowboy boots opened it. I asked whether he was Ed Nowicki, and he immediately slammed the door shut. I waited down the block with my camera crew for a couple of hours, and Nowicki finally came out of the church and headed up Tenth Avenue. We caught up to him, and I asked, "Where's Dennis Malvasi? Who's protecting him?" He became visibly upset, and I had the crew stop filming. Once they did, Nowicki told me, 'This is gonna cost me my job at the church and get a lot of people in trouble.' I responded, 'We just want to get Malvasi to stop planting bombs and surrender.' He and I spoke further, and I agreed not to reveal his identity or mention the church in my story if he promised that, by Monday, he would tell me where Malvasi was. The next Monday, Nowicki

Chapter 14

telephoned and said he'd contacted certain persons in the veterans' network and that I could be assured that, if John O'Connor, the Archbishop of New York, appealed to Malvasi, he would turn himself in."

Shortly thereafter, with the assistance of a monsignor, Miller, accompanied by his camera crew, met with Cardinal O'Connor at the archdiocese headquarters on First Avenue. "The Cardinal and I sit down, and he asked me, 'How do you want to do this? Am I talking to you?' I responded, 'No, please look into the camera and speak directly to Malvasi.' And the Cardinal, without a prepared script, looked into the camera and said, 'Dennis, what you're doing is very wrong. You need to stop this violence. And we need you to come in and talk to the police. If you want, you can call me directly first.'"

Miller aired the Cardinal's plea on that day's five, six, and eleven o'clock Channel 4 news. The next afternoon, wearing sunglasses and a disguise, Malvasi strolled into the lobby of 90 Church Street, which was the ATF's Manhattan headquarters. When none of the law enforcement agents waiting in the lobby recognized him, an impatient Malvasi announced his presence to a U.S. Post Office police officer. During his interrogation by Alex D'Atri, the lead ATF agent on the case,[52] Malvasi admitted, "It's hard to turn down the Cardinal. He's a prince of the church. If the Cardinal says something and you don't listen, when you stand before the magistrate in the celestial court, you got problems. And I got enough problems without God being mad at me."

Rendered Safe

After several months, Malvasi cut a deal whereby he pled guilty to committing two of the attacks. He was sentenced to seven years' imprisonment, which took into account that, whatever Malvasi's intentions, he had not seriously hurt anyone. In Miller's view, "Malvasi's relatively lenient sentence must be seen in the context of its time. New York City then was a cesspool of crime and violence, with the crack-cocaine epidemic in full force. And bombings for a social cause were not at all unusual. So, the tolerance for wrongdoing was greater. Plus, this was pre-9/11, and terrorism was not taken nearly as seriously as it is now."

CHAPTER 15
Mickey Mouse Stickers

We figured the greater danger was the heat. In that enclosed space, if anything went off, we'd be dead whether we had protective gear on or not.

—Donald Sadowy

AS PART OF HIS PLEA DEAL, Malvasi agreed to give up the location of his bomb-making-equipment stash, which was in a locker in the Chelsea Mini Storage, a timeworn ten-story corner warehouse on 28th Street by the West Side Highway and next door to where John Miller had found Malvasi's rooftop lab. The August day prior to the search warrant for Chelsea Mini Storage being issued, Glenn approached Donald to ask if he would be willing to accompany him to the warehouse. "Glenn was concerned that Malvasi, a strange and devious character and a talented bomb-maker, might have planted a booby trap as the last twist of his knife. He knew I was good with detecting and handling those kinds of devices. So, the following day, which was a really hot, humid one, Glenn, me, and another bomb tech, Tony Ruggirello, drove to the building, with a police escort, and took the service elevator to the sixth floor. We had our dogs. Several ESU guys joined and brought the bomb bell [a total-containment vessel for carrying explosives]. Some FBI agents came along, but we asked them to remain outside. Lieutenant Boser also was with us and read the warrant to the men who managed the place and who had no clue about what was going on."

Before cutting the lock on the gate of the 12-by-12-by-12-foot storeroom, which was walled in by floor-to-ceiling cyclone fencing, Donald and his colleagues, wearing bomb suits, checked it for trip wires that might indicate a booby trap. The space was a crammed tapestry of boxes, briefcases, five-pound cans, mounds of clothing, and suitcases, including two decorated with Mickey Mouse stickers. "Those stickers," Donald recounted, "indicated those were the suitcases where Malvasi had placed the high explosives. And they were a reminder of what a loony tune we were dealing with."

Within minutes, the dogs responded positively to the presence of IED material. "There was no ventilation or air conditioning, and the temperature in the building was more than 110 degrees. The ESU men broke open the windows, which were shut and painted over. Still, it was so stifling the dogs went into heat exhaustion. And we bomb techs weren't far behind. We had the dogs led out, and we took off our face shields, helmets, and bomb

Chapter 15

suit jackets. All we left on were the leggings, which had ballistic inserts, and our T-shirts."

Donald, Glenn, and Tony asked not to be relieved, in order to maintain continuity and to ensure that every item was examined. The men took breaks every 45 minutes. "We'd go downstairs and the ESU guys, who had gotten empty coffee cans and filled them with water from a fire hydrant, would pour water on our heads and necks or give us the cans to drink from. Sometimes they'd douse us with a spray straight from the hydrant."

The three Squad members spent most of the next two days crawling on their bellies and methodically probing and X-raying every item in the storage room. They found 78 sticks of deteriorating dynamite, electric matches, more than 150 blasting caps, smokeless powder, gunpowder, wires, switches, tubular containers, and pipes. Among the collection of clothes was an assortment of wigs and makeup kits. Each item had to be separated, marked, tagged, bagged, and stored, destined for analysis by the NYPD crime lab. "The ESU officers had gone to a local bodega and returned with heavy-duty plastic milk crates and padded them with cushioning material from an old life vest to create makeshift containers. We put thirty-nine sticks of deteriorating dynamite into each of two containers and, with a police and helicopter escort, took them in the Bomb Squad's total containment vessel up the West Side and over to Rodman's Neck for disposal."

Their work completed, Donald, Glenn, and Tony heard from the captain who headed the NYPD crime lab.

149

"He was an angry, nasty man," Donald recalled, "who had seen on TV that the three of us had removed our protective gear, and wrote us up for disciplinary action for violating the NYPD Patrol Guide Manual. My God, the Patrol Guide is just that, a guide. It has hundreds of 'rules,' and some are routinely violated so you can do your job well. As a bomb tech, you must be prepared to think out of the box. What good would it have been if we'd passed out from the heat? Bosses almost never enforce minor violations."

The three men challenged the captain's accusations by demanding a trial. "We called our union reps," Donald remembered, "and then the media. At the very least, the captain would be embarrassed publicly." The morning of the trial, the men arrived at the NYPD courtroom at One Police Plaza expecting to meet with their union-appointed attorneys. Instead, they sat and watched as the head of the Bomb Squad, Lieutenant Walter Boser, a six-foot-two-inch former Navy submariner of German heritage, along with the Chief of Detectives Joe Borelli, took to the podium in front of reporters and TV cameras and lauded them for risking their lives to successfully dispose of Malvasi's bomb-making arsenal. "John Miller was there with his film crew. He came over to congratulate us and told us that he had cautioned Borelli, who was old school and tough as nails but, also, a thoughtful, compassionate guy, that the press for the Squad and the NYPD would be horrific. So, instead of being disciplined, we received medals."

CHAPTER 16
Sniper

I could have married Loretta, but I was married to my work.

—James Kopp

AFTER BEING RELEASED from prison in 1992 subject to supervised probation, Malvasi lived in a tiny apartment above a bodega on Myrtle Avenue in Brooklyn under various aliases while working odd jobs. Donald took it upon himself to keep tabs on Malvasi. "I'd call him periodically at night, to make sure he was home and not prowling around. I also spoke regularly with his work supervisor."

Malvasi's bride was Loretta Marra, thirteen years younger and the daughter of William Marra, an active anti-abortion lecturer who for many years hosted a New York City radio program titled "Where Catholics Meet," and was the Right to Life Party candidate in the 1988 U.S. presidential campaign, gaining more than 20,000 votes.

Rendered Safe

The couple would have two children and, unbeknownst to Donald or his NYPD colleagues, become active in a Christian extremist group named "Army of God," which advocated violence toward abortion providers and clinics.

On the evening of October 23, 1998, in Amherst, New York, a suburb of Buffalo, Barnett Slepian, an obstetrician and gynecologist who routinely performed abortions, was shot in the back with an assault rifle through a rear sunroom window after he had returned home with his family from a synagogue service in honor of his late father. The bullet severed his spinal cord. Slepian died in front of his wife and four young sons. The murder received national attention, with President Bill Clinton publicly denouncing it and, after the funeral, flying with Hillary to Amherst to meet the family.

The Justice Department and FBI launched an international manhunt for the sniper. Lieutenant Michael White, the new Bomb Squad head, concerned that Slepian's murder would spur copycat shootings in the city, called a Squad meeting. Donald was an attendee. "We went around the room giving our opinions as to who might be the perpetrator. The consensus was that Malvasi was the prime suspect. But I spoke up, telling them I didn't think he'd done it, and why. Not only because I had kept tabs on him but, also, because he wasn't known to have ever used a high-powered weapon. A bunch of people disagreed with me and were openly pissed."

Donald was proven correct, at least in part. What none of the Squad officers knew was that the Malvasis

Chapter 16

were closely connected to the man who had done the shooting—James Charles Kopp. Kopp, a construction worker, carpenter, and welder, was a prominent member of the Army of God, known as "Atomic Dog" within the group. He was an admirer of William Marra, and he and Loretta had been close. Kopp had been arrested more than twenty times between 1984 and 1997 for civil disobedience outside abortion clinics. In January 1991, he and Loretta were arrested together at a protest outside a Long Island abortion clinic where they had locked their feet together in a steel, doughnut-shape device that Kopp had designed and welded to block the door.

Within days of shooting Slepian, Kopp was identified as the prime suspect through a tip to police from a woman out on a jog who noticed a beat-down Chevrolet Cavalier parked in the upscale neighborhood and copied down its out-of-state license plate number. A material-witness warrant was issued for Kopp, and he was placed on the FBI's Ten Most Wanted List.[53] A $500,000 reward was offered for information leading to his capture, which soon was doubled.

After the shooting, Kopp took refuge in Malvasi's Brooklyn apartment. Then Loretta drove him to Mexico, from where he flew to London and on to Ireland and France. While on the lam, Kopp and Loretta exchanged emails and spoke on the phone in code. Loretta and Dennis wired Kopp money and planned his secret return to the United States.

Rendered Safe

In late March 2001, based largely on intercepted e-mails and cell-phone wiretaps, Kopp was located and arrested in the medieval French village of Dinan.[54] Days later, Dennis and Loretta were arrested at their home in Brooklyn. Ultimately, both were convicted of harboring, concealing, and aiding the flight of a fugitive. After agreeing to a plea deal, each served two-and-a-half years in a federal prison. They were released in October 2003. Kopp is serving a life sentence without any chance of parole.

CHAPTER 17
Gorbachev

> *I was only about twelve feet from Gorbachev. I could hear him asking questions. He was curious about Americans and America, and listened to people in the crowd politely. The problem was that it was almost impossible to fully protect him in those circumstances.*
>
> —Donald Sadowy

THE LAST OFFICIAL MEETING between President Ronald Reagan and USSR General Secretary Mikhail Gorbachev—after four summits that commanded worldwide attention at Geneva, Reykjavik, Washington, and Moscow—took place in New York City on December 7, 1988. Dan Smolanick regards the Gorbachev visit as his most challenging assignment. "It was a hugely important and sensitive event. The Gorbachevs arrived in Manhattan on the evening of December 6 with a packed schedule. We asked Donald to head the Bomb Squad contingent assigned to protect Reagan, Gorbachev, and Bush."

Preparation for the summit was coordinated among USSR, Secret Service, State Department, and NYPD officials and Aly Teymour, the Egyptian-born head of U.N. protocol. Donald knew Aly from when he'd worked at the U.N. "Aly reminded me of Waldheim, as he was well over six feet with his hair combed straight back, a ramrod posture, long strides, and always in a three-piece conservative suit. Aly wasn't himself a security guy. Rather, his job was to make sure every visiting dignitary is graciously received, that security arrangements are made for him, that the appropriate guests are invited, and even that the elevators arrive on time."

The security effort surrounding the Gorbachevs required mobilization of vast resources. "Mikhail and Raisa Gorbachev," Donald clarified, "had somewhat separate agendas, and every place they were scheduled to be at was searched, swept, and secured for the day. That included various areas in the U.N. such as offices, elevators, the delegates' lounge and dining room, and the General Assembly hall. His plane at JFK Airport was protected and serviced for the length of his visit. Numerous threat assessments were done, considering what groups were likely to protest and, more importantly, present a physical threat.[55] We plotted out the best route from one locale to another, and the best alternates. Every manhole along the main and alternate routes was physically checked and then welded shut. And every mailbox along each route was inspected by U.S. Postal Service officials, emptied, and then locked. We determined what, in case

Chapter 17

of an attack or if Gorbachev had a medical emergency, would be the nearest trauma center or safe area. We even had a supply of his medications."

The Gorbachev procession was composed of more than fifty vehicles. "Each one had a different purpose," Donald explained. "There was a backup if his Russian-made ZIL limo broke down. There were advance cars, a motorcycle escort, and an armored, blackened-out Chevy Suburban packed with a group of Secret Service agents in black jumpsuits ready to swarm out with shoulder-held weapons, loaded vests, and body bunkers. And right behind them was an ESU van holding a highly trained and heavily armed counter-assault team. And there was always a helicopter above."

Donald was assigned to a Bomb Squad response vehicle that held a robot, canine, two bomb suits, a portable X-ray machine and developer, and various hand tools. With him was a frequent partner, Steve Berberich. Berberich, short, heavy-set, balding, and with large wire-rim glasses, had been dubbed "Ziggy" by his Squad colleagues, a reference to the diminutive character in the longtime cartoon series. Berberich had dropped out of high school at 16, lied about his age, and took a job sinking shafts for the third stage of a water tunnel in the Bronx. "I spent ten years as a 'sandhog' doing commercial high-explosives work. The money was good, but it was tough, dirty, dangerous work. The saying was you'd lose one man per mile. After four guys that I knew had been killed, I figured my time would be coming, so

I left to join the NYPD." Berberich was one of Donald's favorites—"a great guy, enormously knowledgeable, and funny as hell."

December 7 was a physically strenuous day for the two Squad members. "The motorcade formed outside Gorbachev's hotel at 5:30 a.m., and Ziggy and I were with it all day. And when the Gorbachevs returned to their hotel at night, we had to go back to the Bomb Squad and return the equipment and dog and do some paperwork. You couldn't count on an opportunity to get food during the day, so Ziggy went to Arthur Ave. in the Bronx the day before and bought from a mom-and-pop store cold cuts, cheeses, snacks, bread, and all sorts of drinks, which we kept in a cooler."

After several stops in the morning, Gorbachev's convoy arrived at the U.N.[56] "We pull through the main gate to the delegates' entrance, where Aly Teymour is standing with the Soviet delegation to welcome him. Gorbachev goes inside and up the escalator while dozens of agents, cops, and Soviet secret service rush out of vehicles and motorcycles and race down the stairway to a gigantic men's room on the 1-B level, with dozens of urinals and commode stalls. After several hours, it's our first chance to pee. Ziggy's got a fat white Lab named 'Scamp' with him and, sure enough, the dog has to pee also. Ziggy points to a round, brass drain in the center of the pitched-down floor and lets go of the leash. Scamp rushes over to the drain, lifts up his back leg, and pisses a gallon down it. By now, everyone's looking at the dog.

Chapter 17

Then Ziggy taps me on the elbow, smiles, and as he's standing at a urinal, raises his right leg like the dog. I did the same. Everyone turns to look at us, and suddenly you hear roaring laughter."

The Gorbachevs split up for several hours. The Soviet leader dined with Reagan and Vice President (and President-elect) George H.W. Bush on tiny Governor's Island in New York Harbor, which houses stone forts that never fired a shot in battle and a nine-hole golf course.[57] Meanwhile, Raisa Gorbachev, Nancy Reagan, and Barbara Bush lunched at the Secretary-General's Sutton Place residence with a star-studded lineup highlighted by Barbara Walters and Brooke Astor. Gorbachev's motorcade then glided through numerous stops in midtown and lower Manhattan, cheered by adoring onlookers. "What drove us and the Soviet security agents nuts," Dan Smolanick made clear, "was that three times—at Bloomingdale's, Grand Central Station, and at Broadway and 50th Street—Gorbachev insisted on stopping, getting out of his limo, and engaging the throng. Gorbachev spoke English well enough to communicate with the locals."

In the late afternoon, the Gorbachevs arrived at the World Trade Center, where a crowd in the lobby shouted, "Gorby! Gorby!" They were escorted to the indoor 107th-floor observation deck in the South Tower, presented with a silver bowl from Tiffany's and a crystal eagle from Steuben, and shown the sights."

In the meantime, Donald, along with dozens of other agents, waited at ground level. "It was a rule, one unwritten but set in stone, that you never physically leave the motorcade unless you're sure the principal will be at the site for a period of time. Gorbachev was scheduled to be in the Trade Center for ninety minutes. After Gorbachev entered the complex, Bill Valentine, a respected sergeant in the Detective Bureau, went to grab a fresh cup of coffee from inside the Trade Center. But Gorbachev decided to cut his visit short. He marches out, waves to the crowd, gets in his limo, and speeds away. So, when Bill came out with his cup of coffee, the street was empty."

With the help of other cops, Valentine flagged down a police mounted unit truck used to transport horses. "There was no way for Bill to sit up in the cab, so he had to ride in the back trailer, which was filled with hay and horse shit. And Bill was a guy always immaculately dressed. The truck charges ahead in search of the motorcade and catches up to it at one of Gorbachev's unscheduled stops. Once Bill jumps out, all eyes go over to him, as everyone's wondering what a horse trailer is doing here. Bill stands there embarrassed, knowing he's gonna get crap from the guys for days. Finally, someone gives him a hand tool to scrape all the shit and hay off of him."

The Gorbachevs were scheduled to stay in New York for two more days but cut their visit short because of a massive earthquake that had occurred in Armenia (then part of the Soviet Union), causing an estimated 25,000 to 50,000 deaths. On Thursday, the day of Gorbachev's departure, Donald was assigned to the advance team

Chapter 17

that traveled fifteen to twenty minutes ahead of the Gorbachev procession. "I'm standing at the airport in a perimeter around Gorbachev's plane created by four-foot high metal fencing. I was wearing a suit, tie, scarf, gloves, topcoat, and a big, furry Russian hat, which someone had given me as a gift, but still I was freezing my ass off. Some guys from Secret Service and the State Department who I knew, who were standing inside the cordoned-off area, call me over. We're all chatting when Aly Teymour comes over with the chief of protocol for the Soviet mission. Aly starts singing my praises to the guy, who suddenly says to me, 'Donald, how would you like to come on board? I'll show you his plane.' So I'm walking up the ramp in disbelief, and I could hear guys saying, 'Where's Sadowy going?' But just as I step in, the motorcade comes flying up with Gorbachev. The press are there, and Gorbachev agrees to give a quick, impromptu briefing, during which he thanked America for the great hospitality. I got pushed together with others toward Gorbachev, to the point where I'm only a few feet from him. When he finishes speaking, everyone's following him up steps, with me in the midst. They start pulling the chocks out from the wheels and moving the gates back. Luckily, I decide to follow Aly as he says goodbye to Gorbachev with a vigorous handshake. Gorbachev looks at me, smiles, and nods his head, and I do the same. Then I discreetly make my way around the metal fence, where the guys start razzing me and calling me a sleeper agent."

Rendered Safe

*

A year later, Donald accompanied Bernard Johnson, his longtime mentor from the State Department's diplomatic security service area, to meetings at Langley Air Force Base. "I'm being introduced to various people. One guy who has been staring at me comes over carrying a bunch of photos. He pulls one out and shows it to me. It's a photo of Gorbachev at the press briefing, showing everyone standing near him. The guy points to me in the photo and says, 'Is this you?' I nod my head, and he proceeds to tell me how the intelligence people have been going crazy trying to figure out who I was. Bernard stood nearby, quite amused with our conversation."

CHAPTER 18
Jaws of Life

We realized she was crazy and would use IEDs if she had them, but we couldn't tell what really was in the van. And every argument the hostage negotiators made, she had an answer for.
—Richie Hackford, NYPD Bomb Squad

PREVALENT DURING THE 1980s in New York City and throughout the nation were car bombings. "We saw a few of them," Donald noted, "right after John Gotti took over the Gambino crime family in December 1985 by assassinating Paul Castellano." A bombing capturing nationwide attention occurred the following April, when Frank DeCicco, Gotti's second-in-command, was killed by a bomb that exploded when he opened the door of his Buick in Bensonhurst. The device was so powerful it blasted a hole two feet wide in the street and shook buildings for several blocks. Investigators later determined the intended victim was Gotti himself, who'd been

Rendered Safe

targeted by rival families because they hadn't sanctioned his murder of Castellano.

According to Donald, "Back in the 1980s, bosses at the social clubs used young wannabe organized crime guys as runners. They'd be sent to various locations to collect envelopes filled with money. Sometimes, if an envelope seemed too small to a boss, he'd have the runner find a live IED 'gift' in his vehicle. Usually, it was meant to be found. The message being, if it happens again, the next IED will be carefully hidden."

"Car-bomb cases tended to be frustrating from an investigative point of view," Donald reflected, "because everyone interviewed would lie, saying things like, 'I have no idea who might have done it,' or 'I have no enemies.'

Rendering safe a pipe bomb planted in a car

Chapter 18

But they were interesting technically. For example, we learned there are many ways to complete the circuit for triggering the explosion other than starting the engine, like lifting the trunk, opening a door, or stepping on the brake pedal. One new method, put in practice mostly in Europe, was to use a light-beam trigger, which cuts down significantly on the human-error factor.[58] We also learned a lot about the damage caused by devices to humans and vehicles."

A seminal incident occurred on a late Sunday morning in April 1992, when Linne Gunther, a 41-year-old woman from California, drove a white Ford van at high speed through the 45th Street entrance to the United Nations grounds, almost running over a U.N. security guard. She sped two blocks south along a driveway adjacent to First Avenue and parked in the circle surrounding the plaza fountain, thirty yards from the Secretariat tower. Gunther, the daughter of Owen Chamberlain, a Nobel Prize-winning nuclear physicist who'd worked on the Manhattan Project and later turned peace activist, got out of the van, poured gasoline over herself, and climbed back in, locking the doors. A sign in the windshield claimed there were explosives in the vehicle. Gunther, who was protesting the use of taxes to support the 1990–91 Persian Gulf War, held a cigarette lighter in each hand and threatened to set herself on fire and detonate the explosives.

The police deflated three of the van's tires while ten emergency vehicles, including Bomb Squad and fire trucks, stood nearby. Throughout the day, several officers from the Police Department's hostage-negotiating team, wearing silver heat-retardant suits, spoke with Gunther through the driver's window, trying to coax her out. The standoff went on for 23 tense hours before Gunther emerged and surrendered. Bomb Squad members, prepared to flood the van with water, discovered there was nothing in it that would explode except for several three-gallon cans of gasoline.

Donald and Richie Hackford studied the handling of the Gunther matter. "We felt in hindsight," Richie explained, "it was a mistake for law-enforcement agents to have gone up and talked to her. They were getting too close and too casual, and could have been seriously injured or killed. Donald and I spoke to Lieutenant Boser, who was one of those who'd spoken with Gunther. We told him we thought that vehicle-IED investigations weren't being handled appropriately. For example, if there was a truck in the middle of Times Square potentially with thousands of pounds of explosives in it, we couldn't all stand by and wait, yet emergency responders also couldn't just walk up to the truck to examine it. Boser, who was approachable and open to out-of-the-box ideas, agreed we needed a smarter approach."

Boser allowed the two men to take time off from their regular jobs to research and develop the best means of remote mechanical vehicle entry. "We had a budget of only $1,200," Richie remembered. "The first thing we did was go to breakfast to hash out the task.

Chapter 18

Donald always looked to take things one step further to find a better mousetrap. He told me we needed to operate like MacGyver [from the 1980s TV series, who was a secret agent educated as a scientist and carried a Swiss Army knife and a roll of duct tape]. We complemented each other, because I had come from the ESU and had a mechanical bent, while Donald was good at looking at problems from an explosives mindset."

The two men spent much of their time at Rodman's Neck. "Richie and I got vans and cars of various types from the Sanitation Department and exploded them, exploring different worst-case scenarios and ways of addressing all sorts of conditions." They spoke with welders from the New York City Transit Service, who showed Donald and Richie how best to drill a hole into the vehicle for placement of a fiber optic cable to view the inside. They also consulted with experts at the FBI and with friendly foreign techs such as the Brits, Germans, and Israelis.

Ultimately, they devised two methods of dealing with a possible vehicle IED. One, which arose from Richie's experiences in the ESU, was to disarm it remotely by robot. His idea piggy-backed on the availability of "Jaws of Life"—giant hydraulically powered shears—by George Hurst in the early 1960s after he viewed a stock-car-race accident in which it took workers more than an hour, using crowbars and circular saws, to remove an injured driver from his car.[59] "We were able to implement Richie's innovation," Donald noted, "with the help of Hurst Company engineers. Basically, we armed the bomb robot's arms with lightweight but super-powerful and pointy "stiletto" tips, similar to the ones used at the time for fixing aircraft. Then we ran the robot up to the car. Using its tips, it would cut its way through the vehicle like opening a can of vegetables."

The other method, suggested by Donald, was a technique known as "remote positive use of explosives," which means using an explosive to disable a more powerful one. "That term sounded like an oxymoron, and a lot of folks didn't care for it, but it was accurate. We used a robot to deliver a 'Tupperware shot,' which was a water-filled plastic container sealed with epoxy and wrapped with sheet explosives, with the blasting cap underneath. The robot would place the container on the rear hood of the car. It would rupture and blow open the gas tank, creating a fireball that would be quenched by the water. Eventually, we got to a point where we could predict how far the hood would fly and its arc."

Lieutenant Boser would visit Rodman's Neck weekly to gauge the two men's progress. "We kept a detailed log book of our experiments, findings, and failures," Donald recounted, "which he would review. We also gave him videotapes of our work. I felt we were highly successful, despite having only a small budget and getting no encouragement from others in the Squad. Some, even Squad supervisors, claimed we were chasing our tails and on a 'fool's errand.'"

After a year, Donald and Richie knew they had taken their research and development as far as it could

Chapter 18

go. "We needed tens of thousands of dollars to purchase equipment like a customized Hurst tool. But we couldn't get another dime. So, reluctantly, we ended the project."

*

By the early 1990s, Donald had become a senior member of the Squad and a team leader, respected for his knowledge and experience and tasked with regularly training other bomb techs. "I taught about the numerous types of IEDs and booby traps, how bombs might be disguised, never to enter a suspicious area through the main or obvious entrance if possible, and the like. I emphasized not just charging in and cutting a wire. Just the opposite—use remote techniques if at all possible. For a potential suicide-bomber situation, I told them you've got to take him out in the right way. If he's wearing a vest, shoot him in the head, not the chest."

One time, Donald brought his young son Donnie to a lecture. "I didn't understand most of what my father was talking about, but it was cool anyway. During one scenario that Dad ran, which required finding the hidden replica of a pipe bomb, he had me sit on it, to demonstrate the extremes to which some would go."

The early 1990s was a relatively tranquil time period. On January 3, 1993, in Moscow, George H. W. Bush and Boris Yeltsin signed the second Strategic Arms Reduction Treaty. Ten days later, 165 governments entered into the Chemical Weapons Convention, which outlawed the production, stockpiling, and use of chemical weapons.

Rendered Safe

And on January 20, 1993, Bill Clinton was sworn in as the 42nd President of the U.S. Looking back, Donald admitted that "it seemed not much of significance from a terrorism perspective had happened in our country in years or was liable to happen. Like most, I had no clue about what was lurking out there."

CHAPTER 19
Prelude

Americans are the descendants of apes and pigs who have been feeding from the dining tables of the Zionists, Communists, and colonialists.
—Omar Abdel-Rahman (the "Blind Sheikh")

THE MASTERMIND OF the February 26, 1993 World Trade Center bombing was Ramzi Ahmed Yosef. Born in April 1968 to a Sunni Muslim family in Fahaheel, outside Kuwait City, his birth name was Abdul Basit Mahmoud Abdul Karim. (Yousef used more than a dozen aliases during his terrorist career.) In 1986, after Yousef graduated high school, his parents returned to his father's native Baluchistan, a remote province in southwest Pakistan, while Yousef was sent to Wales to continue his education at the Technical College of the Swansea Institute, where he studied electrical engineering, became fluent in English, and joined a local chapter of the Egyptian Muslim Brotherhood.

Rendered Safe

In 1990, the urbane Yousef graduated and returned to Kuwait, where he obtained a job at the National Computer Center in the government's Planning Ministry. He also married and became a father. But the sedate life of an engineer and family man was not his calling. In late August, three weeks after Iraqi forces invaded Kuwait and began a seven-month occupation, Yousef traveled via Iran to the Pakistani city of Peshawar. In the 1980s, Peshawar, close to the border with Afghanistan, had been the base for the *mujahideen* struggle against the Soviet occupation of Afghanistan. It remained a lawless hotbed of Islamist extremism and hospitable to Osama bin Laden's newly formed al-Qaeda group, which pledged to bring the jihadist cause to other parts of the world such as Israel and America.

Yousef's mother's brother was Khalid Shaikh Mohammed Ali Fadden, who would later become the principal architect of the 9/11 attacks. Only three years older than Yousef, KSM had been an Islamic guerrilla fighter in the Soviet-Afghan War. With his uncle's help, Yousef joined the infamous Camp Khaldan terrorist camp, located in the mountains of Afghanistan's Paktia Province near the Pakistan border and the Tora Bora cave complex that bin Laden would escape to after 9/11.[60] At Camp Khaldan, Yousef received training in hand-to-hand combat, weapons and explosives use, bomb-making techniques, and the construction of firing circuits for bombs.

In the spring of 1992, the wiry, dark-haired, and bearded Yousef, who had a bulging nose, long ears,

Chapter 19

and a "horse face," met twenty-six-year-old Palestinian-born Ahmed Mohammad Ajaj at Camp Khaldan. The two agreed to apply their collective expertise to bomb targets in the United States. A year earlier, Ajaj had lived for a few months in Houston, where he filed a petition for political asylum, claiming the Israeli government had imprisoned and tortured him in retaliation for his peaceful opposition to the "occupation" of Palestine. Ajaj, who supported himself by delivering pizzas, failed to appear at the scheduled Immigration and Naturalization Service hearing on his asylum claim. He later left the country under an assumed name, ultimately arriving in Saudi Arabia. There, he obtained a letter of introduction to Camp Khaldan, which stated that the bearer, Ajaj, had come to the "land of jihad" for training in weapons and explosives use.

On September 1, 1992, Yousef and Ajaj traveled first class to New York on a Pakistan International Airlines flight from Karachi, although the two sat separately and pretended not to know one another. Upon arrival at JFK International Airport, Ajaj presented a stolen Swedish passport, as a traveler bearing a valid Swedish passport would not have needed a visa to enter the U.S. But it had been crudely altered by affixing his photo on top of the original one, immediately raising suspicion among Immigration and Naturalization Security officials. A secondary inspection of Ajaj's baggage uncovered additional stolen passports, bomb-making manuals, instructional videotapes on making explosives, letters referencing his attendance at terrorist training camps, and anti-American and anti-Israel propaganda. One of the agents brought in to search Ajaj's luggage was Steve Veyera of the FBI's New York City International Terrorism Squad. "I had with me an Arabic-speaking agent who read through the documents. It was the first time I ever heard the name 'al-Qaeda.' It was clear something was very wrong about Ajaj. To my mind, he was some kind of mule. My gut now tells me that the World Trade Center plotters had been looking to pull off the bombing earlier, around Christmas-time. But nabbing Ajaj, who had all the instructions, forced Yousef to delay."[61]

After his arrest, Ajaj pled guilty to passport fraud and was sentenced to six months' imprisonment. During his incarceration, he remained in contact with Yousef through an intermediary and continued to be involved in the bomb plot.

Yousef presented an Iraqi passport but lacked the visa needed to enter the country.[62] Moreover, his boarding pass was issued in a different name from his real one. Yousef requested political asylum, claiming he was fleeing Saddam Hussein's forces and had recently been beaten by Iraqi soldiers for being a member of a Kuwaiti guerrilla organization. He was arrested for entering the United States without a visa. The INS officer who questioned Yousef recommended he be detained, but she was overruled because the detention center's cells were full. Yousef was released on his own recognizance and given a hearing date, which he disregarded.

Chapter 19

Yousef contacted another Camp Khaldan comrade, a thirty-three-year old Egyptian-born taxi driver named Mahmud Abouhalima. Tall, beefy, with red hair and a fierce disposition, Abouhalima, who had fought with the *mujahideen* against the Soviet occupation in Afghanistan, was known as "Mahmud the Red." Reflecting a consistent theme among the plotters—manipulation of the U.S. immigration system—he had overstayed a tourist visa and later received amnesty under the 1986 Immigration and Reform and Control Act by falsely claiming to be an agricultural worker. After receiving his green card in 1990, Abouhalima made several trips to Pakistan for combat training.

Abouhalima at the time was the chauffeur for Sheikh Omar Abdel Rahman, a sightless Egyptian-born Muslim cleric who came to be referred to by law enforcement as the "Blind Sheikh." Abdel Rahman, known for his maroon-and-white fez, oversized dark glasses, and scruffy beard, had been in and out of Egyptian prisons during the 1980s. In May 1990, in spite of his name being on the State Department terrorist watch list, he found refuge in the United States and began preaching at the Al-Farouk Mosque in Brooklyn. He remained a leader of *Al-Jama'a al-Islamiyya* ("The Islamic Group"), a militant movement in Egypt responsible for numerous acts of violence, including the November 1997 Luxor massacre, in which 58 foreign tourists and four Egyptians were killed.

In November 1990, one of Abdel-Rahman's followers, El Sayyid Nosair, shot and killed Rabbi Meir Kahane, founder of the Jewish Defense League, in a Manhattan hotel. Abouhalima was the driver of Nosair's getaway car but botched the job, allowing for Nosair's capture. NYPD detectives found in Nosair's rented house in Cliffside, New Jersey, boxes of notebooks and other papers written in Arabic that revealed the existence of a terrorist cell operating in the New York City area. Among the papers were plans to attack a number of targets in New York City such as the World Trade Center. That evidence was largely ignored, and the papers weren't translated into English until after the 1993 Trade Center bombing.

Abouhalima helped Yousef obtain a livery license as a means of identifying himself and found him a rented room in the "Little Cairo" section of Jersey City, New Jersey, where a large concentration of Egyptian Muslims lived.[63] Many worshipped at the *Masjid al-Salaam* ("Mosque of Peace") located in a set of third-floor rooms above a Chinese restaurant and seedy variety store. The mosque was led by a radical Palestinian named Sultan el-Gawli, who had served time for conspiracy to smuggle 150 pounds of explosives to a member of the Palestine Liberation Organization in the Israeli-occupied West Bank.

Abouhalima pulled Yousef into the Blind Sheikh's clan of devoted followers, one of whom was twenty-five-year-old Mohammad Salameh, another close associate of El Sayyid Nosair. Salameh, whose last name means "peace" in Arabic, was a slightly built man with dark hair and a neatly trimmed beard. Born in 1967 in the

Chapter 19

Jordanian-controlled West Bank, he had entered the United States on a six-month tourist visa in 1988 but overstayed, remaining in the country illegally.

Salameh, widely considered an intellectually challenged bumbler, fell under Yousef's spell. The two men moved to another Jersey City apartment and began attending the Blind Sheikh's sermons, in which he spoke of destroying the "edifices of capitalism" and appealed to Muslims to assail the West, "cut the transportation of their countries, tear it apart, destroy their economy, burn their companies, eliminate their interests, sink their ships, shoot down their planes, and kill them on the sea, air, or land." During that fall, Yousef and Salameh scouted out Orthodox Jewish neighborhoods in Crown Heights and Williamsburg in Brooklyn with the idea of planting bombs there. But Yousef changed his mind, deciding they should "do one big explosion" at the World Trade Center after he concluded that most of the people who worked there were Jews. Their reconnaissance missions shifted to the Trade Center, with attention focused on its massive underground parking garage. The new goal was to topple the North Tower and have it fall onto the South Tower, killing the occupants of both buildings, which they estimated to be approximately 250,000 people.

Joining them in the purchase of chemicals and equipment and the assembly of an immense explosive was their former downstairs neighbor, Abdul Rahman Yasin. Yasin, a graduate student at City College who had spent most of his life in Iraq, was an American citizen by virtue of being born in Indiana while his father lived in the country as a foreign student. Another conspirator was Salameh's good friend Nidal Ayyad, a twenty-five-year-old, well-spoken graduate of Rutgers University with a Bachelor of Science degree in microbiology and chemistry who lived in nearby Maplewood, New Jersey. Ayyad, born in 1968 in Kuwait to Palestinian parents, immigrated to the United States in 1985 and was, by 1992, a U.S. citizen. He worked as a research engineer at AlliedSignal, a large New Jersey chemical company, which put him in an ideal position to help procure the necessary chemicals using company stationery. In October, Yasin and Ayyad opened a series of joint and individual bank accounts, to which Khalid Shaikh Mohammed and others from various Middle East countries wired funds.

There are a sizeable number of materials that can be made to explode. Because of its ease of purchase, the group determined that urea nitrate would be their bomb's main ingredient. By mid-November, Salameh and Yousef had contacted a series of chemical companies to obtain commercially manufactured urea (most often used for fertilizer) and nitric acid. From one Jersey City company alone—City Chemical Corporation—Yousef purchased 1,000 pounds of technical-grade urea, 105 gallons of nitric acid, and dozens of pounds of chemicals to be used as bomb boosters, including concentrated sulfuric acid to produce nitroglycerin cylinders. Steve Dodge of the Bomb Squad, among other investigators, later would comment that, given how unstable and volatile

Chapter 19

nitroglycerin is, they were "lucky bastards" not to have blown themselves up during bomb production.

Abouhalima, who was in daily contact with Salameh and Yousef, purchased smokeless powder to create detonators. Ayyad procured three red metal cylinders of compressed hydrogen, to enhance the bomb's destructive force, a trademark of Middle Eastern terrorists.

In late 1992, Salameh, using an alias, rented a ten-by-ten-foot shed on the second floor of one of the four pre-fab buildings constituting the Space Station Storage Company in Jersey City. It became the delivery and storage site for beakers, funnels, jars, glass tubes, transfer pumps, and vats of chemicals. The group also leased a ground-floor apartment near the storage shed for use as their bomb factory. (Terrorist groups often conduct operations out of a ground-floor space to facilitate escape.) Another conspirator, Eyad Ismoil, who grew up with Yousef in Fahaheel, flew in from Dallas, Texas. Ismoil was a Jordanian who had entered the United States in 1989 on a student visa to study engineering at Wichita State University and subsequently dropped out of school. He, too, overstayed his visa.

In late January 1993, the timing of the bombing was delayed when Salameh, who had failed the New Jersey driving test four times before succeeding in New York, skidded off a wet road, totaling his car and putting Yousef in the hospital for a week. The implementation date was reset for the beginning of the holy month of Ramadan. By that time, the group had been able to amass and

Rendered Safe

properly combine the ingredients necessary to assemble, without detection by law enforcement, a 1,300-pound bomb. No explosive device of anywhere near that size had ever before been detonated on American soil.

CHAPTER 20
February 26, 1993

It was pitch black. I thought I was blind. I crawled into a fetal position, and began to pray.

—Timothy Lang

ON TUESDAY, FEBRUARY 23, 1993, in the late afternoon, Salameh visited DIB Leasing, Ryder Company dealership on Kennedy Boulevard, in an industrial section of Jersey City a mile from the Bayonne city line. Using his real name but a fake New York driver's license, he put down $400 in cash as a deposit to rent a ten-foot yellow Ford Econoline panel van, which bore an Alabama license plate. The group had been struggling with financial issues, and Salameh used discount coupons to defray part of the rental cost.[64]

Two days later, Yousef, Abouhalima, and Salameh loaded the bomb into the van. The next morning, Friday, February 26, was marked by bone-chilling cold and a light falling snow. With Yousef in the passenger seat, Salameh drove the van to Manhattan, where they picked up Ismoil, a taxi driver, who traded places with Salameh behind the wheel. Salameh followed in a red Lincoln Town Car. The group headed to the World Trade Center complex. Located on a 16-acre site in lower Manhattan, the World Trade Center complex consisted of two 110-story office towers (North and South—only fifty yards apart), the 22-story New York Vista hotel (3 WTC) that at the time was owned and operated by Hilton International, two nine-story office buildings (4 and 5 WTC), the eight-story U.S. Customs House building (6 WTC), and a 47-story office building (7 WTC). On any given day, an estimated 150,000 workers, commuters, and visitors traveled through the complex.

Shortly after noon, Ismoil drove the van into the basement parking garage and down to the B-2 level (the public parking level), passing an enclosed area where the New York office of the Secret Service kept most of its vehicles.[65] He stopped the van on a ramp a hundred feet from the street entrance, beneath the Vista Hotel and along the south wall of the North Tower.[66]

Although parking in that spot was prohibited, delivery vehicles would routinely do so because it was wide enough not to block trailing vehicles. Yousef calculated that this site was ideal for using the internal geometry of the building to focus the force of a blast. With a match, he lit four 20-foot fuses that were threaded through and protected by surgical rubber tubing (which took twelve minutes to burn), locked the van and, with Ismoil, jumped

Chapter 20

into Salameh's car, which sped off to Canal Street, a mile away, from where they watched the events unfold.

At 12:18 p.m., the fire that raced up each of the fuses reached the blasting caps of gunpowder, igniting four containers of nitroglycerin. Those, in turn, detonated the compressed hydrogen canisters and the main bomb with a force of 800 pounds of TNT. An immense shrieking fireball of heat and gas burst out of the van. As depicted by FBI's Rick Hahn, "First there was a deafening roar that sounded like freight trains colliding at full throttle. It went on for several seconds, six, seven, eight and more. Simultaneously there was a shudder, one violent shake, and then continuing jolts of lesser magnitude."

The sound of the blast, which reverberated throughout the Wall Street vicinity and a mile away on Ellis and Liberty Islands in New York Harbor, baffled many. Joe Connor, working a half-mile away on the 36th floor of the 60 Wall Street skyscraper, heard what he assumed was thunder. "I looked out my window, which faced the World Trade Center, and saw it was snowing. I thought it weird to hear thunder during a snowstorm."

The two soaring towers and the Vista Hotel each swayed noticeably, but held. The blast tore out from concrete and steel an L-shaped crater six stories deep and 130 feet wide, destroyed portions of the above B-1 level (the hotel parking level), set fires from the plaza level down to the B-6 level, showered broken glass into the towers' lobbies, blew out walls and ceilings in the hotel, severed miles of power and communication cables,

183

crushed the Trade Center's air-conditioning units on level B-6, and propelled an 18-foot, seven-ton steel cross beam 75 feet from where it braced part of the parking structure into the North Tower. The steel and concrete ceiling of the PATH station on level B-5 collapsed, leaving dozens trapped under rubble. Plumes of hot, thick, toxic black smoke emanated from fireproofing material, gasoline, insulation, burnt vehicles that had been hurtled about as if they were toys, and other sources. The smoke made its way from the basement into the elevator shafts and emergency stairwells, turning them into giant chimneys. Two million gallons of water gushed from severed pipes into the sub-grade levels. Nearly all electricity to the complex was cut, and the remaining power lines had to be cut to avoid electrocution, plunging both towers into darkness.[67] Most non-cable television stations in the greater New York region were blacked out when the transmitters atop the North Tower lost power. The bomb compromised, though not disastrously, the ability of the bathtub-like Trade Center basement to keep the New York Harbor waters out.

The complex's telephone lines remained intact, and reports of those trapped in the buildings soon overloaded the city's 911 system. First responders from the New York Fire Department (including 130 fire engines and dozens of pumpers), EMS, NYPD, and Port Authority police swarmed the scene within minutes. By the end of the day, the NYFD had sent to the Trade Center close to

Chapter 20

half of its on-duty firemen, representing its first 16-alarm response ever.

The blast resulted in the largest building evacuations ever recorded, of 60,000 workers and visitors. (The towers were relatively full when the bombing occurred, as wintery conditions kept most inside during lunch hour.) Those evacuations were conducted in an atmosphere of panic magnified by the loss of each tower's public address system. People fleeing the towers and hotel into the streets of lower Manhattan made their way with improvised light sources such as cigarette lighters or mini-flashlights through pitch-black, smoke-clogged stairwells, many emerging gasping, bent over, retching soot, and with raccoon-eyed faces. Two hundred elementary school children were stranded on the 107th floor observation deck, forcing them and hundreds of others on the upper floors to hike down over a quarter of a mile, a trek that took as long as ten hours. Among them was a class of kindergartners from Brooklyn, who on the way down were encouraged to sing to keep up their spirits. Many others had to be carried out by first responders, who strode up dozens of flights of stairs or down through rubble.

Damage to the WTC Command Center made communication with most of the stalled elevator cars impossible. Carl Selinger, a 46-year-old Port Authority manager who worked on the 65th floor of the North Tower, was trapped alone in an elevator for five-and-a-half dark hours, worrying the smoke seeping in from the elevator shaft would choke him. He blindly wrote a goodbye letter to his family on a piece of loose-leaf paper. When the lights went out, he paced, sang, and waited, all the while holding a handkerchief over his face. Selinger was rescued by an NYPD ESU officer, Timothy Farrell, who had rappelled from a helicopter to the roof of the North Tower.

Gene Fasullo, a Port Authority chief engineer, summarized his experience being trapped in an elevator with nine others:

> After 10 minutes, we smelled smoke. After 20 minutes, smoke began pouring into the bottom of our elevator. During this time, we pressed the emergency button. We only got a recorded message over and over again that said, "Message received; please be patient." Since we didn't know how long it would be before help arrived, we decided to force the elevator doors open with our hands and used our nail files and car keys to dig. It took us two hours to dig through that wall. When we broke through, we were able to gulp some fresh air from the first hole we had made. Then we came upon a second, plasterboard wall. After an hour, we dug into a ladies bathroom and stepped out.

To firefighter William Duffy, finding an elevator packed with people who had collapsed from smoke "was like opening up a tomb."

Chapter 20

Many other eyewitness accounts were equally harrowing. Timothy Lang, a stock trader who had parked his car on the B-2 level, was lifted into the air by the explosion. Suffering from a large gash on his head, a broken nose, and a concussion, Lang, who at first believed he'd been blinded, began groping in the dark fumes. Climbing over a wall, he fell onto a dead body. Panic-stricken, Lang crawled in every direction until he came to the lip of the bomb crater. He backed off and curled up, believing "I would have to lie there until I was saved, or until I died." Hearing voices and banging, Lang cried out. A boot lit by the beam of a flashlight appeared, and Lang was lifted to safety by two first responders.

One firefighter, Kevin Shea, fell into the crater:

> Suddenly the floor underneath me gave way, and I fell 45 feet straight down, from the B-1 level onto rubble piled on the B-5 level. When I fell, I grabbed onto reinforcing bars sticking out of concrete, but I couldn't hold on. I hit debris on the bottom at a 45-degree angle, feet first, then fell on my back. My leather helmet saved my life: My face smashed into the concrete when I fell. I was conscious the entire time. I landed a few feet away from fire. My shoulder was slightly burned from being so close. I didn't realize how far I had fallen or how big the crater was. I saw bright lights of fire all around me. I also heard explosions that were so loud I could feel them in my chest.

Rendered Safe

The explosion, which was estimated to have caused $500 million in property damage, was pronounced by the FBI as the "largest by weight and by damage of any improvised explosive device we've seen since the inception of forensic explosive identification." More than a thousand were injured, including dozens of responding police, firefighters, and emergency medical services workers, with many suffering from smoke inhalation. Other injuries were major trauma and burns from the blast, cardiac problems, cuts from falling glass, and bruises, and internal harm from the press of the crowd, generating the greatest number of hospital casualties of any domestic terrorist event to that time. Scores of people on the upper floors, including a pregnant woman, fled to the roofs of both towers and were airlifted by NYPD helicopters.[68] Search and evacuation of the towers were completed eleven hours after the incident began.

The identities of five murdered persons quickly were determined. One was 35-year-old Ecuadorian-born Monica Rodriguez Smith, a secretary working for the Port Authority who was at her desk having lunch and studying time sheets for the Center's janitorial staff. The yellow van had been parked on the other side of her windowless office wall. She was seven months pregnant with her first child, a boy whom she and her husband had already named Eddie. That Friday was going to be her last day of work before going on maternity leave. She was in the World Trade Center to train the person who would be her replacement.

Chapter 20

The others were 45-year-old John DiGiovanni, a dental-products salesman headed to a client meeting who drove into the garage at the wrong time, 61-year-old Bob Kirkpatrick, an Air Force veteran and the Port Authority's senior locksmith for the towers, who was planning to retire later that year, 47-year-old Steven Knapp, married with two children who was the Trade Center's Port Authority's Chief Mechanical Supervisor (he was Monica Smith's boss), and 57-year-old Bill Macko, an ex-Marine and the Assistant Chief Mechanical Supervisor for the Trade Center, married with four children. In the final minutes of their lives, Kirkpatrick, Knapp, and Macko were eating lunch together in an employees' break room next to Smith's office, and DiGiovanni was parking.

An FBI agent at the scene pronounced the relatively low number of fatalities as "a miracle." Had the bomb gone off at the beginning or end of the work day, the number of dead likely would have been exponentially higher.[69]

CHAPTER 21
Devastation

The door slides back and I get two taps on my shoulder, signaling me to jump. But, just then, a violent cross wind pulls the copter to the right. All of a sudden, I'm looking straight down 110 stories.

—Donald Sadowy

DURING LUNCHTIME ON February 26, 1993, Donald and Steve Berberich were reviewing old case files in the basement of the Bomb Squad's headquarters. Those archives hold the records of every known bomb ever set or exploded in New York City, and Squad detectives often spend time reviewing files to learn as much as possible about past IEDs and how they were handled.

"We heard on the SOD city-wide frequency," Donald recalled, "about an enormous explosion at the Trade Center, only two miles away, supposedly caused by a transformer or gas explosion. [At the time, underground explosions caused by non-terrorist issues were relatively frequent.] Then Lieutenant Boser rang us. He'd gotten calls from Chief of Detectives Joseph Borelli and from Ray Kelly, and he ordered us down there ASAP.[70] We changed into jumpsuits and boots, got our black bags, and rushed down, gathering at the command center that had been set up outside the North Tower."

They and many other Squad officers arrived to find people streaming out of the towers, scores of police, firemen, paramedics and other first responders milling about, and emergency vehicles double- and triple-parked blocking traffic on West Street, the eight-lane north-south highway that runs past the Trade Center. Black smoke emanated from blown-out gates on a ramp leading to the garage. Berberich asked a nearby Con Ed supervisor if there had been a transformer explosion. "The guy shook his head and said, 'No fucking way.'"

Also racing to the scene were FBI and ATF agents. The ATF's National Response Team was a group of close to one hundred investigators, chemists, and explosives experts who worked on large-scale bombings around the country, with separate teams covering the East Coast, West Coast, Midwest, and South. "The ATF," Donald recounted, "came in force, bringing large command vans with phones, communication systems, computers, shovels, generators, suits, and other stuff."

Quick crime lab chemical analysis revealed traces of nitrates. However, the FBI waited two days until announcing it had established that a bomb was responsible for the blast. Months later, a party was held for an NYPD cop who

Chapter 21

had been promoted. Several FBI and ATF agents were invited. At one point during the raucous celebration, an NYPD detective took the microphone and deadpanned, "By the way, are there any FBI agents here tonight?" Several men raised their hand. The detective yelled out, "Good. We have breaking news for you guys. It was a bomb!"

The Squad members stood around in the staging area on West Street for hours waiting for the smoke to clear enough to begin to investigate. As described by Donald, "they were shivering and frustrated, with little to do except watch firemen and policemen going in and out in their search for people still stuck in the buildings. Some people on higher floors followed the instructions of news broadcasters to break windows to get fresh air. That broken glass struck and injured people exiting the building. We also worried that people in the building would fall out, but fortunately none did."

While Donald and other Squad members waited, Sergeant Mark Torre, in his first week with the Squad, showed up at the site. (Years later, Torre, who previously had been the commanding officer of the NYPD Arson and Explosion Squad, would assume command of the Bomb Squad.) "I was a brand-new, baby-faced Squad member," Torre admitted. "Nobody wanted to talk to me because I didn't come from the Bomb Squad and didn't belong. Even though I outranked most of the veterans, I had no standing. That's just the way things were. Fortunately, I had gotten to know Donald and Richie from observing their R&D work on vehicle bombs, which impressed me. They weren't like the others. They always were very welcoming. It was those two guys who recommended to Lieutenant Boser that I be accepted into the Squad."

"Mark stood there," Donald remembered, "in brand new shiny black leather boots and a Nomex jumpsuit with the NYPD Bomb Squad logo, borrowed because he hadn't been in the Squad long enough to have his own. A few of us guys looked at each other, smiled, and walked over to Mark. Before he could protest, we picked him up and playfully tossed him into a pile of building debris. To get dirt on him, so he didn't look like a rookie. We all had a laugh, including Mark."

Once the smoke died down, Donald and other Squad detectives, holding portable box lights, hiked down toward the B-2 level, finding stairways and portions of the ramp gone, tons of debris strewn all over, massive walls either blown down or severely cracked, burst steam pipes, buckled support columns, miles of electrical cables dancing about, and huge slabs of concrete clinging precariously to steel reinforcement rods. "We fought the wind," Donald recalled, "which was whipping through the openings. Your sense of the enormity of the destruction was heightened as you made your way down the layer-cake levels. The damage had been magnified because the bomb had gone off in a somewhat contained area, allowing the pressure waves to bounce off the concrete walls, floors, and ceilings."

Chapter 21

Steve Dodge was among those who ventured into the destruction. "For the cars we initially saw, which were relatively intact, the blast shock wave had turned on every headlight and alarm. In hindsight, we were foolish, in that we were looking for evidence, but not for any secondary explosive devices that may have been left there. It wasn't yet part of the established protocol."

At one point, the men were stopped by several firemen. Decades later, in a hushed tone, Donald related how "beyond them, there was nothing except a dark pit the size of a football field and deep like a canyon. Fires continued to burn. The box lights we carried allowed you to see more than 150 feet, but you still couldn't make out the other side of the crater. Water was cascading down from the broken water lines. Even worse, the waste lines had been shattered, so waste was pouring down also, which later led to guys getting ill from ear and throat infections. I was glad it was so cold, cause that reduced the bad smell. There were fires all over, which mixed with the chemical residue left by the bomb and caused acrid smoke that hurt your nose and throat to breathe in. Some of the large red metal support beams were bowed out and leaning heavily, and parts of the floor foamed with dust and felt unstable. I knew we each had an unstated fear the building would collapse on us."

Nearing the blast center, Donald took note of all the vehicles that were "burnt and pulverized, many turned upside down, with all their tires melted and paint

Rendered Safe

incinerated by hot gasses. Some were no more than two feet high, and looked like the Jolly Green Giant had stepped on them. You couldn't tell a Mercedes from a Chevy. And forget about license plates. But they provided clues. As you get closer to the seat of explosion, the cars should become more mangled and the fragments smaller."

Anticipating the need to find the origin of the blast and to recover evidence, Donald mentioned to Mark Torre and others that he wanted to rappel down into the yawning void of the crater. "For the first time," Torre recounted, "I acted like a boss. I told him 'No,' because he easily could impale himself on some jagged rebar, have a piece of steel go in a leg and come out a cripple. He wasn't happy."

Around 9 p.m., a call came over the citywide radio that emergency responders who were continuing to search the North Tower had found on the 86th floor, lying in a stairway next to a vertical support, several heavy, bulky boxes sealed with tape. Sticking out of the boxes were wires twisted together. "Given the circumstances," Donald observed, "there was enormous concern, which paralyzed the search."

Lieutenant Boser worried about the difficulty of having bomb technicians hike up dozens of stairways with equipment. He asked the Aviation Unit to fly one of their larger helicopters from the landing zone, a ball field off of West Street, to a nearby parking lot, to carry a team of Squad officers to the roof from where they would walk down. Boser asked for volunteers. Donald

Chapter 21

quickly stepped up, along with Squad Detectives Tony Ruggirello and Steve Berberich, and two men from the Emergency Services Unit. For Berberich, it was only his second helicopter ride ever. Already inside were a pilot, co-pilot, and crew chief. "We tossed in 85-pound bomb suits, a 45-pound military tool box, and X-ray equipment," Donald remembered. "The motor and blades were so loud that you couldn't hear, so the crew members each wore a headset sealed around their ears that had a microphone. We hunkered down on bench seats as the copter took off."

In the star-pierced darkness, the helicopter rose to the top of the North Tower which, unlike the South Tower, had no helipad and whose roof was covered with antennas. As described by Rick Hahn, "The tower held a huge mast that rose 362 feet above the roof of the building. It supported a number of television and radio antennas. Stabilization for the antennas depended on guy wires, tensioned thick steel cables attached from points on the antenna to various outlying points on the roof. As the pilot approached the northwest corner, he studied the wires, searching for a way to get the craft close enough to the roof to deposit his cargo without hitting the wires."

Unable to land, the pilot hovered six feet above, signaling to Donald and the others that they would have to jump out. Donald was to be first. "I'm sitting disoriented on the open deck with the balls of my boots on the landing skid. I've got a canvas bag slung over my shoulder with my bomb suit in it. Tony crouched behind me, one

197

hand braced against the fuselage and the other holding my backpack. The copter is bucking back and forth like a ship in heavy seas because of the winds. I'm top heavy because of the bag and teetering out. I had been out of sorts from the moment we took off, but now I was scared shitless. I hear the crew chief yelling into the microphone in the headset that Sadowy is not secure, and then sets of hands pulled me back in like Humpty Dumpty."

The pilot leveled the helicopter off and opened the throttle, heading toward Battery Park and the Statue of Liberty, giving time for ESU personnel on the roof to cut hold-down cables. Donald watched apprehensively as the copter made its second approach. "We came in at a different angle and hovered over the roof corner. I couldn't hear the crew chief, but I stepped up on the landing-skid deck and, under the spinning blades, jumped the six feet, followed by the other guys. The four of us gathered the equipment and marched down. We were overweight detectives, not athletes, and I was exhausted by the time we reached the 86th floor."

The Squad team set up a safe area to assemble equipment and the X-ray machine, where Donald and Tony suited up. "Tony and I checked out the boxes, and they turned out to contain spare parts for high-tech computers. We gave the all-clear signal, and ESU continued doing its sweep of the building. Fortunately, by then, we were able to take the elevator down from the 78th floor sky lobby. Around 11 p.m., as the late-tour guys were arriving, I headed back to the office, signed out, and drove

Chapter 21

home in my shitty, twelve-year-old Chevy Nova in which nothing worked well, including the heater. I had such a level of unease that I barely slept."

CHAPTER 22
Futility

There were no stairways available because they'd been blown out or filled with crushed concrete and debris. You'd get to the bottom of a ramp and the floor would end. So, you'd have to carefully climb down, without the benefit of a secure line or rope.

—Donald Sadowy

CONSTRUCTION CREWS WORKED through the night in the wrecked basement to secure the structural integrity of the towers. On Saturday morning, lower Manhattan was barricaded, nearby hospitals were overflowing with wounded, and jittery officials were trying to calm a fearful public. Donald returned to the Trade Center garage entrance at six thirty, joining Lieutenant Boser and others who were huddled with several Port Authority engineers. "There was no more smoke," Donald recollected. "And no pedestrian vehicle traffic. We stood around with coffee and ham and egg sandwiches reviewing large blueprints

Rendered Safe

rolled over the hood of a police van as the engineers reviewed the structure of the buildings. The lieutenant left to brief Commissioner Kelly and Governor Cuomo at 26 Federal Plaza."

Officials from the Occupational Safety and Health Administration had arrived and insisted that no one be allowed to enter the sub-basement until an acceptable amount of structural shoring up had been done by Port Authority engineering and construction personnel to ensure stability. "We were on standby for hours," Donald recalled, "getting increasingly antsy. Then we heard that there was a person, William Mercado, unaccounted for, who might still be alive and trapped under rubble and debris."

To assess the damage, develop a plan for working the crime scene for evidence, and assist the effort to rescue Mercado, several Squad members—Donald, Steve Dodge, Pete Dalton, and Denis Mulcahy, who would form the core Bomb Squad group assigned to the Trade Center investigation, plus three FBI bomb techs—Donald Haldiman, Steve Veyera, and Kendrick Williams—donned jumpsuits, work boots, and construction helmets and headed into the menacing, cavernous lower levels. Each carried an oversized, rechargeable Portalight hung from a shoulder-to-hip strap. Donald also brought a set of Blasters tools (specialized tools commonly used by bomb squads and military agencies) held on his leather belt in place of his gun. "Someone asked me what we were looking for. I answered, 'I'll know it when I see it.'"

Chapter 22

The men spread out as they carefully made their way down. "It was super cold and felt like entering a wind tunnel," Donald remembered. "And the quiet was eerie. Every couple of minutes, I took out my K-bar, which I still had from my Marine days, tapped on a piece of pipe or metal, yelled out 'Wilfredo' or 'Mr. Mercado,' and then held motionless and listened carefully."

Donald and the other law-enforcement officers navigated the hostile sub-basement environment several times that day, making their way to different areas, and trading information on where they traversed and what they observed. "We'd come up to street level to pee and get some hot food," Donald recalled, "and be checked by EMS [Emergency Medical Squad] personnel to make sure we were okay. Reporters were everywhere, desperate to uncover anything remotely newsworthy and giving interviews to anyone, mostly people who knew nothing about what was really going on. One of them was overheard telling a reporter that no one was searching for Mercado because he was Hispanic. That got us all livid."

By the end of the day, the searchers had found nothing of significance. Donald arrived back home around midnight, filthy, exhausted, and hungry. "Kathy made me a meal as I sat thinking about all the time spent down in the lower levels. I would be up and back at it only a few hours later, but the effort seemed so futile."

CHAPTER 23
Chassis Frame

Detective Sadowy's ability to recognize the potential of this piece of evidence was astounding given the massive destruction of numerous vehicles, the extremely dangerous structural condition of the parking-garage ramp, and the lack of lighting.
—Malcolm Brady, Assistant Special Agent in Charge, ATF National Response Team

EARLY SUNDAY, BEFORE THE sun touched the morning, Donald and his Squad colleagues again were conferring with Lieutenant Boser, the Squad's liaison with the ATF and FBI, inside a large police van, to plan for the day. Given the enormity of the task, there was no small talk.

After the meeting broke up, Donald wandered off and sat alone in the middle of a broken slab that had been part of the garage floor. "I pulled my knees up, folded my hands over them, and put my head down. The situation seemed hopeless. Much of the vital evidence, including what remained of the vehicle that had delivered the bomb, likely was buried under rubble.[71] Where do you start to find clues as to how the bombing was done and who did it? It was a needle in a haystack. I thought of my old boss, Jack Kelly, who had taught me so much about how to be a bomb tech. Jack had passed away months earlier from a stroke and aneurism. I said a prayer to him, and tried to figure out how Jack would have approached solving this case."

Donald overheard that members of the Joint Terrorist Task Force were gathering in the Vista Hotel's ground-floor Grand Ballroom to examine the damage there. He joined them. The JTTF is an interagency investigative group that was originally formed in the early 1980s to combat a rash of bombings by Puerto Rican independence groups. At the time of the Trade Center bombing, the JTTF consisted of approximately 50 agents from the FBI, NYPD, State Department, Secret Service, Immigration and Naturalization Service, Federal Aviation Administration, U.S. Marshals Service, ATF, New York State Police and Port Authority.

Donald entered the room, two stories above the blast, to find it "filled with rubble from shattered walls and floors. Broken furniture was strewn about. Stretching out from its center was a huge hole. All of the clocks were stopped at 12:18. Decorating the walls of the ballroom were banners and bunting for a sports-award luncheon that had been scheduled for 1 p.m. on Friday for dozens of teachers, coaches, students, and parents. Many of them

Chapter 23

would have been injured or killed had the luncheon begun at noon. It was a sobering thought."

Initially, when the origin of the explosion was yet to be determined, the ATF led the inquiry. However, once the cause was determined to have been a bomb, the FBI, among whose missions is to protect against terrorist threats, assumed the top role. "That caused tension," Rick Hahn recalled, "because the ATF came in raring to go with their pre-organized national response teams. The FBI had no similar component." In fact, many ATF agents resented the FBI's lead role because, as summarized by John Goetz of the ATF, "the FBI didn't know its ass from its elbow when it came to large-scale bomb investigations."

Neil Herman, the Supervisory Special Agent in charge of the JTTF, headed the investigation, code-named "Tradebom." James Fox, affable and avuncular, who ran the FBI's New York office at 26 Federal Plaza, became its face, appearing regularly on television to report on progress. The FBI had initiated use of the JTTF to ensure coordination among the agencies. But the Bureau's heavy hand was evident. As Ray Kelly would later comment, "With the FBI running the investigation, we knew only what they told us . . . They held the information closely, and they seemed to like it that way."

Donald mixed in with the dozens of FBI and ATF agents milling about and bumping into each other, many in their logo nylon jackets. "We had heard there was an

Rendered Safe

unfriendly competition between the FBI and ATF. They seemed to me like players from opposing football teams." (ATF-FBI feuding, which led to racing each other to crime scenes, failing to share information, and refusing to train together, was common knowledge and continued for decades.[72])

Heading the meeting was David Williams, an FBI Laboratory Division technician who had arrived the day before to assume the Case Agent role. Williams, the agency's senior bomb expert, had worked on the 1983 bombing of the Marine barracks in Beirut and the 1988 Pan Am Flight 103 disaster, known as the "Lockerbie bombing." Williams impressed Donald as "a big, alpha man with a real physical presence. A no-nonsense guy who wanted leads ASAP."

Williams asked the group in the ballroom to gather together. "We pulled up chairs," Donald recounted, "and sat in a large circle. He told us the FBI couldn't handle this alone and that he needed everyone's help, working shoulder to shoulder. Which made sense given the depth of expertise of the Bomb Squad and the ATF National Response Team folks. Then we went around and each person announced his or her name, rank, agency, and field of proficiency."

Afterward, the FBI's Steve Veyera, who had worked with the Bomb Squad on numerous occasions, suggested that a multi-agency team composed of people with varying skill sets be sent down to the B-2 level to take photos, videos, sketches, measurements, and chemical

Chapter 23

swab samples.[73] This enabled them, according to Veyera, to "gain an initial idea of what was there, identify the presence of forensic evidence, and determine the limits of the explosion so we could understand what could be released back to the Port Authority. It was important that the basement begin to be restored. That plan followed the basic tenets of bomb-technician work—to protect life and property, collect evidence, and to try to get the scene back to normal."

Williams questioned how, without passable stairways and ramps, the team would make its way through the sub-basement. Veyera pointed out that Donald "had been crawling around in the basement's bowels for the past two days like a groundhog." Donald piped in that he already had an area in mind on the B-2 level.

Williams selected twelve people from the FBI, ATF, NYPD, and Bomb Squad. Among them were a sketch artist, photographer, lab tech, chemist, and explosive experts. He asked Donald to guide the group to where they would have the best opportunity to locate the origin of the blast, from where investigators later would work outward in a circle.[74] Williams also ordered in no uncertain terms that nothing was to be removed from the scene until ground rules and protocols were established. "Dave was a tough guy with a big ego," Hahn explained. "'Super Dave' was his nickname. If you crossed him, you paid for it. But his order made good sense. Dave didn't want anyone 'showboating' and in the process destroying evidence or making it inadmissible in court. He had the long-range view that this massive case could be solved if everyone cooperated and worked in a meticulous manner as a team."

As the group readied to head down, Donald cautioned that the trip would be risky. "No one hesitated. There was a combined sense of patriotism I'd never seen the likes of before. We all had the feeling that this was our generation's Pearl Harbor—a sneak attack on our country—and we needed to pull together."

One of those chosen for the group was Jessica Gotthold, a certified explosives specialist with the ATF's National Response Team who specialized in post-blast investigations. Gotthold had been an undercover agent and competitive power lifter who at the time was married to a former New York City cop and working for a local police department in Monroe, New York.[75] She was at a retirement luncheon in the Bronx on the day of the bombing. "At the same time, everyone's pager went off, so we knew they were mustering the National Response Team and that it must be something big." Gotthold, known for her expertise in evidence collecting, arrived at the Trade Center on Sunday morning and remained in the vicinity for weeks. She was pleased to be following Donald into the bomb scene. "Donald was experienced and capable in a way that none of the FBI guys seemed to be. Plus, he was a nice person, low key, and without the arrogance or macho ego a lot of those guys had. Law enforcement was a good-old-boys club back then, but Donald was very inclusive."

Chapter 23

Each of the twelve donned a two-piece white jumpsuit, helmet, gloves, and boots, along with a small tool bag strapped around their waist. Every person also carried a large rectangular flashlight with a powerful battery strapped over their shoulder and chest. Several brought thermal-imaging cameras.

"It's hard to put into words what the environment that we entered was like," Gotthold recounted. "The sub-basement was the largest crime scene any of us had ever been to. It was an adrenaline rush from an investigative point of view. But it also was surreal, frightening, creepy, and dark. This was early on, before the engineers and construction guys put in lights, so you couldn't easily tell what was ahead. You needed to crouch a lot because of all the loose communications cables. And be extremely cautious with every step you took, not only to avoid getting hurt, but because the basement was so structurally compromised. I also was worried about sucking in asbestos."

Another ATF National Response Team member who joined the group was John Goetz, a certified fire investigator (colloquially known as a "digger"). "The environment we entered was unbelievable, even for those of us who had seen a lot of major bombings. The best way I can describe it succinctly is that it looked like a war zone. What really frightened me was when you heard chunks of concrete fall. For years, I had nightmares from being there that day. Thinking about it still raises the hairs on the back of my head."

Donald was given an FBI radio for emergency use. "Off we went, each of us nervous, but with a sense of urgency. I asked everyone to follow me closely. Once we started down the ramp, the banter stopped." They trekked slowly, single file on the narrowest of paths through a phantasmagoria of broken concrete, steel, reinforcing bars, light fixtures, and cable, all the while on the lookout for items that appeared out of place as well as for IED components. Shining a light on where he wanted them to step, Donald guided the group to the B-2 level and proceeded carefully around the crater's edge to a far side. "My reasoning was that not only was this beneath the ballroom of the New York Vista Hotel, the most likely site of the bomb's origin, but it was a relatively pristine area. You could see that from the dust. No one had been there because it was hard to get to. Once we arrived, everyone spread out, took out their gear, and started doing their thing." (At the time, before environmental concerns stopped the practice, urea pellets were commonly used to de-ice surfaces. As a result, when swabs were taken, it wasn't at first indicative that urea nitrate had been the key bomb ingredient.)

Donald teamed up with Joe Hanlin, a senior ATF enforcement official based in Atlanta who had been an explosives-ordnance-disposal officer in the US Army, experienced in disarming all types of bombs globally. The two men spotted a loose pinion gear, ordinarily a part of a car's rear-differential-gear assembly, designed to move a larger gear that turns the rear axles. Making their way further, they noticed parts of the undercarriage

Chapter 23

of a vehicle and sat to examine them. "What caught my eye," Donald remembered, "were two curved pieces of metal that looked like an eggshell when you put them together. I recognized this as the outer housing of the differential or gear train [which transmits power to the wheels while allowing them to rotate at different speeds] for a larger vehicle. Bending down carefully on our hands and knees, we picked up pieces and tried to put them back together hodgepodge in the bell housing shell. It was like working on a giant Rubik's Cube. I would have had no chance if not for what I'd learned in high school. I told Joe that I'd never seen such damage to an undercarriage, and that it was really significant, because we're dealing with cobalt steel that had been put under tremendous pressure. High-explosive damage [a "high explosive" decomposes rapidly and with much destructive force—examples are nitroglycerin, TNT, and dynamite] is unique and can't be duplicated with machinery. It's only seen on materials very close to the explosion. Everything else was burnt, bent, and mangled, but still in one piece. This had been blown apart. I thought it had to have come from the vehicle that carried the bomb."

Further on, at the edge of the crater, the two discovered a four-foot-long piece of metal jutting out of debris at an angle. "We gently tugged and pulled it back, and removed bits of concrete. It was scary because the pieces would fall into the crater and you wouldn't hear them hit for several seconds. With Joe holding his light on it, I examined the metal and saw that it was a mangled piece of chassis frame."

213

Rendered Safe

Donald remembered what Larry Riccio had taught him years ago about every vehicle's unique 17-digit vehicle identification number. The automotive equivalent of DNA, the VIN reveals where the vehicle was manufactured and when, and its body type, make, model, and options. "Larry had worked in the NYPD's auto crime unit. Whenever we got together after I stopped working with him, we were like two old yentas, talking about everything we did. Once, I'd ask him how he figured out where a burnt-out car came from. Larry told me that confidential VIN codes are stamped by the manufacturer into various metal objects in places such as the frame, rear wheel well, underneath the spare tire, inside the driver-side doorjamb, and the engine block. It's not always a complete VIN but, rather, a code that can be used to find the full, public VIN."

With that in mind, Donald searched for more parts that may have come from the same vehicle. He studied a 15-feet-by-15-feet slab of concrete that hung precariously at the edge of the abyss suspended by threads of steel reinforcing bar. On it was what appeared from its unique shape to be another part of a damaged chassis frame rail from a car or truck. Crawling on his stomach, Donald inched his way out onto the hanging slab. Reaching the five-foot long piece of metal, he ran his fingers through its inner surface, feeling the "peened" numbers and letters typical of identifying marks on vehicles. Donald carefully moved himself and the metal piece back onto the secure floor that remained.

Chapter 23

The two men, holding their prize on each end, examined it. "The forged steel was twisted like a piece of licorice. It had signs of 'bluing,' the result of intense heat scorching blue spots on the steel. And there was a lot of carbon on it." Donald took the glove off his right hand and, with his thumb, rubbed the underside of the metal back and forth. "When I got halfway, I felt a series of raised dots followed by a long series of letters and numbers that ended in a star shape. I looked up, smiled, and said to Joe, 'This is the C-VIN [confidential VIN number] code. And I think it's from the vehicle that held the bomb, because otherwise it wouldn't have been blown away from under the vehicle.'"

Their hearts racing, Donald and Joe carried the various parts to the far end of B-2 level and gathered together the team. Donald announced, "I know that Dave Williams specifically said not to touch, remove, or bring any evidence out, but we believe this stuff is important. Debris could fall and cover them, and it might take weeks to find them again. So, they're too valuable to leave behind." Several were skeptical given Williams' admonition. Donald asked for everyone's help, making clear that he would take the heat personally. A consensus was reached in support of removing the vehicle parts.

At that moment, Donald's FBI radio crackled. The female dispatcher came on to inform him that the Port Authority would be pulling a crushed train out of the damaged PATH station underneath the towers. "That could cause falling or shifting debris," she cautioned

Donald. "You all have fifteen minutes to get out of there." The prospect of a rumbling train causing a secondary collapse clinched Donald's decision.

The team members scrambled to pack their gear and helped Donald and Joe gather the evidence and move it to higher ground. Donald and Joe rushed up to street level and toward several ESU men. "We asked them to bring over two Stokes baskets [wire stretchers with sides and a removable cover designed to transport an adult in a search-and-rescue operation—best known from Korean and Vietnam War images of rescues of the injured] and two body bags." Donald and Joe hustled back down with them. "We laid one body bag in the basket and took all those metal parts from the undercarriage and chassis frame and placed them orderly on the body bag. Then we strapped the body bag to the basket. We put the other body bag on top and strapped it down. Several of us each grabbed a piece of the basket, and we cautiously made our way to street level, just beating the deadline."

Before the team arrived at a point at street level where they could be detected by the hovering media, Donald jogged ahead to speak with two nearby NYPD officers sitting in a station wagon. "I asked one of them, a sergeant who I'd previously worked with, to ask cops to use their cars to shut down the West Side Highway going south and not allow any press vans with film crew to follow us for five minutes. The cops quickly swung their cars into place. Another officer backed a station wagon down the ramp. We loaded the basket into it, and the station wagon came

Chapter 23

rolling up the ramp with lights on and siren blaring. It hauled ass on the West Side Highway, swung underneath the Horn [the curved tunnel that connects the east and west sides of lower Manhattan] and onto the FDR Drive, and headed for the underground garage of the Police Academy building on 20th Street that housed the NYPD crime lab. I heard that the media guys went crazy and cursed at us, but there was nothing they could do. Some sped north on the highway to the Medical Examiner's Office, wrongly guessing that we had found the body of Mercado."

That the pendulum had swung in law enforcement's favor still was unknown in the early evening when Donald, physically and mentally drained, headed through the corridor connecting the Vista Hotel and Trade Center. "I saw a livid Dave Williams and his FBI entourage coming toward me. He started screaming at me from a distance, so loud that the sound of his voice reverberated through the corridor. He ripped into me for authorizing the removal of evidence against his specific orders. I waited for him to get out of breath, but he never stopped yelling. He called me a 'cowboy' and threatened to throw me off the investigation and to contact the Chief of Detectives. 'You're gonna be persona non grata,' he ranted. I realized I wasn't going to have the chance to explain myself, so I put my head down and walked away." Richie Hackford was an observer. "I think Williams would have hanged Donald from a nearby tree if he could have."

Donald trudged across the street to the section of the World Financial Center garage that Merrill Lynch had provided the JTTF for use as a temporary headquarters.[76] "I kept mulling over my actions. It was the only time in my life I could recall disobeying an order. But this was different."

Donald entered the headquarters, which was enclosed with cyclone fencing and fitted with landline phones, radios, and other equipment. "It was a good place to report to and start and finish each day. I took off my boots, helmet, gloves, and jumpsuit, and put them in a black bag. I heard someone whispering that I was in trouble."

Once in street clothes, Donald hurried out without speaking to anyone. "As I drove home, all I kept thinking about is that I'd get my ass reamed by the Chief of Detectives for disgracing the NYPD. That I'd be transferred out of Bomb Squad to some outer city precinct, never to be heard from again. I didn't tell Kathy anything, not wanting to burden her."

*

Unbeknownst to Donald, later that Sunday, the FBI's Steven Burmeister, one of the chemists he had led into the cavern, found himself back at the same area at the edge of the crater. He took note that the slab of concrete Donald had inched himself onto to retrieve the frame rail had been "pancaked," crushed by another large slab of concrete and steel that had fallen onto it. Had Donald not made the decision to claim the frame rail when he did, it may never have been found.

Chapter 23

Chaotic scene outside World Trade Center shortly after the blast

B2 level after the blast

Rendered Safe

Bottom of crater after lights installed

Chapter 23

Car near the seat of the explosion

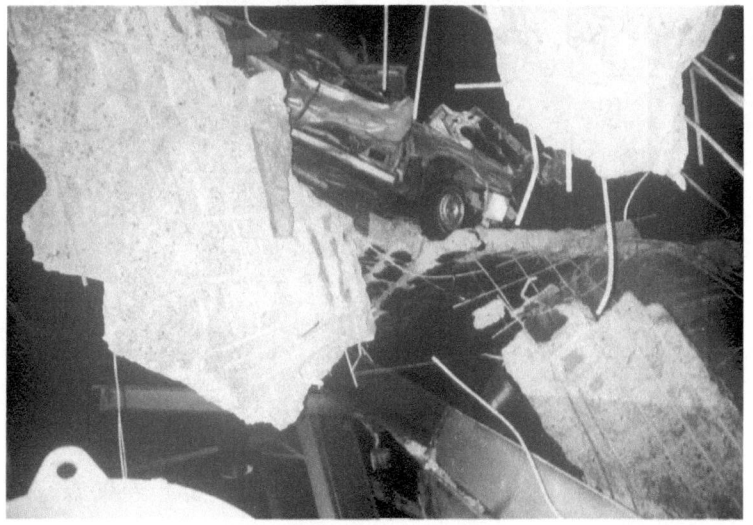

Wrecked car amid chunks of concrete clinging to rebar

Rendered Safe

ATF, FBI, and NYPD agents sifting for evidence

Examining wrecked cars

Chapter 23

In the front row kneeling, from the far left, are John Goetz (ATF), Marshall Littleton (ATF), Kevin Washington (ATF) holding a small American flag found by Donald in the rubble that had been the engineering room, Richard Coccaro (ATF), and Donald. In the back row from the far left are Peter Dalton (NYPD Bomb Squad), Brenda Molloy (ATF), Dan Boeh (ATF), Tom Waskom (ATF), Larry McCune (ATF), and Denis Mulcahy (NYPD Bomb Squad)

CHAPTER 24
Capture

Had Sadowy not recovered those critical pieces of evidence when he did, the conspirators who were plotting follow-up bombings in New York may well have succeeded in carrying out their planned attacks on tunnels, the U.N., 26 Federal Plaza, and the George Washington Bridge.
—Rick Hahn, FBI

LATE THAT SUNDAY AFTERNOON, one of the NYPD crime-lab techs, Detective John Sardone of Ballistics, received a call from Donald, who he had worked with in the past, telling him he'd soon be receiving something "real important." Soon after the parts in the body bag arrived, while Sardone was sorting through them, ATF and FBI representatives appeared. Jessica Gotthold slapped an ATF evidence sticker on the twisted metal left chassis frame rail, filling out the date, time, and location and angering the FBI agents.

That evening, after the FBI agents left for dinner, Sardone surreptitiously carried the chassis frame rail into a back room and placed it into a bench vise. With help from NYPD Detective Edward Masin, he bent it using two 24-inch plumbers pipe wrenches and cleaned the exposed section with acid wash, revealing the partial VIN code. Sardone took Polaroid pictures of the raised number and faxed them to the National Auto Theft Bureau, whose computerized data base traced it to a yellow E-350 Ford Econoline van with an Alabama license plate that had been reported stolen. The owner was identified as the Ryder Truck Rental Company's Jersey City dealership, which advised the FBI that the renter was Mohammad Salameh, whose name already was known to the Bureau because of their investigation into the murder of Meir Kahane.

The dealership also informed the FBI that Salameh had shown up on the past Friday afternoon, two hours after the bombing, to claim his $400 deposit.[77] When asked whether he had reported the van's theft to the police, Salameh replied that he didn't know that was required. He was instructed to obtain a police report and fill out an insurance application, as prerequisites to the agency accepting his account of the loss.

Salameh rushed to the local police station and claimed that the van had been stolen the night before from the parking lot of a Pathmark supermarket on Route 440, known as "the back highway' in Jersey City. In making this false report, Salameh proffered a handwritten

Chapter 24

statement that incorrectly represented the license number of the van. This mistake would delay the issuance of the necessary police report.

A Ryder official, working with a script provided by the FBI, called Salameh, informed him the agency needed to close out its books for February, and asked him to return to the dealership with the necessary forms to receive his deposit back. When Salameh arrived at the dealership in the morning of Thursday, March 4, Bill Atkinson, an FBI agent posing as a Ryder manager, handled his request in an attempt to gain information and root out the remaining terrorists. The operation was led by John Anticev, who had been assigned to the Trade Center bombing because, initially, the Bureau's working hypothesis was that Serbian terrorists had carried out the attack in revenge for U.S. support of the republics that had broken away from the former Yugoslavia. Anticev's parents were Croatian, and he spoke Serbian.

After chatting up Salameh innocuously, the FBI agent gave him $200, with the rest being "deducted for the rental." FBI agents had intended to follow Salameh after he left the dealership, but their cover was blown by reporters who arrived at the scene after hearing about the operation over a police scanner. Instead, Salameh was arrested outside the Ryder office.

The FBI promptly raided a Jersey City apartment at 34 Kensington Avenue that had been traced through a telephone number Salameh had listed on the rental agreement. In the apartment, agents found photographs of Salameh and his friends, bomb-making materials, and a telephone, whose records helped them to identify Yousef, unknown to law enforcement, and the other plotters. In the apartment, they also found Abdul Yasin, who they arrested. Yasin would provide a wealth of information, including the location of the storage unit and bomb factory.

When FBI agents stormed the Space Station Storage Company building, Steve Dodge accompanied them. "We found barrels of viscous nitroglycerin liquid, a sight I had never seen before. It was as if the plotters were preparing to fly a rocket to the moon. The FBI guys brought in their chemist, Steve Burmeister. Burmeister entered the storage unit but then ran right out. Seeing that, Donald Haldeman of the FBI telephoned a senior Bureau official in Washington. After a brief chat, Haldeman told Burmeister that the Washington guy wanted him to take a sample of the liquid. Burmeister responded, 'If he wants a sample, let him get his ass over here and take it himself!'"

The FBI brought in Jersey City Bomb Squad officers, who asked the New Jersey State Police to provide a NABCO total-containment-vessel trailer. "We used the trailer to bring all the barrels to Liberty State Park. It was nerve-wracking. The FBI stopped all traffic into the park and even asked the FAA to halt all flights from coming over. Then we blew up the trailer. The FBI had to buy the state police a new one."

Viewed as a cooperating witness, Yasin was released by the FBI and allowed to leave the country the next day

Chapter 24

via a Royal Jordanian flight to Amman, Jordan. From Amman, Yasin flew to Baghdad. In 1994, *Mukhabarat*, the Iraqi intelligence service, arrested and imprisoned Yasin. The Iraqi government, headed by Saddam Hussein, sent an emissary to the State Department to inform them they had captured a perpetrator of the World Trade Center attack and were prepared to hand him over in exchange for the lifting of U.N. sanctions. The State Department declined the offer. After 9/11, the Bush Administration placed Yasin on the FBI's most-wanted list. In response, Iraq began negotiating extradition protocols via Egypt. On May 23, 2002, the Iraqis allowed Lesley Stahl of CBS News access to Yasin to interview him for a segment on *60 Minutes* in which Yasin appeared in prison garb and handcuffs. The extradition negotiations hit a snag, and Yasin hasn't been seen or heard from since the interview, even though the State Department has offered a reward of up to $5 million for information leading to his arrest and conviction.

The other plotters were, over time, rounded up. Ajaj had been released from prison on Monday, March 1, but was rearrested on March 9 at an INS center. A month later, his asylum request was denied.

Ayyad, a tall man with wavy black hair, a mustache, and gold-rimmed glasses, whose 18-year-old wife was pregnant with their first child, instead of fleeing became the undercover spokesman for the group. He called the *New York Daily News* tip line and left a message claiming responsibility for the bombing in the name of the

Rendered Safe

"Liberation Army."[78] He also sent a letter to the *New York Times* from the Liberation Army demanding a stop to all military, economic, and political aid to Israel. Ayyad was discovered through a number of clues, including a business card found in Salameh's possession when he was arrested. Ayyad was taken into custody the day after Ajaj was rearrested.

As for Abouhalima, on Tuesday, March 2, he fled to Sudan via Jeddah, Saudi Arabia, leaving behind his wife and young children. From Sudan he returned to his native Egypt, where he stayed with his parents. Less than a month after the bombing, Abouhalima was captured by Egyptian police, tortured, and extradited to the United States.

On October 4, 1993, trial opened for Abouhalima, Ajaj, Ayyad, and Salameh. 208 persons testified. The following March, each defendant was convicted of a variety of felonies. Two months later, Federal Judge Kevin Duffy imposed the extraordinary sentence of 240 years on each, with no possibility of parole. In doing so, he consulted actuarial tables to ascertain the life expectancies of each of the six persons who died in the blast, and added the years that each of them presumably lost, arriving at a figure of 180, which involved the first six counts of the indictment. Two other counts, including assault on a federal officer, carried mandatory sentences of 30 years each, adding another sixty years to the 180, totaling 240 years.

But where was the mastermind of the plot? Ramzi Yousef, hours after the bombing, left his expendable

Chapter 24

comrades behind and boarded a flight from JFK Airport to Amman, with a connecting flight to Karachi, Pakistan. From there, he proceeded to Quetta, located at the mountainous border with Afghanistan. In the summer of 1993, Yousef participated in a failed plot to assassinate the Prime Minister of Pakistan, Benazir Bhutto, that was initiated by members of *Sipah-e-Sahaba*, a Sunni Muslim extremist organization and political party that Yousef's father had been a member of and which later was banned as a terrorist organization.[79]

Now the world's most-wanted man, Yousef began plotting the slaying of major figures, including Bill Clinton and the Pope, as well as bombings of airliners. In December 1994, traveling with an Italian passport, he planted a liquid nitroglycerin bomb under his seat on a Philippine Airlines plane flying from Manila to Tokyo before leaving the plane during a stopover in the Philippine city of Cebu. An hour and a half from Tokyo, the bomb exploded, ripping in half a young Japanese businessman, injuring ten others, and nearly downing the plane.

On January 6, 1995, a fire broke out in Yousef's Manila apartment, where he had set up a bomb lab. Investigators found in Yousef's laptops and computer disks details of a plan, code-named "Bojinka" (Serbo-Croatian for "big explosion"), to detonate time-delayed bombs on eleven U.S. long-haul flights over the Pacific. Bojinka had the financial support of Osama bin Laden and the logistical involvement of Khalid Sheikh Mohammed.

Rendered Safe

The following month, based on information from an informant, Yousef was captured in Islamabad by agents of Pakistan's Inter-Services Intelligence and the U.S. Diplomatic Security Service. During the raid, agents found Delta and United Airlines flight schedules and bomb components in children's toys. (In August 1995, Ismoil, who also had flown out of the U.S. the night of the Trade Center bombing, was captured in Amman by Jordanian authorities and extradited to the United States.) The final leg of Yousef's trip was via helicopter. As they flew over lower Manhattan at night, an FBI official pushed up Yousef's blindfold and pointed at the glowing lights of the Trade Center towers. "Look down there," he told Yousef. "They're still standing." Different versions of Yousef's reply have been reported. In the scene in the 1997 HBO Studios film *Path to Paradise: The Untold Story of the World Trade Center Bombing*, starring Peter Gallagher (as John Anticev) and Marcia Gay Harden, in which this event is depicted, Yousef presciently says, "Next time we'll bring them both down."

U.S. prosecutors produced two separate indictments against Yousef—for the bombing of the Trade Center and for the bombing of the Philippines airliner. The Trade Center trial came second. On November 12, 1997, at the end of that trial, Yousef was found guilty of a number of charges including engaging in a "seditious conspiracy." The star prosecution witness was Emad Salem, a burly former Egyptian army officer and security guard for the Blind Sheikh who had been a paid FBI informant and who

Chapter 24

"lived, ate, and slept" with the plotters for a time. "Salem was recruited by the FBI after Kahane was murdered," explained Anticev, who was Salem's handler. "We dangled him in front of that radical group and got him accepted by them." Unfortunately, the FBI dropped Salem as an informer in July 1991, while Anticev was temporarily out of work because of a medical condition. "My boss's boss didn't like Salem, and was pissed that he wouldn't wear a wire. So, he fired him. The person who came on the scene and took Salem's place in the cell was Ramzi Yousef. I believe that, if Salem had stayed undercover, he would have learned of Yousef early on, and we likely could have prevented the bombing."

Judge Duffy could not impose the death sentence on Yousef because there was no Federal death penalty in terrorist cases for acts done before 1994. Instead, Duffy gave Yousef the same sentence he'd handed out to the other conspirators, 240 years in prison. The judge recommended that Yousef's entire sentence be served in solitary confinement, calling Yousef an "apostle of evil who wanted to kill for the thrill of killing human beings." Yousef's response was, "I am a terrorist and proud of it." In April 1998, Ismoil also was sentenced to a 240-year incarceration, in spite of his argument that he had been unwittingly pulled into the conspiracy.

After the Trade Center bombing, based on the Blind Sheikh's ties to the bombers, the FBI investigated him and his followers more closely. Salem was rehired and asked to infiltrate the Sheikh's followers for a payment of $1.5M. Salem, who became the Sheikh's bodyguard again, wore a listening device. As Salem would later state in one of his books:

> For the sake of the six people and unborn child who were savagely blown away in the World Trade Center bombing, I made the choice to put my neck on the line, jeopardizing the American dream I had for my family. I acted as a private citizen who loved my adopted homeland country in order to save thousands of lives.

Salem recorded Abdel-Rahman saying he preferred attacks be concentrated on U.S. military targets, but acts of violence against civilian targets were not illicit. Uncovered by Salem was the Blind Sheikh's most alarming plan—to set off, within ten minutes, bombs at the United Nations, the Lincoln and Holland tunnels, the George Washington bridge, and the Federal building housing the FBI. Backed by videotapes showing the Sheikh's adherents mixing bomb ingredients in a garage, Abdel-Rahman, along with nine of his followers, were arrested in late June 1993. On October 1, 1995, Abdel-Rahman was convicted of seditious conspiracy, conspiracy to murder Egyptian President Hosni Mubarak, solicitation to attack a U.S. military installation, and conspiracy to conduct bombings. He was sentenced to life in solitary confinement without parole, and died in prison in February 2017 at the age of 78.

CHAPTER 25
Redemption

Dave Williams asked me to take a walk with him in private. 'Sometimes in life,' he told me, 'you have to go with your gut feeling. You did the right thing.'
—Donald Sadowy

ON THE MORNING OF Monday, February 26, World Trade Center buildings 3, 4, 5, and 6 reopened, and commuters were able to take the PATH train to the World Trade Center stop. "All the walls were blown away," Joe Connor remembered, "but the station reopened anyway. I was so proud, thinking this gives the finger to these bastards."

When Donald arrived at the temporary headquarters, he found the space packed with senior officials and staff from various agencies. "I walked to the back of the room to grab my gear, and sat on a bench facing the back wall as I put on my jumpsuit and boots and got my equipment together. I was waiting for the ax to fall. My spirits couldn't have been lower."

Rendered Safe

Donald heard yelling in another part of the room among Williams, several ATF agents, and two Bomb Squad detectives—Pete Dalton and Steve Dodge.[80] The ATF's John Goetz was nearby. "They were going at it hot and heavy, with the ATF and NYPD guys defending the removal of the evidence. It almost came to blows."

Rick Hahn persuaded the enraged Williams to leave and allow him to conduct the morning briefing. Hahn updated the group and gave out assignments. "Rick kept me as a team leader," Donald recounted. "He was being kind, but I was concerned because Williams had the last word." No one approached Donald. "I was glad to go back to work. I spent the morning on my hands and knees like a coal miner clearing the office where Monica Smith died and looking for more evidence, which gave me a sense of purpose."

Around noon, Donald and his co-workers set aside their equipment and headed up top for a break and a "central booking sandwich"—baloney on stale white bread with chips and a can of soda. "I was the last guy up the ramp. I didn't want to talk to anyone. My lower back, arms, legs, and feet all ached."

Donald emerged slowly, head down. "I was stunned to find that everyone was clapping, applauding, and whistling. Guys started coming over to shake my hand and slap me on the shoulder. I had no idea what was going on. Finally, an ATF official said to me, 'They traced the VIN number to the place it was rented from. We know some of the players. We're gonna get those guys. I can't

Chapter 25

tell you more, but you and your team cracked the case wide open!' Then people on my team came over and hugged me, which meant the most. The rest of the day, I was in a dream-like state. That night, I slept like a baby."

*

By Tuesday, Rick Hahn and Dave Williams had worked out an arrangement. "I would establish a crime-scene command post down at the site," Hahn explained, "and operationally run the crime scene for Dave. He would stay with the heavies at the command post, where he wanted to be."

Hahn had repeatedly asked FBI seniors for additional resources. "On Tuesday, 80 agents arrived at the site. I had each of them sign in, noting their experience, squad, and phone number. Then I sent them all to lunch while I organized the group into joint teams with ATF and NYPD personnel."

As Dave Williams spoke at the Tuesday morning briefing, Donald again sat next to the back wall quietly changing into work clothes and gathering his equipment. "All of a sudden, Williams steps down from the podium and marches all the way back toward me. He stuck out his hand, pulled me forward, and publicly apologized. You could have pushed me over with a feather."

Before Donald could return to the briefing, a JTTF supervisor asked him not to go back down into the hole and, instead, review with him and Rick Hahn video footage of the garage taken during the morning of the bombing. "Rick orchestrated that to give me a break for a day, which I was grateful for. I had planned to explore another pristine area, where I thought more evidence could be found. I learned, later the same day, there was a collapse of concrete pieces from the floor above onto that spot because a rebar broke. It was an avalanche that likely would have killed me."

In the evening, as Donald drove home, his hands and body began to shake. "I got off the Long Island Expressway onto the service road and stopped at a bagel place to buy a can of soda. I dropped my wallet twice. The guys behind the counter were whispering. They probably figured I was a junkie. Although it was cold, I sat on the hood of my Nova for a long time, sipping the Coke through a straw, until I was calm enough to drive home."

*

Over the subsequent decades, many have written about Donald's discovery of the key piece of evidence that led to the capture of the Trade Center bombers. Perhaps the most eloquent summary was penned by Rick Hahn:

> *Out of the hundreds of destroyed vehicles and 125,000 tons of broken debris ultimately removed from the blast scene, and in pitch darkness, Sadowy had found the few pounds of key evidence that would solve the case. What if Sadowy had not spent the time on Friday and Saturday in the bowels of the World Trade Center sub-basement?*

Chapter 25

What if he had obeyed orders and left the car parts in place where, by the next day, they may have been crushed, never to be recovered? What if he hadn't had the training at Brooklyn Automotive High School? That Sadowy was the exact right person with the exact right background to have recognized the crucial car parts, the conviction they were key pieces of evidence, and the willingness to risk his career to recover them, it all was miraculous.

CHAPTER 26
Two Tall Guys

The construction workers mounted a 4 × 6 American flag on a board and kept it with them at all times as they moved along with us on different levels during the clearing operations.

—Donald Sadowy

DURING THE WEEK AFTER the bombing, a giant mobile crane was brought to a cutout section on the plaza level and used to lower equipment and containers for holding heavy debris. Also of immediate priority was repairing the slurry wall that held back water from the Hudson River, which came close to being breached. "Among the unsung heroes of that time," Pete Dalton observed, "were the iron workers, who did a tremendous job shoring things up."

For the next two months, hundreds of law-enforcement personnel from the ATF, Bomb Squad, EMS, ESU, FBI, NYPD Arson and Explosion Squad, and FDNY Fire

Marshals, as well as construction workers labored seven days a week in the sub-basement, now with the benefit of lights powered by generators provided by the New York City Transit Authority.[81] The Port Authority opened up restaurants on the lobby level 24/7 for the crews. Outside, a viewing stand was erected for city and agency officials, diplomats, congressmen, and other dignitaries.

OSHA officials set up a station, with folding chairs and tables, near the hotel banquet room, using a trailer on West Street to hold equipment. "After OSHA came," John Goetz explained, "you couldn't enter the garage without Tyvek coveralls [one-piece garments used for light HAZMAT applications, including asbestos and radiation work] fitted with respirators because of the chemical and cement dust and PCPs. But most of us took off the respirator masks once we got down to the work area, because you couldn't do your job properly with it on. Many came down with bronchitis and pneumonia, including me. I was out for three weeks."

As Donald remembered, "The OSHA woman in charge was deeply serious about compliance with safety requirements. The game plan was that each of us intending to enter the sub-basement had to get sized by an OSHA staffer for a Tyvek suit. All the agents lined up to get fitted. By this time, everyone knows everyone else. Steve Veyera is first in line, and I'm behind him. The woman asks Steve, who is tall and heavy set, and me, who was at least ten pounds overweight and bursting out of my Nomex jumpsuit, for our sizes. We don't answer right away, and she looks at

Chapter 26

us puzzled. Finally, someone in the back yells, 'Just get them two fat-guy suits.' Her face gets red while everyone else starts howling in laughter. Her equally strait-laced assistant asks her, 'What size do I put down?' She finally stutters out, 'Just put down two tall guys.'"

Four Bomb Squad members—Donald, Pete Dalton, Steve Dodge, and Denis Mulcahy—worked daily at the scene on twelve-hour shifts, with other Squad members appearing on a rotational basis. "After such a roller coaster of emotions," Donald admitted, "I felt a warm happiness working there. The four of us always arrived by 6:30, suited up, and took a golf cart from the temporary headquarters to the crime scene." During that time, Donald acquired the nickname "The Human Q-Tip" from his Squad colleagues. "Donald was big into cleaning the floor and ducts to uncover evidence," Steve Dodge recalled. "He'd come out of the sub-basement dirtier than I've ever seen a human being."

Each day began and ended in the same manner. "The morning briefing," Donald noted, "focused on what was going on topside, while the evening briefing covered developments below ground." They also would read reports filed by the other teams and attempt to discuss with the FBI and ATF what areas we would explore as part of the post-blast investigation." As Dodge recounted, "The FBI guys were less forthcoming, so we had to do a lot of evening drinking with them."

The wind and cold affected all involved in the investigative and repair efforts. "Fortunately," Donald explained,

243

Rendered Safe

"Pete Dalton, who spoke fluent Spanish and Italian and could talk to anyone and make them laugh, bonded with the construction workers. Pete wore construction clothes, boots, and a hard hat and guided those men as they worked right behind us clearing debris. At his request, they brought in halogen lamps on stands connected to generators that ran quite a distance away so we wouldn't breathe in fumes or hear the noise. Those lamps gave us light and some heat. They also brought us space heaters so we could warm up our hands and feet periodically."

The construction workers built rough wood benches and work tables for use by law-enforcement agents to log in evidence. Six locations for the collection of evidence were established, each administered by Jessica Gotthold.[82] "We set up a site at each of the entrances to the garage. Almost the entire garage initially was deemed part of the evidentiary perimeter, which was a massive area when you considered all the levels. Every piece of debris and rubble on each sub-level was examined, with agents using screens to inspect miniscule pieces. Every item collected that was deemed to be of evidentiary value use was numbered, tagged, bagged, photographed, and brought to one of the evidence sites before being placed onto trucks for removal. A duplicate Ryder van was lifted into a space in the basement to help identify parts that might have come from the van used by the plotters. One of the biggest challenges was that all of us law-enforcement folks had to manage alongside the diggers, cement layers, steel workers, and others who were shoring up the hotel

Chapter 26

and other areas.[83] They were doing things like placing steel beams between support columns to prevent them from twisting and to keep them upright. That required hundreds of people, so the coordination process was difficult. It also presented a security problem, as other people, particularly reporters, tried to mingle in and gain access. The NYPD finally set up a badge system, with different colors for different levels of access, and the area was sealed off tightly."

For seventeen days, law-enforcement agents and construction workers dug by hand, aided by jackhammers, through tons of broken cement and mangled steel searching for the body of William Mercado, a 37-year-old immigrant from Peru, who lived in East New York, Brooklyn, with his wife and their two young daughters. Mercado worked two jobs at the World Trade Center: weekdays as Windows on the World's purchasing agent and weekends as a security guard. At the time of the explosion, he was at his desk in the basement checking in supplies. His wife, Olga, had returned to the site each day to monitor the rescue-and-recovery effort. One day, the searchers stopped their shoveling and joined Olga in a hopeful prayer.

To assist the searchers, cadaver dogs were brought in. "The NYPD had stopped keeping cadaver dogs," Steve Dodge recalled, "so we contacted the Connecticut State Police, who came down to the site with a few of theirs. One problem we had was that Mercado's body was near the Trade Center's meat lockers, which confused the

245

dogs. We also used heat-detecting cameras, but that didn't work well because the body was buried so deep in the wreckage."

On March 15, Mercado's body was discovered on the B-5 level by a mix of construction workers and law-enforcement agents. One was Steve Dodge. "Mr. Mercado's body, still sitting in his chair, was pretty much intact because of the cold and because he had died from the blast pressure and not from falling debris. All work stopped, and everyone stood respectfully with their helmet off. We covered the body in a blanket to make sure no photos were taken by the media. Then we put it on a gurney and had it taken by ambulance to the Medical Examiner's office. I also asked that the notification to his family state that he was killed immediately and didn't suffer."

On that day, Port Authority Police Department Captain Joseph Martella led Olga Mercado to the crater, which he pronounced as "the most heart-wrenching thing I've ever done."

The investigative process lasted two months. Much of it involved sifting for evidence through debris brought by wheelbarrows to stations specially made by carpenters, similar to how an archeologist would search for artifacts. "It was a massive task," Donald remembered, "given the size of the crime scene. Our saying was that the work will be finished when the last shovel is sifted." As described by Denis Mulcahy, "The search for evidence largely was a process of elimination. As you cleared out an area, you found stuff you felt worth taking a closer look at. Most

Chapter 26

times, on a second or third review, you then disposed of it as not valuable."

The law-enforcement unit providing the largest manpower during those two months was the Emergency Services Unit, which did the bulk of the "grunt work." One of the many ESU officers involved was David Burkart, Kathy's younger brother. David had been inspired to join the NYPD by listening to the many stories told over the years at family gatherings by Donald and by his sister Kim's husband, Kevin, who was a member of the Nassau County Police Department. "It was eerie," David recalled, "seeing the giant crater and feeling that the bomb, had it been bigger, might have taken down the North Tower."

By the end of April, an estimated 2,500 cubic yards of debris, weighing 4,000 tons, had been examined. A wall was broken to gain access to the PATH station, from where a train of flatcars removed the fragments. Anything of evidentiary value was stored in a warehouse on North Moore Street in Tribeca that the FBI had rented, with the more valuable items periodically shipped to Quantico.

Among the items removed were more than two hundred wrecked vehicles. "The ESU guys used a Jaws of Life to cut apart what was left of each vehicle," Donald explained, "to find a VIN number or code. The car or van was marked by spray paint, and lifted by a front loader onto a container that had been lowered into the pit. Each container, which also held any loose auto parts, was lifted topside, which was no easy feat. Then a flatbed truck took the vehicles to a central place in the plaza

Rendered Safe

set up by the auto-crime guys, where it was examined for items of evidentiary value. Afterward, based on the VIN numbers, the owners of the destroyed vehicles were notified so they could file an insurance claim."

As winter turned to spring, media stories of the bombing and subsequent investigation abounded. On April 1, ABC's *Nightline* news show, anchored by Ted Koppel, aired a half-hour report. Walter Boser, James Fox, Joe Hanlin, and Dave Williams each appeared. During the episode, Hanlin was filmed inside the basement pointing out where the key piece of evidence had been discovered. He made no mention of Donald, nor did any of the others. And, at the end of the show, Koppel spoke of the success of the investigation and capture of the perpetrators as "all initially flow[ing] from Joe Hanlin's discovery." This, of course, enraged many in the Bomb Squad and NYPD. Donald was less angry than many of his buddies. "I knew the truth. And I figured, since the ATF had gotten a lot of bad publicity from the Waco siege, showcasing Hanlin was their way of trying to make up for it."[84]

At the end of the investigation, FBI photographers were brought in. "They called my name and handed me a shovel," Donald recounted, "for a photo on a lower level with one of the FBI agents. The caption read something like, 'Down to the Last Shovel.'"

During the investigation and in its wake, Donald received much individual publicity. One example was an April 1993 article entitled "How the New York Bomb Squad Cracked the World Trade Center Terrorist

Chapter 26

Bombing," published in *The City Sun*, a now-defunct Brooklyn weekly newspaper. The article described Donald as a "supersleuth" and "top-notch bomb expert" who "broke the case of the World Trade Center bombing."

"After I returned to the normal routine," Donald recalled, "some of the guys made clear they were jealous of the four of us who had worked full-time on the Trade Center bombing, and me in particular. One of the sergeants approached me and said, with an attitude, 'Were you hoping to get a medal?' I said to him, 'That doesn't put food on the table or help pay the mortgage.' I just wanted to fall back into my usual routine."

In late April, Lieutenant Boser summoned Donald into his office. "The lieutenant was on the phone, but he motioned for me to come in. He says, 'Hold on, he's right here,' hands me the phone, and sits back and smiles. I say, 'This is Detective Sadowy.' It felt like I was being set up. The voice on the other end, who sounded as if he were an in-charge person, said, 'Detective, make sure your dress uniform is in good shape. And get a good military-style haircut, cause the media will be there.' And then he hung up. As I handed the phone back to Lieutenant Boser, he laughed and asked me, 'Don't you know who that was?' Being sharp as a marble, I said, 'Nope.' 'That was Commissioner Ray Kelly. You're being promoted tomorrow at 11 a.m. at One Police Plaza! Someone will meet you there with a new set of white gloves.'"

On Friday, April 30, 1993, Donald was promoted to Detective Second Grade, as were Pete Dalton, Steve

Rendered Safe

Dodge, and John Sardone. (Denis Mulcahy was promoted to Detective First Grade.) "That was big for me," Donald admitted, "including financially. As a Detective Third Grade, I made more money than a patrolman but less than a uniformed sergeant. As a Detective Second Grade, I made the top pay of a sergeant." Commissioner Kelly presided over the ceremony in a packed first-floor auditorium."

In the audience were Donald's wife, Kathy, six-year-old son Donald Jr., and five-year-old daughter Kaitlin. "We were married nine years before we had our first child," Kathy explained, "because we first wanted to get settled and buy a home. After we had Donnie, we were so excited to have another kid. Soon, I became pregnant with Kaitlin." Also present were Kathy's parents and Aunt Louise. Donald was struck by the fact that the Commissioner, in his remarks, couldn't, for legal reasons related to the upcoming prosecutions, express why the men were being promoted. "He just referred to something huge we had done that affected the entire city. Everyone knew what he was talking about. At the end of the ceremony, we marched to the end of the stage. One at a time, our names and new rank were announced. We saluted the Commissioner, and he presented us with our certificates. Then we turned for a quick photo as we got a standing ovation." Later, Donald's extended family posed for additional photos with Commissioner Kelly. One shows Donnie wearing his dad's detective's hat, which presaged Donnie's future career with the NYPD.

Chapter 26

Donald receiving his promotion

*Denis Mulcahy, Steve Dodge, Joseph
Borelli, Donald, Pete Dalton*

Rendered Safe

Donald and his family being congratulated by Police Commissioner Ray Kelly

Chapter 26

Donald, Donnie, and Kaitlin

Rendered Safe

Later that afternoon, Donald was relaxing in front of the TV, emotionally spent. "I'm half watching channel 4, and suddenly I see John Miller doing a story on me. I yell to Kathy to come in. Miller had gone to my old high school and interviewed two of my shop teachers about my knowledge of car parts. I literally slid off the couch on my butt." As John Miller described, "I decided to build a story around Donald and how a great mystery got solved. And also illustrate the law of unintended consequences, which in that case meant that Donald's actions throughout his life led to unanticipated, and happy, effects."

*

Donald's role in solving the 1993 bombing has been represented in various books and films. One is the four-hour 2006 ABC miniseries *The Path to 9/11: The Untold Story of the World Trade Center Bombing*, a 1997 HBO Studios film in which Donald is portrayed by Al Sapienza, best known for playing the character Mikey Palmice, a violent sociopath, in the *Sopranos*. The discovery of the chassis frame by Donald and Joe Hanlin (who is incorrectly called "Steve"—perhaps in reference to Steve Berberich) and Donald's dressing down by Dave Williams are depicted. That miniseries, which was nominated for seven Emmys, was shown only once on TV and is near impossible to obtain on DVD. The film's writer and producer, Cyrus Nowrasteh, has alleged that Bill and Hillary Clinton used their influence at Disney/ABC to effectively

Chapter 26

ban the miniseries because it exposed, only months before Hillary announced the exploratory committee for her original presidential campaign, Bill Clinton's failure to capture and kill Osama bin Laden.

CHAPTER 27
TWA Flight 800

It was fascinating work but, also, particularly challenging and frustrating. With a plane crash, everything looks like potential bomb damage because of the mangling, burning, charring, and other damage that results from impact with water. In the case of TWA flight 800, there was damage to the metal structure of the luggage container that looked exactly like the damage found in the 1988 Pan Am 103 plane crash where a bomb had been placed in a piece of luggage and blown out a side of the plane.

—Mark Torre, Bomb Squad commander

BY MID-1993, WORK LIFE had returned to normal for Donald. One particularly enjoyable day was when he brought his son Donnie to Rodman's Neck. "Dad showed me the firing range," Donnie recalled, "and I got to play with the dogs and robots. Dad also did a scenario showing how a dog sniffs out an explosive. That was really, really cool."

Rendered Safe

In October 1995, in Rijeka, Croatia, *al-Gama'at al-Islamiyya*, an Islamic terrorist organization based in Egypt, drove a bomb-laden car into the wall of a police station. Twenty-seven employees in the police station and two bystanders on the street were injured. The only person killed was the attacker. John Anticev was sent to assist in the investigation. "I picked Donald's brain a lot before I went over, to know what to look for. When I came back, I shared with Donald all the information I had found about the bomb and the means of attack. He was eager to use that knowledge for the benefit of the Bomb Squad. What particularly struck me was, in spite of how knowledgeable he was, Donald listened to me quite carefully and took it all in."

The two men would work together again the following year, on a much-higher-profile event. On July 17, 1996, at 8:31 p.m., TWA flight 800, a Boeing 747, exploded in a fireball and crashed into the Atlantic Ocean near East Moriches on Long Island twelve minutes after takeoff from JFK Airport headed to Rome via Paris. All 230 on board were killed. At the time, it was the third-deadliest aviation incident to occur in U.S. territory.

The subsequent four-year accident investigation, shrouded in controversy to this day, would be headed by the National Transportation Safety Board, with the FBI initiating a parallel criminal inquiry. A widespread speculation was the plane had been the target of a missile strike, as more than 250 witnesses essentially testified they observed a "streak of light" rising toward a point where

Chapter 27

a large fireball appeared. The missile-attack theory was challenged by CIA weapons analysts, who, in an animated video re-creation, argued that what the witnesses saw was the plane itself temporarily ascending several thousand feet before erupting. The CIA's position, in turn, has been widely disparaged.

The Nassau and Suffolk Bomb Squads took an active role, as well as investigators from the Federal Aviation Administration and the ATF. (As with the 1993 World Trade Center bombing investigation, there was palpable tension between the FBI and ATF agents.) Every day, at least one NYPD Bomb Squad member was assigned on a rotational basis to the investigation.

Also on the scene was Ed Kittel, an FAA official who had spent more than two decades as a Navy Explosive Ordnance Disposal Officer and served the NTSB as a specialist on suspicious plane crashes. "Under controlled testing circumstances, I had blown up a lot of airplanes. I also had done testing on the effect of MANPADS [portable shoulder-launched surface-to-air missiles] on planes. I became an expert in post-blast causes and effects on aircraft. I also knew the rules for collecting evidence for criminal prosecution and was able to help bridge the gap between the NTSB and FBI folks, who had different cultures and spoke different languages, because the FBI is all about solving a crime and prosecuting perpetrators, while the NTSB is focused on finding the probable cause of a crash and preventing future crashes."

259

Rendered Safe

The investigation was the most expensive and complex air-disaster probe in U.S. history, with the FBI estimating the cost to itself alone as being close to $20 million. At its heart was a lengthy and extraordinarily difficult salvage effort labeled the greatest one since Pearl Harbor. To reassemble the airliner, FBI and Navy divers searched a 40-mile patch of the ocean floor. Divers would eventually recover the remains of all 230 victims and more than 95 percent of the plane. One of the last bodies to be recovered was that of a woman strapped in a seat near the front of the plane, 105 feet beneath the surface. A remote-controlled probe was used to unbuckle her seat belt. She was found still clutching her handbag.

Kittel described the recovery operation:

> We took over a huge facility in Calverton, Long Island, for storage, examination, and reconstruction. It was a former Grumman F-14 Tomcat production plant that was vacant once the F-14 went out of production. We did a 'flat laydown' of all the recovered wreckage, meaning a three-dimensional reconstruction from nose to tail and wing tip to wing tip, and investigated every aspect of what may have caused the crash. We also did a three-dimensional reconstruction of the front 93 feet of the fuselage and the center fuel tank. Side-scan sonar that can detect debris in mud and silt, underwater metal detectors, miniature subs that send real-time color video to the surface for on-the-spot identification,

Chapter 27

and laser scanning equipment all were used to map the area. Divers, cranes, dredges, and remote-operated vehicles were used to scour the ocean bottom and pull up wreckage. All the pieces, some of which were as small as a fist, were marked, placed in wooden crates on barges, and delivered to a Coast Guard station on the Shinnecock Canal, where they were loaded into cargo nets and trucked to a Calverton hangar. The bomb techs examined every one of the more than a hundred thousand pieces recovered. We left no stone unturned. Every one of us had authority to submit a piece for chemical or metallurgic lab analysis. The operation went on for months, well into winter.

The hangar in which the main reconstruction of the plane took place wasn't large enough to fully lay out the wings, so another hangar was taken over. "We put down wooden supports that looked like big railroad ties," Kittel recalled, "to set the wings on so you could examine both underneath and on top. One day, Donald and I were looking them over. We crawled under the left wing with our flashlights and found a large hole caused by intense heat that seemed as if it could have been caused by a rocket-propelled-grenade-shaped charge. We went nuts, thinking we might have solved the case, until someone came and told us what we saw was a test burn for an acetylene cutting torch used to cut the wing into manageable pieces."

Rendered Safe

The FAA Explosives Unit members (from left to right—Ed Kittel, Larry Gallatin, and Roy McClain) who helped piece together the Boeing 747

"On a normal day out at Calverton," Donald recounted, "guys from the different agencies would gather for the daily briefing organized by the FBI to review developments from the past twenty-four hours. It was a procedure similar to what had been developed for the 1993 Trade Center investigation, although in this case the FBI agents seemed to take a back seat to the other investigators, who worked together quite cooperatively. Most days, wearing boots, jeans, a sweatshirt, and gloves, I did a twelve-hour shift in one of the gigantic hangars, which were powered by outside generators. A hoist connected to an overhead I-beam and controlled by a winch

Chapter 27

was used to move the pieces as they came off the trucks. Saltwater would be dripping off them. Of particular interest was technical equipment like gauges. I was amazed at what survived and what didn't. We recovered a uniform-flight-crew hat undamaged. Half of a toilet intact. Even round white bulbs from one of the kitchen areas and bottles of champagne that weren't broken. In the hangar in which the interior of the aircraft was laid out, you could see where the plane had broken and flames had come up in the passenger compartment. Another hangar had the stringers, which were the structural elements supporting the plane's skin. It looked like skeletal remains of a dinosaur."

On certain days, Donald would join men from other agencies in reviewing the video footage taken by the mechanical submarines that methodically swept the debris fields with a spot light. "The video always showed the date, time, course, longitude, latitude, and depth. Several of us would watch intensely for items of interest."

Recovered bodies were placed into body bags and, once they arrived at the East Moriches Coast Guard station, taken by ambulance to the Suffolk County morgue. "Protocol required," Donald explained, "that representatives from four separate agencies be present at the morgue to observe each autopsy, to ensure proper protocol was followed and to look for evidence. I was asked to do that occasionally. It was perhaps the most unpleasant task I performed in my entire career, including the Marines. I had been present at autopsies before, but now at times

I was seeing the dissection of corpses of children. We would remove each body bag from the ambulance by gurney, bring it inside the morgue, and unzip the bag, from which saltwater would come pouring out, and help the Medical Examiner's staff slide the body onto the exam table. Crabs that had eaten into the body would run out of the mouth, eyes, and stomach cavity. They'd scurry on the table and fall to the floor. The sight and horrid smells tore at each of us present. It became important to rotate law-enforcement staff so no person was there repeatedly."

As the plane was reconstructed, it became apparent something had caused the center fuel tank to explode, leading the forward section of the plane to rip away. Among the explanations proffered were a bomb left on board or carried by a passenger, a missile from a terrorist source or a nearby Navy military exercise, electromagnetic interference caused by military aircraft in the area at the time, pressure of jet-fuel vapor built up in the tank, or a spark or transient voltage causing arcing in the wiring across the center tank. The NTSB ultimately determined the explosion occurred because of ignition of the flammable fuel-air mixture in the tank, most likely a short circuit, possibly resulting from damaged wiring. The FBI found no conclusive evidence of a criminal act.

As related by Kittel, "When the center fuel tank was finally reconstructed, the question became whether the explosion started on the inside or the outside. Eventually, while the investigators weren't able to determine with

Chapter 27

certainty precisely what had caused the tank explosion, we knew damned well it wasn't a high explosive from a bomb or missile. There was no evidence of that." Pete Dalton agreed. "It definitely was not a rocket or missile. The explosion happened from inside the tank. You could see the metal protruding from the inside out."

Donald respected these views but remained with doubts. "I'm far from an expert on plane crashes, but I could never get out of my head the report of the two Air National Guard pilots in a Black Hawk helicopter who had witnessed a streak of light moving from east to west moments before seeing the plane explode. They filed their report with the FAA the same night. We asked to read the interview done with them by the FBI, but they wouldn't show us. And there was an expert from Scotland, who had worked on the Lockerbie bombing, who was flown in. He brought scaled-down models of similar aircraft. I wanted to ask him questions but was shooed away by the FBI. Plus, it seemed to me that not all of the physical evidence supported an internal explosion. The Flight 800 case has always gnawed at me."

265

CHAPTER 28
Letter Bombs

If the letter bomb had gone off in an enclosed room, where the blast-pressure wave acts more powerfully, it could easily have killed or seriously injured everyone there. So, we knew we had to act quickly and forcefully.

—Donald Sadowy

ON JANUARY 13, 1997, two unique 5 × 7 white greeting-card-sized envelopes arrived at the main mail room in the United Nations Secretariat building. Both were addressed to Raghida Dergham, a reporter for the Arab-language daily newspaper *Al-Hayat*. That publication, owned by members of the Saudi royal family, had an office in the building, and Dergham was stationed there.

Each envelope contained a musical greeting card within which were paper-thin sheets of Semtex, a plastic explosive manufactured in Czechoslovakia during the Cold War, the usual lithium button battery, a leaf-switch detonator designed to be triggered when the envelope was opened, and metal pins meant to rip through a human body. As noted by Steve Chiarini of the NYPD Intelligence Division, who focused on dignitary protection, "Those devices were pretty clever and well designed. Suspicious packages usually have characteristics that evidence something is wrong. No return address. Numerous stamps. Oil stains or leaking. But these were prepared meticulously. The sheets of Semtex were carefully wrapped in cellophane. The bomb-maker knew what he was doing."

Michael McCann was head of U.N. Security at the time. "Every piece of mail delivered to the U.N. was put through an X-ray machine. In the case of certain notable persons, like the Secretary-General, and high-risk offices, like *Al-Hayat*, their mail was routinely segregated and screened a second time. *Al-Hayat* previously had been the target of letter bombs."

By good fortune, McCann had run into Raghida Dergham that morning while both were grabbing coffee. Dergham informed McCann that, hours earlier, two mail clerks at the paper's London headquarters had been injured while opening envelopes with the same writing, postmark, size, and color.[85] Based on that information, McCann oversaw the second X-raying of the newspaper's mail, which took place in an isolated basement area. Once the envelopes were confirmed to be of a suspicious nature, McCann ordered the evacuation of the U.N. mailroom and nearby floors, and called in the NYPD Bomb Squad.

Donald and Riche Hackford arrived with a robot, which was used to carry the envelopes to an outdoor

Chapter 28

parking garage. The bomb techs then placed sandbags around the packages and used a water cannon to disarm them. Meanwhile, McCann ordered his security personnel to walk through each of the 38 floors and collect every piece of unopened mail in each office's in- and out-box, desk, and trash can for further examination. "They used the cleaning-staff dollies with heavy, metal wire rods," Donald explained, "to transport the material by freight elevator to the lobby. The pile of mail, which was more than 50,000 pieces from all over the world, eventually stretched a block and a half in length."

Donald and Richie found a working X-ray machine and, aided by three other Bomb Squad teams, examined each piece of mail. "We stayed there for three days and two nights," Donald recounted. "Each morning, Lieutenant White had a dozen coffees, ham and egg sandwiches, and doughnuts brought in. By the end, we looked like homeless people. But it was worth the effort. We identified five more suspicious envelopes, each with a Paris postmark. They were rendered safe with a water cannon that took out the firing system without the device blowing up, and then marked, bagged, tagged, and placed into a containment vehicle to be taken to the lab. Afterward, the lieutenant had us go over what we'd done with Chief of Detectives Pat Kelleher, Police Commissioner Howard Safir, and Mayor Rudy Giuliani. By then, I couldn't keep my eyes open. The FBI, which had taken all of our evidence, case folders, and notes, held a press conference. Senior FBI guys, in their Brooks Brothers suits, reviewed the outcome of the case, making no mention of NYPD Bomb Squad. That caused a lot of animosity and resentment. We did the grunt work but got no acknowledgment. It was just like that in those days."

CHAPTER 29
Israel

Suddenly, it felt like I was kneeling not in front of an altar but at the beach, and that a wave had come over me. I began to weep.

—Donald Sadowy

IN 1993, THE SQUAD'S INTELLIGENCE coordinator retired. It was a position that had interested Donald for years. "You liaised with the Intelligence Division of the NYPD and with federal and foreign law-enforcement agencies on security developments involving IEDs. I also liked that it would give me weekends off, so I could spend more time with my family. In that role, you weren't on an active team unless one was short-handed or there was an emergency. Before I could apply, Lieutenant Boser offered the job to me, saying I was good with people and had a knack for that kind of work. But I had my reservations. I told the lieutenant I'd take the position on one condition—he let me handle the job the way I think it should be run. That I wanted to be allowed to be proactive."

Donald spent two years obtaining the necessary clearances with the FBI and State Department. "After that, I was able to speak with every federal law-enforcement agency. Old-timers from those agencies took me under wing, making me realize that, just because you have clearances doesn't mean anyone will talk to you. You need to establish yourself personally. To be trusted on a gut level to keep information confidential and seek only what you need. Or else doors will close. So, I learned the best ways to obtain information from other agencies, including foreign ones, without pissing people off."

In 1996, Congress established the U.S. Bomb Data Center, under the ATF's oversight, as a national collection center for information on arson- and explosives-related incidents. The Center gathers data from the ATF, FBI, U.S. Fire Administration, and state and local law-enforcement agencies, plus equivalent sources globally. "That appeared to be a great development," Donald explained, "as the intelligence information was meant to be accessible for insights and analysis by the entire law-enforcement community. But I found that the Feds held on to the information for a long time, sometimes years, before making it readily available to folks like me. Sometimes they would wait until the information was in the public domain. So the new Data Center proved not to be that useful."

More helpful was the deep relationship that Donald developed with the State Department in general and with

Chapter 29

Bernard Johnson in particular. "The State Department typically shared with me information about IED developments internationally within 24 hours. And I had a point of contact with the Department, who I could reach 24/7. That was huge!"

One example of the close cooperation between the Bomb Squad, the NYPD, and the State Department involved the growing threat of explosive-laden vehicles used to bring down a building. "In 1996," Donald recalled, "we received information from the State Department about a very credible threat by Muslim radicals to use a car-delivered bomb against the Israeli mission to the U.N. That had been done the prior year in Buenos Aires, when a suicide bomber drove a van bomb into a Jewish Community Center building [killing 85 people and injuring hundreds]. The building's load-bearing walls were destroyed, which, in turn, led to progressive failure of the floor slabs and the collapse of the building. Our response initially was to line up Sanitation Department trucks in a semi-circle around the building line. Later, the idea arose of placing multi-ton cement planters with flowers in front of the entrance as barriers to vulnerable sites, an approach that was aesthetically far more pleasing and which was adopted by many other cities around the world."

Donald established himself well within the international law-enforcement community. He developed a particularly close relationship with the Protective Security Department of Shin Bet, the Israeli security agency. "Over the years, I had worked numerous cases with them. Things like checking out suspicious mailed packages, a magnetic device under a car, or a briefcase that nobody claimed. Or clearing a room."

"Once at a hotel where an Israeli dignitary was scheduled to speak," Steve Chiarini recalled, "the Squad checked the lobby and hall with one of its Labs. To make sure the dog was working properly, they set down in a corner of a room an explosive without a detonator. The dog signaled the place was clean except for the test IED. But then Israeli agents came and insisted the dog check again. The second time, the dog sniffed around and signaled the presence of another IED. Well, it turned out the Israelis, who didn't trust anyone, human or animal, had put down their own test explosive to make sure the Squad dog was working properly. The Squad guys went nuts. Things almost came to blows. Fortunately, Donald was there and was able to calm both sides down."

"Donald was the face of the NYPD to the Israelis, and they had faith in him," Steve Bernstein of the State Department explained. "The Israelis look to take someone out for a test drive or two before they're willing to buy. After a couple of test drives, they decided they liked the Sadowy vehicle. So, he had juice with them." Donald's close relationship with Israeli officials enabled him to work with them directly. "Like many other cops, I took on part-time jobs outside of my NYPD work to supplement my income. Many of those were for the Israelis, who would call me periodically to work special events. I'd be the one to do a sweep of the location, which usually

Chapter 29

was a midtown hotel, and then join the security detail during the affair."

After Donald became intelligence coordinator, he was in constant touch with senior Israeli intelligence officials. "If, for example, the foreign minister of Israel came to town, I'd get a call asking me to meet at a certain time and place, often the Israeli embassy. There, I'd ask questions like which groups would target him, how they might approach killing him, their track record, how their bomb-makers are trained, and what explosives and detonators they use. Then I'd let the Squad guys know on a confidential basis how to prepare for his security."

Donald decided he'd benefit from attending Israel's IED training school, a premier one, and spending time with their response teams in the field. "Mike White, who succeeded Walter Boser as Squad commander, thought it was a great idea. After the State Department approved the request, he wrote letters to Commissioner Safir suggesting setting up a program to exchange bomb techs with other countries' techs, with my going to Israel being an example. But he got pushback from people in Safir's office who felt this would be some kind of junket."

One day in February 1999, Donald was brought by State Department officials to the Israeli mission to the United Nations, located on Second Ave. "At lunch with the Israeli ambassador and counsel general, I mentioned my request to go to their bomb-disposal school. The next day, I find out that the ambassador had spoken with Mayor Giuliani, that I'd be leaving for Israel the following evening, and that a check already had been cut for my expenses." That was not surprising to Steve Bernstein. "The Israelis like to expose non-Israelis to contacts and programs that bind them closer to viewing the world the way they do. They want people working with them not just because it's their job but, also, because they believe in the state of Israel."

Donald was in seventh heaven until he realized he didn't have a valid passport. "I called Bernard Johnson, who told me a car would pick me up the next morning at seven from the 6th Precinct house. I was driven to the passport office at Rockefeller Center, which didn't formally open until nine. Someone brought me to the back, checked my ID, took photos, and 45 minutes later, as I was having tea and a Danish and reading the paper, he came back with my passport on a tray. The plastic still was hot."

That night, Donald was on an Air France flight from JFK to Tel Aviv via Paris. "I get to the terminal at JFK, and a middle-aged guy in a dark suit standing next to the gate asks me if I'm Donald Sadowy, whispers Bernard Johnson's name, wishes me a safe trip, and gives me the name and phone number of my contact at the U.S. embassy in Tel Aviv. I flew first class, which became comical because I didn't have a clue about how to use the seat."

Arriving in Charles de Gaulle airport in Paris, Donald waded through a sea of humanity to the passport-control line. "The uniformed officer looked at my passport and ticket and asked, 'What's the purpose of your visit to

Chapter 29

Israel?' Being tired and anxious to make my connecting flight, I thoughtlessly said, 'None of your business.' Then all hell broke loose."

Donald was taken out of the line and questioned by several senior French customs agents in a side office. "I pulled out my NYPD ID and asked for professional courtesy, saying I wasn't at liberty to speak about my mission. They took my passport and said they'd have to notify their ministry. I lost it. I raised my arms and said, 'Put me in irons and take me to the Bastille!'" Donald ended up spending the night at the airport police station, but as a guest, not imprisoned. "A couple of the officers took me for a nighttime tour of Paris, which I'd never seen. In the morning, they apologized, gave me back my passport, and handed me a first-class ticket on Swiss Air to Tel Aviv."

The Israeli Police Bomb Disposal Division, which deals with both criminal and terrorist acts, often is dubbed "the busiest bomb squad in the world." It hosted Donald in a former police building built by the British outside Jerusalem. "The training environment in Israel was much less formal than in the U.S. Everyone dressed down. We called each other by our first names, regardless of rank. And senior officers had good personal relationships with the junior staff. There seemed to be no oversized egos or huffy attitudes. Everyone was on the same page. Because they're under serious threat all the time, nothing was considered unimportant. Every call was taken at face value."

Donald found the Israeli methods for handling terrorist and criminal events insightful. "For example, in a hostage incident in the U.S., we were taught to first establish a perimeter, bring in a negotiator, get him talking to the hostage taker, and try to talk it out. The Israeli concept was to immediately launch an assault, because their premise was that any hostage taker was a potential suicide bomber. Over the years, U.S. law enforcement came to adopt this 'active shooter' approach for many hostage-type situations."

In addition to classroom study, Donald traveled with his Israeli counterparts throughout the country, from the northern border with Lebanon to the Sinai Peninsula. "The instructors thought you could do your job best if you had a feel for the different geographies and communities, combined with studying actual events. And Israel is small enough to make that type of travel and study feasible. In each locale, we would be asked to address real-life scenarios. Then we'd be critiqued. All the terrorist attacks that had gone on and were still occurring made what we were doing intensely serious."

While in Jerusalem, Donald was taken by Israeli soldiers on a tour that encompassed the Wailing Wall in the Old City of Jerusalem, viewed by Jews as uniquely holy as the only remains of the Second Temple of Jerusalem. "Because of my escort, everyone was looking at me, thinking I was some sort of celebrity. Out of a group of young religious students, one ran toward me yelling something. Two soldiers grabbed him and pinned him

Chapter 29

down. I asked them to let him go. He shouts, 'Where are you from?' 'Brooklyn,' I tell him. 'I'm from Williamsburg! We're kinsmen!' he responds. We end up hugging and having our picture taken together."

Donald, who all his life had remained a church-going Catholic, asked to be taken to the Church of the Holy Sepulchre, the site of Jesus' crucifixion, burial, and resurrection. "I was guided by a monk to the tomb where Christ's body had been laid. Then we descended stairs to the Armenian Chapel of St Helena [St. Helena was the mother of Emperor Constantine the Great and an Empress of the Roman Empire] and, further down to a rock-cut cistern where St. Helena is believed to have found the parts of the cross and the nails used to crucify Jesus. He left me alone inside. Feeling unworthy and not knowing what was expected of me, I knelt by an altar built in front of a black stone statue of St. Helena holding onto the cross. There was a beautiful old oil lamp nearby. I stared at the flame inside and, with tears flowing and shaking hands, prayed for a neighbor, Marie, who was suffering from cancer. After several minutes, I arose and left. The monk was waiting for me with a big smile. I nodded to him, but I was too overwhelmed to speak."

CHAPTER 30
Ehud Barak

Seated in the front row were a "who's who" of prominent New Yorkers, many of whom were looking at me with a "Who is this guy?" expression.

—Donald Sadowy

WHILE DONALD, DURING HIS travels throughout Israel, was in the northern part of the country, an Israel Defense Forces paratrooper unit on a nighttime patrol was ambushed in the security zone that then existed in southern Lebanon.[86] During a fierce battle, three Israeli soldiers were killed and five wounded by Shiite Muslim guerrillas who attacked them with grenades and machine guns. Israel retaliated with air strikes early the next morning.

One of those who rushed to the border to better understand what had happened was Ehud Barak, the former Minister of Foreign Affairs and Commander of the IDF. At that time, Barak was the leader of the Labor

Rendered Safe

Party and campaigning for Prime Minister. In the election held three months later, he would easily defeat Benjamin Netanyahu to assume that position. The following year, after Israel withdrew from southern Lebanon, Barak met with Arafat at a Camp David summit hosted by President Bill Clinton in an effort to end the Israeli–Palestinian conflict. The summit ended without an agreement.

"I knew Barak," Donald recounted, "from the many pro-Israel functions he'd attended in New York City over the years. And we met again during my training in Jerusalem. A short, stout man, built like a fire hydrant, Barak is very personable. He always addressed me as "Donald." Barak impressed me as being a serious, thoughtful, brilliant guy. When we ran into each other at a border observation post, we chatted briefly. The brutal murder of the three soldiers affected him greatly, as it did all of us. The ugliness of the situation, including Hezbollah posting a video of the blood-soaked clothing of the dead, can't be overemphasized."

*

Later that year, Donald was asked to join the security detail for an IDF fundraiser in the grand ballroom of the Sheraton Hotel in Times Square. The featured speaker was the new Israeli Prime Minister, Ehud Barak. "At the start of the event, I'm standing in the back in my tuxedo," Donald recalled. "The crowd was huge, but I noticed a few Shin Bet agents who I knew. When they spotted me, they smiled, came over, and brought

Chapter 30

me to a seat in the front row, right near the podium. I was really puzzled because that had never happened before. I realized they didn't want me to be part of the security detail. I sat quietly listening to several speakers. Then the Prime Minister is introduced and walks to the podium as he's getting a standing ovation. Having not paid any attention to the Israeli election, I have a 'holy shit' moment as I see it's Ehud Barak. At one point, as part of his thanking the United States for its support of Israel, he made mention of certain Americans who traveled to Israel and put themselves at risk to help his country. As he did so, he looked down at me, made eye contact, and smiled. He did everything but mention my name. I was surprised he even remembered me."

At the end of Barak's speech, a Shin Bet agent walked over to Donald and asked him to remain after the crowd had left. "Much later on in the evening, I ended up having drinks with the Prime Minister. I felt quite honored."

283

CHAPTER 31
Gaza

I told those men, 'Whatever happens, when I go back to America and am asked how I was treated in Gaza, I'll tell the truth!'

—Donald Sadowy

AS THE GAZA STRIP, on the eastern coast of the Mediterranean Sea adjoining Israel and Egypt, was an active source of bomb threats, Donald considered visiting the territory. (In 2007, the terrorist organization Hamas took control of Gaza.) "The Israelis told me not to go. But I'm very curious by nature. I wanted to talk to Palestinians without Israelis around. I tried to follow advice that my old boss, Joe Ahearn, who had traveled a lot to troubled areas, had given me. Try to dress like the locals do. Try not to look at people directly. Walk, look, and act body-language-wise like you belong. Keep to yourself."

Rendered Safe

At the border checkpoint, Donald told the border agents he was a retired American history teacher. Once in Gaza, in spite of being in a crowd and following Joe Ahearn's advice, he soon was approached by several middle-aged women. "They made me out as a foreigner and were angrily pointing and screaming at me. They grabbed sticks as they came toward me. I was scared."

Donald spotted a large, open café, which he raced into, with the enraged women following. "It looked like the inside of Rick's Place [the bar made famous in the movie *Casablanca*]. Large arched doorways, high ceilings with slow-turning fans, beaded curtains separating rooms, and fancy balconies and railings. Arabic music was softly playing. Sitting inside were three casually dressed, serious-looking men sitting at a low, round table having coffee and pastries. I ran in, put my hands up, and said in a loud voice, 'If anyone here understands English, I'm an American. I came here on my own to speak to the Palestinian people.'"

With that, the three men stood, shooed the women out, and invited Donald to join them. "We sat and talked for a long time. They told me about their life experiences. I told them about my U.N. service, which softened up the conversation. I asked them what they really were looking for in this battle with the Israelis. They mentioned having their own independent nation, healthcare, indoor plumbing, a modest little car, and nice blue jeans and sneakers for their kids. When we were done, they walked me back to the checkpoint. Thinking back on it, it was an

Chapter 31

unwise decision of mine. But, on the other hand, I feel good about having made contact."

*

The trip to Israel cemented Donald's relationship with Shin Bet and Mossad, Israel's foreign-intelligence service. "I didn't turn into James Bond. But I developed a flow of useful information to and from the Israelis that I used for the benefit of the Bomb Squad. When an IED incident took place in Israel, they would tell me data like location, logistics, type of package, explosive, and detonator, whether there were any booster charges, whether there was a booby trap, how the IED was delivered and disguised, and whether the event seemed random or planned. I was at the Israeli mission and other consulates so often I got tagged by the FBI's Counterintelligence Division. But I always had Bernard Johnson to help straighten things out."

*

With the passing of the millennium mark and retirement impending, Donald assumed his riskiest days were behind him. But the dangers posed by the 1993 Trade Center investigation and other past cases would be mere mist compared to the torrential rain that soon followed.

CHAPTER 32
9/11

The woman who convinced me to turn around and head down the stairs was my angel. She saved my life.
—Donald Sadowy

BY EARLY 2000, Donald resigned himself to the fact he'd never make Detective First Grade. "An old-timer suggested I go down to the union office and have them work up the numbers for me. A union guy looked at my time records and told me if I left within 90 days, with all the overtime, night differential, and holiday pay, I could retire as if I were a Detective First Grade, which is lieutenant's pay. So, in June, I did. The Squad threw a great retirement party for me at a catering hall in the Bronx. Then Kathy and I took the kids to Florida, where we stayed with her parents and hit all the theme parks. I hadn't been that relaxed in decades."

During that summer, Donald received calls from other retired detectives who were working at Merrill

Lynch. "Long story short, I got a job at Merrill's world headquarters in the World Financial Center as a security supervisor. I had my own parking spot that ironically was near where the temporary headquarters had been set up in 1993 for the law-enforcement agencies. I was fat and happy. I had money to pay the Catholic high school tuitions for my kids and to fix up our house." Life was good for Donald, although his years as a Marine and cop had changed him. "I never was able to get comfortable in the corporate-world culture. In the military and law enforcement, there was much more camaraderie, and people had your back. It seemed like, in the private sector, a lot of folks were petty and shallow."

Donald's role in solving the World Trade Center bombing continued to be publicized in various forums. In July 2001, the A&E channel announced that the premier of its documentary series "Minute by Minute," would revisit the 1993 attack. Donald, along with Steve Dodge and Joe Hanlin, appears in that hour-long show, which, by eerie coincidence, would air only weeks after 9/11. During the last minutes of the program, Donald reflects before the camera on how the event caused him to be more aware of his mortality.

The early morning of September 11, 2001, before the sky rained red, was tranquil and the weather perfect. Donald, dressed in a blue pinstripe suit, white shirt, power tie, and Florsheim dress shoes, sat at his usual post in Merrill's worldwide operations center in Four World Financial Center, a 34-story building that soon would

Chapter 32

suffer major damage to its stepped pyramid roof. "It was a huge room built as a bunker and designed to resist an earthquake, which acted as the global pulse of Merrill. I was with another supervisor, and we were checking to see if everything was good before heading to nearby Pace University to take a computer course. It was going to be kind of a fluff day. Suddenly, our pagers went off. Instead of the usual soft message, this was blunt. 'Report to the Winter Garden Atrium [a 10-story glass-vaulted pavilion in the World Financial Center] forthwith.' I was struck by the use of the word 'forthwith,' which no one uses."

At the entrance to the Atrium, Donald met up with his manager and other Merrill supervisors. "People were sobbing and distraught. We heard differing versions of what had happened. Some thought a bomb had gone off. Others said a plane had hit the North Tower, which we assumed was an innocent accident. Everyone was standing around not knowing what to do, with a deer-in-headlights look. That bothered me. I knew the World Trade Center like the back of my hand, so I decided to go across, find out what happened, and evaluate the threat. Then I could go brief the top Merrill execs." Donald decided to head to the Trade Center, a choice made on the spur of the moment and consistent with the essential instinct instilled by his Marine Corps and NYPD training and experience to run toward danger, not away from it.

Donald hustled through a stairway door and onto the grassy knoll that sloped down to the sidewalk on West Street across from the North Tower. (West Street separates

Rendered Safe

the World Trade and World Financial complexes.) "First, I noticed all these emergency-response vehicles parked haphazardly. The NYPD already had shut down vehicular traffic nearby. Then I looked up and saw that something really big had hit the tower."

Donald recognized an FBI agent, Rod Miller, with whom he had worked on the TWA Flight 800 investigation. Miller had been a chemistry major in college and worked at the Calverton facility for two months assisting with the forensic analysis. On 9/11, he was at the Trade Center managing a public-corruption case involving tax assessors. Miller was sitting on a bench in the landscaped, open-air plaza in the shadow of the North Tower, listening in via radio on a conversation taking place in the hotel (by 2001, owned by Marriott). "All of a sudden, I feel a blast of heat on the back of my neck. I look up and see a huge fireball. My partner and I started running as all these airplane pieces and chunks of concrete start raining down on us. I had my gun in a fanny pack, and I realized that I'd left it on the bench. So, I ran back to get it, and that's when Donald and I met up."

Together, the two men raced across the street while bouncing theories off each other, such as whether a terrorist bomb had been set off. Donald can still envision the scene in the North Tower lobby. "We could see glass broken outward lying shattered, and small fires. Masses of evacuating people were being guided by Port Authority security to go through the Concourse [the first level below the plaza—containing a huge enclosed shopping

Chapter 32

mall] and out at Church Street, to avoid getting hit by falling debris. Firemen were rushing up the stairways in groups. Behind the marble desks that made up the information desk were a crush of law-enforcement and emergency personnel talking to each other and using the bank of telephones there. I saw a poor guy who had been lit up like a Roman candle because a stream of jet fuel had gushed into the lobby after blowing the doors off an elevator. At some point, the second plane hit the South Tower. The North Tower swayed and the marble floor shifted big time, like in an amusement house."

Donald and Rod Miller dashed over to the elevator shaft, whose doors had been torn off. "I asked Rod to grab hold of my belt and the back of my shirt as I leaned in and looked up. A really dumb idea in hindsight. I turned my head, shoulders, and torso and looked up. I could see that the rectangular elevator shaft had been twisted violently, which made a deep impression on me. What kind of force would it take to do that?"

After Miller pulled Donald back in, they quickly discussed the need to assist fire and police personnel and help secure the crime scene. "Ever since I was in the Marines," Donald recounted, "I've been mission oriented. I can't just stand around and do nothing." Given there were no operable elevators, the two men headed up the center stairway.[87] "After 1993," Donald recounted, "it had been repainted in this shiny, battleship-gray color, and better lights had been put in. There was water lightly flowing down the steps because the sprinkler systems

Rendered Safe

had kicked in, so it was slippery. I soon lost sight of Rod, who had an athletic build, while I was thirty pounds overweight and panting like an old dog."

Remarkably, Miller made his way to the 86th floor, offering assistance to fire and police personnel as he climbed. "It was rather orderly in the stairway. Everybody was being nice and helping each other. There wasn't any panic. I was getting sporadic reports on my radio of what was going on, including that the other tower had been hit. When I reached the 86th floor, the passage was blocked. By grace of God, something told me to head back. On my way down, the South Tower collapsed, which set the North Tower swaying back and forth. At that point, the firemen unhooked their gear, and we all made a beeline down to the mezzanine balcony. I got outside to find the landscape white from dust. It looked like a battlefield, with carnage everywhere and body parts like heads, torsos, legs strewn about. I made it a block down the street when the North Tower collapsed. I feel blessed to have survived all that."[88]

Meanwhile, with increasing difficulty, Donald had climbed to the 20th floor. "Unlike in 1993, there was no cloud of smoke, but I could smell and even taste the fumes from the burning jet fuel that were slowly coming down the narrow stairway. They burned my nose, throat, and lungs. It became harder and harder for me to breathe. I must have looked awful, because a middle-aged woman paused and grabbed me gently by the arm. She said, 'Don't bother going up further. Everyone who

Chapter 32

can is getting out. There's nothing you can do for rest of them.' I felt bad, but what she said made sense. On the way down, I stopped on the tenth floor, where someone had broken open a door and people were handing out bottles of water from vending machines. By the time I got to ground level, I must have looked bad because someone grabbed me and led me to a chair. A couple of emergency medical technicians looked me over and gave me water and a shot of oxygen."[89]

Everyone in the lobby could hear the thuds of those dropping from the upper floors, as the Trade Center complex transformed into a tomb. "About 25 feet from where I was, by the blown-out windows facing West Street, there was an awning made of glass and stainless steel that overhung a half-moon sheet driveway. One fellow hit the awning and fell through. His body split in half, with the two pieces of torso coming down right down in front of us. Another fell directly onto asphalt, making a sound like someone took a raw piece of roast beef and slammed it against the surface. His body flattened. When that happened, everyone stopped talking. We had suddenly been thrust into combat, without any expectation or preparation."

Donald observed a group of Port Authority personnel in black vests with white lettering off to the side. "They were building mechanics and engineers, with tool bags, hard hats, and radios. One guy was squatting on the floor by a main panel that monitored the elevators. He was doing some work, and then he yelled, 'There's a car way

295

up that I'm not getting a response from. People probably are trapped up there!' His boss shouted, 'We're evacuating. Just grab your equipment, and get out. All of you!' The group of men looked at each other and one yelled back, 'This is our house. We left no one behind in '93, and we won't leave anyone behind today. We know our building best. We're going up there and get them out. Will call you on the radio.' And, with that, those guys picked up their riggings, tools, helmets, and radios and marched toward the stairwell. I've always assumed they all died."

Donald caught sight of Father Mychal Judge, the FDNY Chaplain, standing in the lobby next to the fire chief, wearing a fireman's uniform. "I knew Father Judge because of security work I had done on the side years earlier at St. Francis of Assisi, where he lived and worked. He was holding Rosary beads in his hand and reciting the Rosary prayer repeatedly. His face was an ash color, and he looked as shocked as the rest of us, which I found really unnerving." (When the South Tower collapsed, debris flew through the North Tower lobby, killing many inside, including Father Judge.)

Jimmy Wong, an FBI supervisor who worked on the JTTF, spotted Donald and approached him. "Jimmy was there with four other agents. He smiled, grabbed me softly by the arm, and pulled me over into a football huddle with the others. I realized he thought I was still with the Bomb Squad." Not wanting to mislead Wong, Donald informed him that he was retired from the Squad. "Jimmy was surprised. And disappointed. We shook hands

Chapter 32

and I turned to head out of the lobby. Just then, a fireman put both his hands on my shoulders and squeezed them. He stuck his face within inches of mine and said, 'Be very careful going outside.' Then he hugged me and said goodbye. That man stayed while I left. One of so many memories that always will haunt me."

CHAPTER 33
Buried Alive

His body fell backwards while his legs kept going for a while. The look of shock and horror in his eyes and face is indescribable.

—Donald Sadowy

Donald was among the last civilians to leave the North Tower lobby, via the entrance on West Street heading toward the World Financial Center. "I was replaying in my mind what I'd just seen and heard, to be able to tell a coherent story to the top Merrill execs about how bad this is. Suddenly, there was a sound I'd never heard before. It was the I-beams on the South Tower twisting and bending, which sounded like metal screaming. I looked up and saw the upper part of the tower starting to break apart and fall. Everyone began screaming and running. My mind raced. I was already out onto West Street, which is eight lanes. What do I do? It was too far to run across the highway back to Merrill's building. I thought to race back toward the North Tower, but realized I'd be at risk from falling debris. Then I spotted abandoned emergency vehicles, including a short, stubby fire truck parked the wrong way on a northbound lane facing south. Half of the truck sat under the north pedestrian walkway. I figured if I could get to that truck, I might survive, protected by the truck and the walkway. So, I ran toward it for all I'm worth, my heart pumping like it was gonna pound out of my chest. But it still felt as if I was moving in slow motion."

As Donald shifted direction, two other middle-aged men, each also in a suit and with the same overweight build as Donald, turned and followed him. "As we neared the truck, the man on my left was only a couple of steps behind me. Then, I heard a scream. I turned to see that a large piece of falling glass had hit him, cutting him in half from his left collarbone to his right hip. Like he'd been placed in a large guillotine. I could see his look of shock and horror. In all my years, that was the worst sight I'd ever seen."

Donald dove underneath the truck, banging up his knee badly and pulling a couple of ribs. "I looked from underneath the truck and watched the second fellow run toward me. He got fifteen feet from truck when I heard what sounded as if a roaring freight train were passing. Thick debris came down and across him in waves. It was the last I saw of him."

Donald pulled himself from underneath the truck and hopped onto the metal steps and then onto the open

Chapter 33

cabin. "I took my suit jacket off and wrapped it around my temples and eyes and the arteries in my neck. I draped fire hoses over my head and shoulders. I turned the left side of my body against the bulkhead and curled into the littlest ball I could. And prayed like I'd never prayed before. I felt I was talking straight to God. Debris was coming down and hitting the front of the truck and pedestrian walkway. Fortunately, it didn't hit me directly but rolled over me. My right side was exposed, and I ended up with a damaged shoulder, knee, hip, and spine from the pounding. My clothes were shredded, and my wallet was gone. I felt buried alive. I began to choke from the toxic dust cloud. Realizing I was suffocating, I crawled inside the front cabin and jammed the door shut, using what was left of my jacket as a shield. Heavy debris kept pelting the fire truck, jolting it in every direction as if it were a toy truck being shaken by a three-year-old. I found it increasingly hard to think as powdery dust continued to pour into my lungs. It seemed too ironic. All those years in the Marines and as a cop, and I'm going to die an ignoble death. I was angry with the world and sad for myself. And I worried that, with my wallet lost, my body wouldn't be able to be identified. Somehow, I remembered I had a ring with a miniature of my detective shield given to me as a retirement present, which I took solace in. Before I lost consciousness, I was at peace, thinking, 'Whatever the next world is, I'm about to find out.'"

The angel of death hovered, but moved on. Donald's memory of his miraculous survival experience understandably is incomplete. Over a decade later, while visiting his cousin Arthur, Donald was shown a portion of the 2011 Smithsonian channel documentary *9/11: Day that Changed the World*. "Kathy, the kids, and I are watching that day's horrible events unfold. About halfway through the film [the 45-minute mark], '10:15 a.m. New York' comes on the screen. Suddenly, I'm looking at the fire truck that I'd taken refuge in. Then I hear myself in a frantic, high-pitched tone saying, 'Can anybody hear me? I'm a civilian. I'm trapped inside one of the fire trucks underneath the collapse that just happened. I can't breathe much longer. Save me!' It was only then that I realized I had been on the truck's radio calling for help. Needless to say, I was blown away by hearing myself as I was back then."

Donald came out of unconsciousness caked in dust laced with concrete, glass and asbestos, temporarily blind, and struggling to breathe. He heard muffled voices. "I thought maybe they're angels bringing me to the gates of heaven. Turned out they were two firemen who had noticed the abandoned truck and decided to salvage it. By sheer luck, they saw my hand moving. The firemen lifted me up and, holding me under my arms, dragged me for blocks over to the corner of Vesey and West Streets. There, they tossed me into the arms of five EMTs. One of those guys came close enough that I could feel his breath. 'We have you,' he said loudly, 'and you're gonna make it.' They cleared debris off me, picked me up, carried me down West Street, and then cut across

Chapter 33

to the North Cove Marina by the Hudson River. There, they gently laid me down on the sidewalk next to several trauma bags. A paramedic rushed over. He put a glove on and, with two fingers and a suction, scooped out debris from my mouth and the back of my throat to clear an airway. I was dry heaving and gagging, but I forced myself to relax and not panic. He cleared my nostrils, ears, and eyes, sat me up, and offered me water. I began to shake like an epileptic, and then I started hysterically crying."

After Donald calmed, he was left alone while the EMTs moved to help others. "I rose and started to walk aimlessly. I saw people I knew, but they didn't recognize or acknowledge me. Then I made out Ray O'Hagan, a retired NYPD lieutenant who was another Merrill supervisor, and walked toward him. As recollected by O'Hagan (who soon would learn that his firefighter brother had lost his life in the disaster), "I saw this dazed figure totally covered in dust walking toward me. He got about fifteen feet from me, and I realized it was Donald. I got some water and washed him off as best I could and tried to help him to breathe better."

The two then heard screaming as the North Tower collapsed. "People began running north," Donald remembered, "including men and women I worked with at Merrill who could have helped me but just fled. Something that rubs me the wrong way to this day. Fortunately Ray stayed in his professional, calm mode. He said, 'Donald, put your arm around me, hold on, and try to move one leg as best you can. We gotta get out of here.' I blurted

Rendered Safe

out, 'The powder is turning to paste in my mouth. If I suck in another lungful, I'm finished!' Ray responded, 'There are no ambulances. Just keep moving. I won't leave you.'"

With no ferries operating, Ray half-walked, half-carried Donald along the Esplanade to nearby Stuyvesant High School on Chambers Street. "There was a medical area set up in the auditorium, with doctors and nurses waiting for the injured. They laid me down on a table while Ray spoke with a doctor quietly, out of earshot. He must have told them I was dehydrated, because someone quickly gave me a quart container of Tropicana OJ, which was manna from heaven."

After a brief respite, Ray helped Donald make his way up West Street and over to a Merrill location a mile away at 570 Washington Street, a nondescript, three-story brick building a block north of the Holland Tunnel entrance. "The lobby was packed with Merrill employees. Ray yelled out for someone to help me. A dozen people rushed over. I was lifted and carried to the basement. Someone helped me take my clothes off—I still had the collar of my shirt and double-Windsor knotted tie but most of my shirt was gone. I took the best shower of my life even though there was no hot water, washing my hair and body repeatedly to try to get off all the toxic stuff deep in my skin and pores. At one point, I started laughing because of the trauma. Someone knocked on the stall and yelled, 'Donald, you okay?' I yelled back, 'I'm alive!' When I finished, they

Chapter 33

gave me a set of mismatched clothes of the wrong sizes. I looked like a war orphan."

*

The morning of 9/11, Kathy Sadowy was teaching a second-grade class in a public school in South Ozone Park, Queens. "Once the second plane hit and we knew it was terrorism, the teachers gathered all the children in the auditorium. We were asked by the principal not to say anything to them. Some parents came to pick up their kids, but a lot of our students were foster children who lived in shelters. They remained with us for the day. I tried but couldn't get Donald on the phone. I knew he didn't work in the Trade Center, but I had this panicked feeling anyway, which increased by the hour. I called Donald's mom, who still lived on Green Street in Greenpoint with a view of the smoke rising to the sky from the Trade Center area, to see if she was okay. She was crying hysterically. I lied and told her I had spoken with Donald and that he was fine. That calmed her a bit."

By mid-afternoon, Kathy was able to leave for home. "I knew that my brother, David, who was an ESU officer, and my brother-in-law Kevin, who was a Nassau County cop, were okay. But there was no message from Donald." David Burkart, who lived across the street from Kathy and Donald with his wife Pat and their four daughters, had been home from work that morning caring for his youngest child, who was a baby then. "Pat was a manager at a construction company," David recalled. "I called her and asked that she hurry home because I wanted to get down to the World Trade Center to help. She was only a fifteen-minute drive away, but she took her time getting home. When she arrived, I was pretty angry. I handed her the baby, ran to my car, and made my way through really bad traffic to the City. As I was driving on the Long Island Expressway in western Queens, honking my horn and flashing my lights, at about the Greenpoint Avenue exit, I looked to the left and saw the first tower come down. At that point, it struck me that Pat had delayed coming home on purpose."

A day later, David would play a dramatic role in the rescue effort. His boss gathered together a number of ESU officers and informed them there were broken air shafts discovered that potentially could contain either a person still alive or a body. He asked for a volunteer to search them. "Most of the ESU guys," Donald observed, "were built like linebackers and could fill a doorway. My brother-in-law was short and thin, and easily the smallest of them. So, Davy raised his hand. They tied a rope around his waist, gave him a portable light and a radio, and slowly lowered him down several levels of two separate shafts. There were fires still burning under the debris at the time, and the heat in the shaft was so intense that it burnt Davy's arms, knees, and hands right through his gloves. And it melted his boots. After he came up from the second shaft, an inspector ordered the procedure stopped out of fear for my brother-in-law's life."

Chapter 33

In the afternoon of 9/11, while Kathy waited anxiously, along with her children, to hear from Donald, family members as well as numerous neighbors and friends arrived to provide comfort. "People started streaming into the house," Kaitlin, then an eighth-grader, recalled, "including some of mom's co-workers whom I hadn't seen in years. Nobody said much of anything. Every time the phone rang, we all were frantic. Mom tried to be hospitable to everyone, offering drinks and food, despite being freaked out herself. At one point, I walked by myself into the backyard and said a prayer for my dad. And I thought about how my parents had taken Donnie and me to church every Sunday and that all the prayers we'd said over the years were for a moment like this."

In the late afternoon, a techie brought Donald a briefcase containing a cell phone. "All the landlines and cell phones still were out. This one transmitted over satellite. I just stared at it, because I couldn't remember my number. Or even my address. I started to cry until Ray, God bless him, came over. 'Calm down,' he told me. Ray dialed my number and then left. My daughter picked up. She heard my voice and started crying hysterically. I heard my son, then in high school, in the background saying, "Katie, what's the matter?" He took the phone and started crying. Kathy, who had fallen asleep on a couch, came on the phone and said, 'Who is it?' and started bawling. Of course, I am blubbering the whole time."

307

CHAPTER 34
Recovery

I cried my eyes out during every session with the psychologist. But I came out of them more relaxed and with fewer nightmares.

—Donald Sadowy

AFTER A COUPLE OF SLICES of pizza, a can of Coke, and two Tylenol, Donald lay down on cushions underneath a desk in a corner of a room and fell into a deep sleep. The next morning, with assistance, Donald walked north to Canal Street and made his way home via subway and bus. "I was in the hurt locker. I couldn't go up steps to the front door, so I went around to the side door and leaned on it while ringing the bell." Kathy opened the door and looked her husband over. "He had on misfit clothes. The shirt was too small and his belly was hanging out while his pants were too short and falling down. I smiled and said, 'You came home looking like this?' We hugged and cried for quite a while." Kaitlin was struck by how "beat up" her father appeared, and the "different look in his eyes."

That afternoon, after helping Donald to dress and walk, Kathy brought him to a medical center. "When the nurse asked him what had happened, he just sobbed. No one there seemed to know what to do for him."

Donald recuperated for months. "I had major breathing problems. It was as if I had pulled a plastic bag over my head and sealed it. Often I would panic as I gasped for air. And I was in constant pain, sometimes off the charts in intensity. I couldn't raise my right shoulder more than ten degrees. My back, right hip, and right knee all were damaged. All the Vicodin I'd taken tore up my stomach, so I switched to OxyContin, which I took like M&Ms. But they didn't help me much with the pain. They just made me feel like I was drunk. I ended up getting several epidural injections in my spine, which finally allowed me to sleep well."

During his lengthy recovery, Donald suffered spasms of guilt, flashbacks, emotional detachment, and a bottomless pool of anger. Donald's and Kathy's bedroom was next to their son's. "On many nights, I would hear my dad crying uncontrollably. It was shocking and upsetting because all my life, he had been so mentally and physically tough."

Haunted day and night by images of 9/11, Donald became a recluse. "I didn't want to speak to anyone, not even on the phone. It seemed all I did was watch TV and go to medical appointments. With the help of a wonderful,

Chapter 34

kind chiropractor, Emil Tocci, who refused to take any money from me, I avoided surgery initially. I was in physical therapy for eighteen months and, in the end, got back much of my ability to move without pain. I also went for psychological counseling, which was the best thing I could have done. Finally, I was able to tell the story of what happened and move on with my life, although I continued to struggle with all sorts of physical ailments, including asthma, lung damage, and acid reflux. We tried to shield my troubles from the kids, but they knew."

One of those helping Donald recuperate mentally was his former NYPD colleague, Richie Hackford, who also had retired. "Richie often would call me up," Kathy explained, "and say something like, 'Get Donald's fat ass off the couch, and get him dressed. I'll be there in thirty minutes.' Then Richie would take Donald out on his boat that was docked in Freeport. A beautiful 24-foot fiberglass one with an inside cabin. They would go fishing but not really try to catch anything. They'd just drop anchor and sit at the edge of the boat staring at the water, listening to mellow music, and chatting for hours. To this day, when Donald hears Van Morrison songs, he'll remark about how it reminds him of those peaceful times on the boat with Richie." To that description, Donald added, "Richie would get me talking about everything, like things I was worried or angry about, during a time when I wasn't talking about anything."

For decades, Donald had been intimately acquainted with the prevalence of suffering and death. Yet his grief for those killed on 9/11 was, at times, unbearable. One was a good friend, Claude "Danny" Richards, who perished while searching for victims in the Customs House building, which was destroyed when the North Tower collapsed.[90] "Danny had been an Army Airborne Ranger prior to joining the NYPD. You couldn't find someone with higher character or integrity. I helped get him into the Squad and recommended him for the intelligence-coordinator position, which he got. Because of that, although it wasn't rational, I felt enormous guilt about his death."

Another of Donald's friends who lost his life was Thomas Langone, an ESU officer who posthumously received the NYPD Medal of Honor. (His firefighter brother, Peter, also died in 9/11.) In April 2015, Donald joined Tom Langone's daughter, Caitlin, in relating their 9/11 experiences before an audience at the 9/11 Tribute Museum as part of a pilot program entitled "We Were There." In response to a question as to whether America had lost its innocence on 9/11, Donald responded, "For us in law enforcement, we lost our innocence back in 1993."

*

St. Paul's Episcopal Chapel stands directly across the street from the World Trade Center site. On 9/11, miraculously, the sanctuary suffered no physical damage, although its exterior and yard were covered in debris. In the ensuing months, the chapel served as a place of rest,

Chapter 34

nourishment, and solace for rescue-and-recovery workers, police, firefighters, National Guardsmen, construction and sanitation crews, and others, who also would participate in the daily Eucharist. The wrought-iron fence surrounding St. Paul's spontaneously was turned into a memorial, filled with banners, posters, personalized t-shirts, flags, letters, religious items, and other mementos that held personal meaning.

In March 2002, the sanctuary reopened to the public. Donald watched the ceremony on TV. "I felt my soul was wounded. I needed to be there. A week later, on a Friday night, a friend drove me to the chapel. I couldn't get in because it was packed, so I stood outside with the help of a cane, crying like a baby. A black clergyman with a deep, clear voice walked up behind me and put his hand on my shoulder, which gave me a sense of peace. Then he stepped in front of me, smiled, and spoke words of comfort to the crowd. Although he was addressing everyone, I felt he was just talking to me. When he finished, he wrote something on a piece of paper and tucked it into my shirt pocket. The words were from Joshua 1:9: 'Have I not commanded you? Be strong and courageous. Do not be afraid; do not be discouraged, for the Lord your God will be with you wherever you go.' I read that quote every day afterward. It was the beginning of me coming back emotionally and spiritually. I used to go to church for my kids, and kind of went through the motions. Afterward, I became confirmed in the Episcopal Church and joined a Bible-study group so I could genuinely participate in the services. It took a building falling on me to wake me up."

After one study session, Donald asked his priest, who knew Donald's 9/11 story, "Why did God save me?" In response, the priest challenged Donald with his own question, "What are you going to do with your second chance?" This prompted Donald to return to work at Merrill Lynch. "I needed help from Kathy getting dressed, and someone had to drive me to lower Manhattan. But I came back too soon. The area still was desolate, and there wasn't much to do. I walked around with a bottle of Vicodin and a cane, chatting with the guards who were there to prevent vandalism and feeling completely useless."

The priest's question also compelled Donald to start a list, which grew beyond what he initially expected. "I wrote down the name of each person I loved and felt close to, but who I had never said those words to, going back to my youth. People who had done things for me well above and beyond what I could have expected. And then I reached out to each one of them and told them how I felt. I needed to do that, and I made it my new mission."

CHAPTER 35
Shooter

This was only a year after 9/11, and everyone was really concerned about what else was in the suitcase.
—Donald Sadowy

IN 2002, DONALD LEFT Merrill Lynch and returned to the U.N., this time as an independent consultant for Michael Stapleton Associates, a private security firm composed mostly of retired NYPD Bomb Squad and ESU officers. Among other services, the firm provides dogs trained to sniff out explosives.

One October morning, after an argument with Kathy over an insignificant matter, Donald left his house distracted, failing to notice he hadn't taken his revolver. With him was an explosives-detecting canine that was living with them. Donald's assignment that day was a fixed post at the East 45th street entrance to the U.N. garage off the FDR Drive, where delivery trucks entered. "My partner, a former U.S. Army sergeant who also had a canine with him, and I would check the manifest against the cargo to ensure everything was correct, search the vehicle methodically, and have a dog smell for IEDs. More than a hundred trucks would enter each day, so a lot of work had to be done. Around 1 p.m., just as a truck arrived at the gate, I got a frantic call on the radio from another security guard, John Caliendo, who was posted in a booth in front of the Secretariat building by the circular pool with a fountain in its center. He was yelling that shots had been fired. We locked the gates so that no one could go in or out. I handed off my dog to another guard, told the driver that there was an emergency, jumped into his truck, and we raced up the ramp. Nearing the main entrance, I hopped out and ran toward Caliendo's post. I saw John, crouching behind his booth with his gun drawn. I reached under my jacket for my gun, and there's this huge, 'Oh shit' realization it's not there."

Marching toward the Secretariat building was Steven Kim, a 57-year-old naturalized American from North Korea who was a postal worker in a Chicago suburb. Seeking to draw attention to human-rights abuses occurring in North Korea under its ruler, Kim Jong-Il, he had entered U.N. property by climbing a five-foot security fence. Using a .357-caliber Magnum revolver, Kim fired seven shots at the building façade. One bullet passed through a window into a desk space where a U.N. staffer ordinarily worked. Fortunately, she wasn't present that day.

With diplomats and visitors running to take cover, Donald and the other security guards watched as Kim

Chapter 35

stopped in the traffic circle, opened a suitcase, and flung leaflets into the air that appealed to the U.N. to "destroy the false and evil" Kim Jong-Il regime. The day was windy, and the papers flew everywhere. Kim then closed the suitcase and resumed walking until a NYPD detective and Secret Service agent, who were there to provide protection for a foreign minister, ran over and tackled him. "They cuffed Kim," Donald remembered, "and dragged him inside the building into a security office. We didn't have a dog readily available, so amid the chaotic scene, I crawled over and did a 'hand entry,' cutting observation holes. Doing a hand entry was the last thing I wanted to do, but the circumstances called for it, given the large number of people nearby. I saw no IED, only papers and personal items, and cleared the suitcases."

The next concern was the perpetrator himself. "This was not long after the Shoe Bomber incident [In December 2001, Richard Colvin Reid, a British Muslim, attempted to detonate peroxide explosives packed into his shoes while on a flight from Paris to Miami], and this guy had shoes with thick soles and stitching that looked new. We stripped him down to his boxer shorts, and I searched him and his clothing exhaustively, including the linings. I cut open his padded belt from end to end. Then I noticed that the stitching on his shoes around his thick soles appeared new. I took the shoes, ran to the lobby's Heimann X-ray machine, and examined them, including the laces, thinking there might be a fuse lined with powder. Then I cut the soles open. Finally, I reported he was clean. I'd examined and cleared a lot of suspicious packages over my career, but that was my most nerve-wracking experience."[91]

CHAPTER 36
The Marshal's Office

One day while we were riding in the special prisoner elevator, Gotti looked at me and said, 'Don't take this the wrong way, but why do you wear such ugly shoes?'

— Donald Sadowy

SEEKING PERMANENT employment, and not ready to close the curtain on his career, in the summer of 2003, Donald joined the U.S. Marshal's office for the Southern District of New York, which was headed by Joseph Guccione. "I knew Joe," Donald explained, "from the Malvasi bombings. I became one of a dozen or so of his staffers."

Donald's responsibilities, among others, were providing security for defendants held in a court cell, traveling by car, rail, and plane to escort an apprehended person to prison, shutting down bank accounts, serving process, and executing warrants. "I did everything but kick doors in."

Rendered Safe

From left to right: Steve Berberich, former U.S. Army Sergeant Paul Carter (a Redstone Arsenal instructor), and Donald at the celebration of the 100th anniversary of the Bomb Squad

One trial for which Donald helped to provide security was, ironically, for Lynne Stewart, a radical-leftist lawyer who gained notoriety for representing violent self-described revolutionaries. One of Stewart's clients was Sheikh Omar Abdel Rahman, who Stewart helped to smuggle messages to and from the imprisoned Sheikh and his violent followers in Egypt. She was arrested in 2002 and convicted in February 2005 of three counts related to her violations of a promise to abide by the "SAMs" ("Special Administrative Measures"—restrictive rules governing selected prisoners in federal jails) imposed on her client, and one count of providing support to a

Chapter 36

terrorist conspiracy. Her prison sentence, initially set at 28 months, was later increased to 10 years after an appeals court ordered the trial judge to consider a longer term.[92]

"The Stewart prosecution," Donald recounted, "drew a huge amount of publicity. Stewart was a short, round-faced woman who looked like your typical grandma. She'd arrive in court wearing a New York Mets cap and a floral-print housedress, dangling a cloth tote bag rather than the lawyer's briefcase and inevitably drawing a clutch of news photographers." Over the course of the trial, Donald became casually friendly with each of the prosecutors and defense attorneys, including those for Stewart's two co-defendants—Mohammad Yousry, the Sheikh's interpreter, and Ahmed Sattar, a postal worker who was a fervent supporter of the Sheikh.

One Sunday during the last few weeks of the ten-month trial, Donald was home watching TV. "I saw this commercial for Grecian formula [a hair-coloring product] and impulsively ran out, bought a bottle, and dyed my hair jet black. When my wife and kids got home and saw me, they were shocked. Called me 'Elvis' and said I looked horrible. The next day, as luck would have it, I got to the courtroom at 40 Foley Square late because of subway delays. The room, which was the largest one in the building, was packed with reporters, sketch artists, family, and law enforcement types. I entered as a female prosecutor was speaking to the jury and headed for my assigned spot sitting against a wall. The floor groaned as I walked, and then I opened up the swinging wooden gate, which creaked. I could hear people laughing and mumbling to each other and see jurors giggling and tapping each other on the elbow. The prosecutor, having lost her train of thought, turned around, saw me, and did a double take. Judge Koeltl, a serious guy, was pissed. He banged his gavel as he stared at me and announced there would be a fifteen-minute break, during which time he hoped everyone could compose themselves. I left the courtroom looking for a chair to crawl under. Several female jurors came over to me, nice as could be. One told me how brave I was to try to dye my hair and suggested I go with a chestnut color the next time. Another rubbed my arm, and a third offered me a homemade cookie she had brought in her pocketbook. My defense to the intense teasing I received was to point out all the female attention it got me."

Donald also provided security for two of the four trials of John Gotti, Jr. for mob-related charges, one of which was ordering attacks on radio-talk-show host Curtis Sliwa. Each trial ended with a hung jury. "We'd sign Gotti out of his cell block in the Metropolitan Correctional Facility and bring him through an underground passage across to the courtroom building, locking and unlocking chambers as we went. We'd give him his court clothes after searching them. Then we'd babysit him all day while he met with his attorneys, had lunch, and attended court proceedings. At one point, Gotti, who dressed in court like his 'Dapper Don' father, in a friendly way started razzing me about how I dressed.

Chapter 36

This led to some amusing back-and-forth between us. One day, after a lengthy trial session, Gotti whispered to his attorney, 'Could you ask the marshal with the ugly shoes if I could use the bathroom?'"

CHAPTER 37
Ghana

The crocodiles had a look that translated into, 'Here comes lunch.'

—Donald Sadowy

IN OCTOBER 2011, a cousin on Donald's mother's side—Sergeant Michael Fernald—was a Marine sergeant and the assistant post commander for the Corps' detachment in Accra, the capital of Ghana. Involved in the planning for the American embassy's upcoming celebration on November 10 of the Corps' birthday, Fernald met with U.S. Ambassador Donald Teitelbaum to inform him of Donald's background and career and pitch the idea of asking his cousin to participate. Teitelbaum bought in, inviting Donald to be a guest speaker at the highlight of the festivities—a diplomatic ball.

"I was thrilled to get the invite, to travel to this exotic place, and to see my cousin. I decided to leave a few days earlier to sightsee. I went to the Ghana Consulate for a visa, thinking it would be a snap, but initially I was denied one. I found out later that the U.S. had declined quite a few visa requests from Ghanaian nationals, and I got caught up in a tit-for-tat fight."

Before leaving, Donald received a call from an official in the American embassy in Accra. "He assured me I'd be well taken care of by the Marines. Then he added, 'By the way, these guys haven't had a taste of American whiskey in a long time.' At a duty-free shop in the airport, I bought the biggest bottle of Jim Beam they had, which was inside a metal decorative container, and carried it with me like a mother carries a newborn."

U.S. Marines picked Donald up at the Accra airport tarmac and drove him to the American embassy compound. "It was a ten-acre fortress, surrounded by thick, fifteen-foot walls that had towers manned by armed personnel. There also were barriers to prevent suicide bombers. Ambassador Teitelbaum greeted me and told me he'd given Mike and a few of his guys time off to tour me around the countryside and jungle. The ambassador warned me the country was beautiful, but perilous, and gave me a list of do's and don'ts. What struck me most was his story of an American doctor killed in front of his wife when a crocodile dragged him from a dugout canoe after he'd sluffed off several warnings."

Mike and other Marines drove Donald in a jeep west along the coast to the edge of a foreboding jungle. "The head of the group was a short, bald, muscular lieutenant colonel whose tone, body language, and facial expressions

Chapter 37

made clear he was a tough piece of work. He reminded me of Gunnery Sergeant Hartman in the film *Full Metal Jacket*. Given the circumstances, I felt especially glad to have him along."

In the evening, the entourage reached their destination, an encampment. After settling down and being sprayed with mosquito repellant, Donald pulled out the Jim Beam bottle from his backpack. "The lieutenant colonel asked, 'Who's that for?' 'For all you guys,' I told him. And, sure enough, the Marines lined up with metal canteen cups, each getting a taste. If I'd have passed out gold bars, that wouldn't have made them any happier."

The next day, Donald and his guides began the trip, which would encompass traveling over two mountain ranges and two rivers in the direction of the bordering nation of Togo. "During the day, we stayed mostly on dirt trails under a thick cover of trees, which filtered the sun and made the 90-degree heat more bearable. We traversed dense vegetation and waist-deep ponds while on the lookout for dangerous wildlife. The soil, black and mineral-rich, broke apart easily in your hands. All the fruits and vegetables seemed gigantic, as if grown on steroids. We ate pineapples that were delicious and twice the size of ones back home."

Throughout the trip, Don was reminded not to touch anything. "As we weaved our way through the jungle, our lead guide paused to slowly point out to me a light green snake only about six inches long and a half inch wide that sat on a leaf hanging to about waist level. He quietly said, 'It's called the 1-2-3 snake by the locals.' Of course, I asked, 'Why?' 'Because,' he replied, 'it's one of the deadliest snakes in the world. If it bites you, you die within three minutes.' Then he and the other guides laughed heartily, with me joining in nervously."

At night, beneath a canopy of stars, the group camped in the jungle. "The next day, while walking along a sandy beach bordered by scrub and filled with seabirds, the ocean whispered our name. The tide was coming in, and the water was warm, so we stopped for a run into the breaking waves and a swim. During that time, a string of wild horses came up, sniffed all around, and then galloped away. Later, we encountered an impromptu barbeque restaurant set up by locals. As the sun set, we ate grilled shrimp the size of a man's fist and other seafood with rice while a keyboardist and a sax player entertained us with jazz songs. It all seemed surreal."

Although the views could be spectacular, the mountain trek was difficult for Donald because of his breathing problems. "But, going over the two unstable bridges was the worst, as I was flat-out scared. Each was about 400 feet long and 200 feet above the water. Made of rope, they looked like giant macramé. Each one swayed easily, so my hands always had a strong grip on the rope line on each side. You stepped on one-inch-thick and ten-inch-wide wood planks laid out in sections, methodically placing one foot in front of other and taking only a half-step. Only two people could be on at the same time. You had to walk at the same pace and be totally in sync

Chapter 37

with the man in front of you, which in my case was my cousin. Only when he moved a foot did you do so. And when he set down that foot, you did also. Mike told me to look only at him. But, of course, I did glance down. What struck me were all the crocodiles, each more than twenty feet long and about five feet wide, staring up at us. At night, we celebrated our safe arrival at the next camping ground with beers. "As we toasted each other, I silently blessed God for my getting there in one piece."

During the hike home, while maneuvering on a dirt trail, Donald spotted nailed to a tree a hand-carved and painted sign that read, "This way to Mrs. Doolittle's Monkey Forest Retreat." His guides led him to the site, which was a hospital for wounded monkeys as well as other animals such as tortoises, snakes, and porcupines, often injured by poachers. "This lovely old-school Netherlands couple—Dennis and Lily—had come to Ghana years earlier and fallen in love with the country. They received a grant from the U.N. and permission from the government to open up the facility. We signed the visitors log and were taken by Dennis on a tour of the compound. Then we sat on the patio of a house built into the side of a mountain, sipping sodas and listening to their stories. At one point, Lily lit a cigarette and held it with her hand all the way back like Bette Davis would. All of a sudden, a monkey about three feet high came swinging down from a tree and snatched the cigarette. He swung back onto the branch and started making screeching noises. I had no idea what to make of this until Dennis calmly said,

'Lily, I've told you again and again that the monkeys are afraid of fire.' Lily turned to the monkey and demanded that he return the cigarette. Instead, the monkey shook his head and tore up the cigarette."

Before arriving in Accra, one early afternoon, the group stopped at a crocodile farm located by a slow-moving river. "As my cousin Mike and I walked in, our tickets were taken by a five-foot-tall, stout native woman with a serious look on her face. She was wearing a uniform and holding an eight-foot thin, tapered pole, attached to which was raw chicken. Under a thatched canopy, there was a snack bar with plenty of drinks and beers. Beyond that was a fence and gate, on which was a metal sign reading 'Not responsible for pets or children.' About fifty yards past the gate was a clearing leading to the river. All around were crocodiles, each taking a nap. They ranged in size from three to nine feet long. Much larger ones, some more than twenty-five feet from nose to tail, were in the deep water in the river."

Mike pointed to a crocodile about eight feet long sleeping on the sand in the shade. "He asked me," Donald recounted, "to go and squat over that croc so he could take my picture. 'No way,' I yelled back. So Mike gave me his camera and slowly walked over to the crocodile. He squatted over the beast and smiled. As I took his picture, the crocodile sensed Mike's presence and stirred. Mike started hustling back toward me as the crocodile sat up and began chasing us. We ran uphill at full speed toward the gate. The woman who took our tickets shouted

Chapter 37

something and began running toward the crocodile. We made it to the gate, completely out of breath, and closed it behind us. We couldn't see the woman anymore, but I assumed it was just a day at the office for her."

The November 10 diplomatic ball was held in the Mövenpick Ambassador Hotel Accra. "That hotel, considered the top hotel in Accra, was beautiful and luxurious but was marred by ten-foot walls and heavily armed guards everywhere. There were more than three hundred attendees, including diplomats and their spouses from various embassies dressed to the nines and being entertained by a military band. As it was a black-tie affair, the ambassador had arranged for me to be fitted for a tuxedo pronto. I spoke for almost twenty minutes, telling my 1993 and 9/11 World Trade Center stories. At the end, I gave credit to God and my Corps training for giving me the fortitude and mindset to have survived."

Donald received a standing ovation and toasts to his continued health. Then, as the oldest former Marine, he participated in a traditional ceremony, using a saber to cut a sheet cake decorated with "Happy Birthday Marine Corps" and the eagle, globe, and anchor emblem. "I took one bite and stood at attention as the band played ceremonial music. The next day, I was on a flight home, contemplating how once again life had dealt me the strangest hand."

Rendered Safe

Donald's cousin Michael squatting over a crocodile

Marine Corps cake-cutting ceremony

CHAPTER 38
Reflections

Bernard Johnson, my big brother, told me, 'Maybe God doesn't want you to work anymore.'
—Donald Sadowy

IN LATE 2011, Donald received an annual medical exam, required by the Marshal's Office. "It took a half-day and was pretty extensive. A week later, my supervisor calls me in, tells me he needs to suspend me, and asks for my credentials and gun. I was shocked. I had failed the exam. He was nice, telling me he'd hold on to my credentials and that I could get retested and gain back my job if I started going to the gym and working my ass off with a trainer, and then my own doctor deems me fit. The union guys were supportive, urging me to fight the suspension. But, the more I thought about my situation, the more I appreciated I had physical issues that couldn't be easily fixed. The weight of my years had caught up to me. I realized that, at the ripe old age of fifty-seven, it was time to retire."

The hourglass of Donald's career having run out, his time over the next several years was taken up with personal- and family-health issues. "I had to undergo a number of surgeries. They took tumors out of me the size of golf balls. But my breathing problems from diminished lung capacity couldn't be fixed. My biggest worry is developing lung cancer."

Donald moved his elderly mother and her younger sister, Aunt Margie, both of whom had developed severe physical problems, from their Greenpoint home to a co-op apartment down the block from him. "With the help of Kathy, who had retired as a teacher, and aides, I took care of my mom and aunt full-time, including paying their bills. It was the right thing for me to do at that point in my life. My aunt eventually developed dementia, and we had to put her into a nursing home."

Donald also volunteered as a docent at the 9/11 Tribute Center and later at the 9/11 Museum. There, while reviewing exhibits on the bottom level, he was stunned to see the fire truck he had taken refuge in. "I thought there were no surprises left." Also, while viewing the section of the museum covering the 1993 attack, Donald took notice of the now-famous piece of mangled chassis frame housed there. "It had been donated to the museum by the Justice Department and FBI. But there was no mention of the Bomb Squad or me. That hurt."

Chapter 38

Donald in 2019 at the 9/11 Museum next to the chassis frame

Donald in 2019 at the 9/11 Museum next to the fire truck

Once his mother and aunt passed, Donald gained more of the precious gift of time. "All those years I worked, taking on second and third jobs like most cops do, I didn't have the opportunity to pursue any hobbies. Now I'm big into all sorts of things. I practice archery frequently with my daughter. Kathy and I belong to a trap-shooting club and travel to competitions. I swim regularly. There are lots of church activities. And I try to make every reunion with the old NYPD crew. Of course, the best is being with the family."

One of Donald's pleasures is watching his son's burgeoning career with the NYPD. "Growing up," Donnie recounted, "my mom's dad would tell me stories about

Chapter 38

being in the Marines and show me videos of Marine boot camp. And, of course, I knew my dad had been a Marine. After 9/11, I really wanted to join up as soon as I graduated high school, but my family convinced me that it would be better if I served my country where I lived, in New York City. When I graduated from the Academy, my dad gave me advice that helped a lot. Like always having your head on a swivel, make sure I know what's going on around me at all times, and try to work with the most street-savvy cops. To this day, he blows me away with all the knowledge he has." Following somewhat in his father's footsteps, Donnie now works in the NYPD's Intelligence Bureau.

The modest celebrity Donald has achieved hasn't changed him. Recollections of past tragedies, particularly those from 9/11, persist, but no longer haunt. Now in his mid-60s, Donald feels blessed. "I'm alive, and my life is a good one, something I never take for granted. I have no regrets. I lived the life that I chose. And I did good. I made a difference."

ACKNOWLEDGMENTS

THIS BOOK WOULD NOT have been possible without the generous assistance of numerous law-enforcement, investigative, and security officials, each of whose service is to be appreciated and admired. They include:

Bureau of Alcohol, Tobacco, Firearms, and Explosives: John Goetz and Jessica Gotthold

Federal Aviation Administration: Ed Kittel

Federal Bureau of Investigation: John Anticev, Rick Hahn, Rod Miller, and Steve Veyera

New York Police Department: Steve Chiarini, Jeff Matlin, John Miller, Marylou O'Brien, Larry Riccio, Dan Smolanick, and Greg Solis

NYPD Bomb Squad: Steve Berberich, Pete Dalton, Steve Dodge, Richie Hackford, Donald Hurley, Dan McNally, Denis Mulcahy, Mark Torre, and Charlie Wells

U.N. Security: John Caliendo, Michael McCann, and Nick Panzarino

Rendered Safe

U.S. State Department: Steve Bernstein and Bernard Johnson

Extra gratitude to Bernard Johnson for suggesting the book's title, and to Steve Dodge, John Goetz, Jeff Matlin, Nick Panzarino, Larry Riccio, and Charlie Wells for the interesting, significant, and sometimes remarkable pictures they shared with me. John also provided me with a treasure trove of original documents prepared by ATF after the 1993 World Trade Center attack.

Rick Hahn is renowned for his work as an FBI agent. Less well known is that he's a talented and prolific author. For this book and my previous one, *Shattered Lives,* Rick kindly shared with me his valuable and comprehensive writings, which deserve to be widely read.

A seminal figure in Donald's Bomb Squad career was Lieutenant Walter Boser, who died on April 26, 2019, during the writing of this book. His wake was attended by Donald, Richie Hackford, Steve Berberich, and many other former Bomb Squad members. "I cried for the loss of a wonderful Bomb Squad commander and, more importantly, a great man," Donald told me afterward.

I'm grateful to Kathleen Murray, the widow of Brian Murray and author of a deeply honest and moving book, *Life Detonated: The True Story of a Widow and a Hijacker,* who provided me with insights on Brian's life and the Bomb Squad.

Thanks to Donna Orminski for her thoughtful and vivid recollections of Greenpoint of a half-century ago

Acknowledgments

and of young Donald and Kathy. Much appreciation to Arthur Katulak, Donald's cousin, who not only furnished colorful descriptions of the Sadowy and Katulak families but, also, provided me with invaluable videos. And my appreciation to Ray O'Hagan for his remembrances of 9/11 and for being one of the thousands of quiet heroes on that day.

Donald's family is a close and loving one. Much gratitude to Kathy Sadowy for her detailed and perceptive recollections and observations about Donald and the family structure he grew up in, as well as for her candid portrayal of life as a wife of an NYPD and Bomb Squad officer. Thanks to Donnie and Kaitlin for sharing their memories of and reflections on their beloved dad, and to Kathy's brother, David, for his recollections of 9/11.

As always, I am grateful to my family's support, especially my wife, Linda, who read multiple drafts and made numerous thoughtful and valuable suggestions, and my talented daughter, Arielle Morris, who designed the cover.

*

I first met Donald Sadowy in 2016, when I was researching my previous book on the 1975 Fraunces Tavern bombing by the FALN, which took the lives of four men, including the father of my co-author, Joe Connor. Donald provided a great deal of valuable information and background on the 1982 New Year's Eve bombing by the FALN that gravely injured three NYPD officers.

I was immediately struck by Donald's comprehensive knowledge of Bomb Squad matters and his power of recall. Cops are known to be good storytellers, and Donald is on the high end of the spectrum. Not only could he relate events from decades ago in detail but, also, he would provide important emotional and historical context. Donald is an impressive student of both people and situations. And when a story involved him, he told it "blemishes and all," to quote Kathy.

I knew Donald was the "hero" of the 1993 World Trade Center bombing, to the extent there was one. But I came to understand that Donald, who all his life was driven to find meaningful pursuits, was a magnet for many other historically significant events and persons, such as Kurt Waldheim, the Abortion Bomber, TWA Flight 800, and 9/11. As Donald put it, he often was "on the fringe of things a lot bigger than me." I found the urge to write a book based on his life irresistible.

Delving into the Bomb Squad and its members also intrigued me. Why do they take on such dangerous work? Donald's explanation is, "It isn't courage that drives a bomb tech. You can call it confidence, pride, or even arrogance—and each of us is a bit of an alpha dog—but we believe that we're smarter, stronger, and mentally and emotionally tougher than others. We believe that we are better able to solve the problem posed by an IED than anyone else and survive. Once you believe that, there is no other choice to be made but to go try to render the device safe."

Acknowledgments

The core of the book is formed by the four dozen interviews I conducted with Donald over two years. During those talks, which Donald would meticulously prepare for based on questions I provided him beforehand, he candidly revealed the people, places, circumstances, and decisions that had shaped his life. I also benefitted from Donald being a well-liked figure in the NYPD and U.N. community, as dozens of former officials were happy to speak with me about him. Because Donald is a pack rat, he was able to provide many historical pictures and documents.

This world needs more people with Donald's qualities—dedicated to the public good, courageous, hardworking, talented, and warmhearted. I am fortunate to have met and been able to collaborate with him, and to consider him a friend.

BIBLIOGRAPHY

Anthea Appel, *The First Responders: The Untold Story of the New York City Police Department and September 11, 2001* (2009)

Eli Rosenbaum with William Hoffer, *Betrayal: The Untold Story of the Kurt Waldheim Investigation and Cover-Up* (St. Martin's Press, 1993)

Emad Salem & Victoria Baxter, *On the Run: Life After Undercover* (2015)

Eric Shawn, *The U.N. Exposed* (Sentinel, 2006)

Fergus Mason, *Before 9/11: A Biography of World Trade Center Mastermind Ramzi Yousef* (Absolute Crime Books, 2013)

Geoffrey Cobb, *Greenpoint Brooklyn's Forgotten Past* (2015)

Henry Holden, *Famous Cases of the FBI—What Really Happened to TWA Flight 800* (2013)

How to Defuse a Bomb: The Project Children Story (Alleycats Films, 2016)

J.E. Fishman, *Dynamite: A Concise History of the NYPD Bomb Squad* (Verbitage, 2013)

Jeannette Remak, *TWA Flight 800: Enigma of an Accident* (Phoenix Aviation Research, 2015)

Jeffrey A. Kroessler, *Urban Terrorism in New York City from the 1960s through the 1980s* (John Jay College of Criminal Justice, 2014)

John Miller & Michael Stone (with Chris Mitchell), *The Cell: Inside the 9/11 Plot, and Why the FBI and CIA Failed to Stop It* (Hachette Books, 2002)

John Parachini, *The World Trade Center Bombers (1993)* (MIT Press, 2000)

Jon Wells, *Sniper: The True Story of Anti-Abortion Killer James Kopp* (HarperCollins, 2013)

Kathleen Murray Moran, *Life Detonated: The True Story of a Widow and a Hijacker* (Amberjack Publishing, 2017)

Laurie Mylroie, *The War Against America: Saddam Hussein and the World Trade Center Attacks* (HarperCollins, 2001)

Lawrence Wright, *The Looming Tower: Al-Qaeda and the Road to 9/11* (Vintage Books, 2007)

Mark Hamm, *Terrorism as Crime: From Oklahoma City to Al-Qaeda and Beyond* (NYU Press, 2007)

Michael Greenburg, *The Mad Bomber of New York: The Extraordinary True Story of the Manhunt That Paralyzed a City* (Union Square Press, 2011)

Minute by Minute: 1993 World Trade Center Bombing (A&E Channel, 2001)

Bibliography

Nightline Investigation: *World Trade Center—Ground Zero* (April 1, 1993)

9/11 (Documentary by Rob Klug, Gédéon Naudet, Jules Naudet, 2002)

9/11: Day that Changed the World (Smithsonian Channel, 2011)

Path to Paradise: The Untold Story of the World Trade Center Bombing (HBO Studio film, 1997)

Paul Sann, *Kill the Dutchman! The Story of Dutch Schultz* (Arlington House, 1971)

Ray Kelly, *Vigilance: My Life Serving America and Protecting Its Empire City* (Hachette Book Group, 2015)

Richard Esposito and Ted Gerstein, *Bomb Squad: A Year Inside the Nation's Most Exclusive Police Unit* (Hyperion, 2007)

Rick Hahn, *Luck, Miracles, and Evil* (2015)

Robert Burgess, *More Tunnel Tales from Vietnam* (Spyglass Publications, 2017)

Robert Daley, *Target Blue: An Insider's View of the NYPD* (Delacorte Press, 1973)

Simon Reeve, *The New Jackals: Ramzi Yousef, Osama bin Laden, and the Future of Terrorism* (Northeastern University Press, 1999)

Statement by J. Gilmore Childers and Henry J. DePippo before the Senate Judiciary Subcommittee on Technology, Terrorism, and Government Information

Hearing on "Foreign Terrorists in America: Five Years After the World Trade Center" (February 24, 1998)

Stephan Talty, *The Black Hand: The Epic War Between A Brilliant Detective and the Deadliest Secret Society in American History* (Mariner Books, 2018)

Susan Sheehan, *A Prison and a Prisoner* (Houghton Mifflin Co., 1978)

The 9/11 Commission Report: Final Report of the National Commission on Terrorist Attacks Upon the United States (2004)

The Path to 9/11 (ABC miniseries, 2006)

Thomas Perry, *The Bomb Maker* (Mysterious Press, 2018)

TWA Flight 800 (Lionsgate, 2013)

U.S. Fire Administration, *The World Trade Center Bombing: Report and Analysis* (USFA-TR-076/February 1993 Homeland Security)

We Were There—Donald Sadowy and Caitlin Langone (9/11 Tribute Center, 2015)

William C. Nagel, *The Law Enforcement Approach to Combatting Terrorism: An Analysis of U.S. Policy* (Thesis, June 2002)

*I hope you enjoyed this book.
Would you please do me a favor?*

Like all authors, I rely on online reviews to encourage future sales. Your opinion is invaluable. Would you please take a few moments now to share your assessment of my book on Amazon or any other book-review website you prefer? Your opinion will help the book marketplace become more transparent and useful to all.

Thank you very much!

ENDNOTES

[1] Hell's Kitchen's moniker was said to have been crafted by Davy Crockett, who upon visiting the area in 1835 (a year before he would die at the Battle of the Alamo) described its inhabitants as "worse than savages, they are too mean to swab hell's kitchen."

[2] Schultz's nickname derived from an earlier gangster of the same name, who was known for his viciousness.

[3] Killed along with Dutch Schultz was his accountant, Otto Berman, a mathematical wizard who was reputed to be the greatest horse-race rigger and handicapper of his day and is said to have coined the phrase, "Nothing personal, it's just business." Known as "Abbadabba," Berman was so colorful a character that his friend, Damon Runyon, the famed author whose short stories were the basis for the musical *Guys and Dolls*, incorporated him into several of his writings under the alias "Regret, the horse player."

[4] Sing Sing, whose name derives from a Native American tribe, the Sinck Sinck, meaning "stone upon stone," dates back to 1826 and is one of the oldest penal institutions in the United States.

[5] Before the United States' entry into World War II, he joined the Merchant Marines as a seaman in order to enjoy a brief period of travel. In 1942, to escape incarceration, John Anthony enlisted in the Army. But the following year, when home on leave, he went AWOL, stole a Studebaker and, while driving drunk, crashed into

Rendered Safe

a police car. He would plead guilty to attempted grand larceny and be returned to Sing Sing.

[6] In the book, Sheehan gives John Anthony the pseudonym of "George Malinow."

[7] As Donald explained, "The first man Margie fell in love with died accidentally while serving in the Merchant Marines. After that, she lost interest in dating. Margie devoted much of her time to taking care of me. It was my aunt who kept our household together. She would take me for a new set of clothes, arrange for my birthday party, and buy me Christmas presents. My aunt also took care of my mom during those times when she suffered from seizures, which would happen at least once a month. Sometimes, my mom and I would be walking in the neighborhood or to church and she would start having a seizure, and we would end up being driven home in a police car."

[8] One of Uncle Alex's tales was of the Battle of the Bulge, during which Alex's platoon was overrun by German troops. Alex was shot in the stomach, suffered shrapnel from a hand grenade, and was bayonetted in the hip and shoulders by two German soldiers whose job was to make sure none of the injured Americans would survive. Alex explained to Donald that, had it not been for the extreme cold, he would have bled out before being found by soldiers from Patton's Third Army. He spent months in a hospital in England recuperating. Heavily sedated most of the time, emaciated, and with unkempt long hair and a beard, he woke up one day in a hospital to find himself being tended to by a pretty blonde nurse. "The walls and ceiling were white," Alex reminisced to Donald, "as was her uniform. I thought I was dead and in heaven, reunited with my loved ones. I instinctively yelled out 'Alexandra!' The nurse, not wearing a nameplate, was astonished. 'How do you know my name?' she asked. 'Because I'm your brother,' I replied. She completely lost it. And that's how I was reunited with my younger sister, whom I hadn't seen in many years."

Endnotes

[9] Donald remembers "sitting on an oak and metal desk broken and so old that you could see where the original ink wells were. Pipes ran across the ceiling. The cars we worked on were 1950s models cut in half and raised on adjustable 'horses.' If you wanted a tool, you had to log it out to prevent theft. The cafeteria in the basement was so decrepit that everyone brought their lunch."

[10] Fort Sill is the site of the Apache warrior Geronimo's grave.

[11] Donald and his fellow Marines were required to take three salt tablets per day to replace salt lost through sweating and to carry at least two canteens of water when traveling during the day. One time, Donald drove into the desert for several hours without a hat. "I was young, cocky, and stupid. I got blisters on my skull and had to go to the infirmary for treatment."

[12] Kathy's father, David, had been born and raised in Charleston, South Carolina. Thin and with short, receding hair, he sported a manicured mustache and dressed immaculately. His bearing revealed an ex-Marine who had fought in the Korean War. To Donald, "Kathy's dad was a God-fearing, Southern gentleman who read the Bible regularly and never cursed. When he first laid eyes on me, he pegged me as a 'Good Time Charlie.'" One night, when Donald arrived at Kathy's family's Dutch Colonial wooden house, David instructed that his daughter was to be home by eleven. "We went to dinner and a movie," Donald remembered. "I had no car, and the bus was late. We got back to Kathy's house after 11:30 and sat on the living-room couch watching TV. I was trying to sneak in a kiss when her dad came down the stairs slowly, wearing a smoking-jacket robe, pajamas, and slippers, and carrying an old rifle. He walks over, looks at me, and says, 'Hey, kid, have you ever seen one of these before? This was from the real war.' He tossed me a Japanese rifle that he'd received as a battlefield souvenir from his older brother. Then he laughed and asked Kathy to go upstairs."

Rendered Safe

¹³ That program had been developed out of concern about the Marines' ill-preparedness for fighting in winter weather during the Korean War battle at Chosin Reservoir, when the temperature plunged to as low as −35 °F, and frostbite casualties and weapons malfunctions abounded.

¹⁴ The tyrant Pol Pot's Khmer Rouge forces had taken control of the capital, Phnom Penh, ousting the U.S.-backed military dictatorship and imposing Marxist-Leninist rule. The American container ship *SS Mayaguez*, with 39 crewmen, was seized by Khmer Rouge naval forces in waters believed to be international sea lanes. The U.S. considered the capture an act of piracy, and responded militarily with Air Force, Marine, and Navy forces, in what certain historians refer to as the last battle of the Vietnam War. The *Mayaguez* and its crew ultimately were released, but not before dozens of U.S. military personnel lost their lives.

¹⁵ Before formally leaving the Marines, Donald "decided to play the re-enlistment game for what it was worth. I asked the NCOs for training to become a military policeman and to be assigned to the base provost marshal's office. Within days, I got a set of orders to be sent to military-police school. As an MP, I was given a four-door sedan and came and went as I pleased. A lot of what I did was checking up on privates and lance corporals, who often would get drunk off base, fight, and end up in a local jail. I got to eat in the enlisted men's club, watch movies for 50 cents in the base theater, and have weekends off."

¹⁶ Ali Bhutto was hanged eighteen months later. In 1988, his daughter, Benazir, became Prime Minister.

¹⁷ Anne Morgan, headstrong and trailblazing, was renowned and adored for leveraging her family's wealth and connections to bring attention to the women's suffrage and workers' rights movements and the plight of immigrants.

Endnotes

[18] The threat from radical Palestinian groups escalated in 1993, when Arafat signed the Oslo Accords. The Oslo Accords were a set of agreements between Israel and the PLO that created a Palestinian Authority tasked with limited self-governance of parts of the West Bank and Gaza Strip and acknowledged the PLO as Israel's partner in permanent-status negotiations about remaining questions.

[19] Dag Hammarskjöld, the second Secretary-General of the United Nations, who revamped the original room, described it as "a meeting of the light, of the sky, and the earth . . . it is the altar to the God of all . . . we want this massive altar to give the impression of something more than temporary . . ."

[20] On July 22, 1946, a militant right-wing Zionist underground organization known as the "Irgun Tsvai Leumi," headed by Begin, bombed the King David Hotel, which was the British administrative headquarters for Palestine, killing 91 people of various nationalities.

[21] In 1987, while Waldheim was president of Austria but, also, an international pariah, he was placed on the Justice Department's watch list of prohibited persons, the first time in U.S. history that the head of a friendly country had been branded as an undesirable alien.

[22] Professor Robert Herzstein of the University of South Carolina, a historian whose archival research was crucial in uncovering Mr. Waldheim's Nazi past, was quoted in Waldheim's obituary as saying, "The fact that Waldheim played a significant role in military units that unquestionably committed war crimes makes him at the very least morally complicit in those crimes."

[23] The CIA's failure to expose Waldheim's wartime record early in his diplomatic career later aroused Congressional resentment. "We now know that our government had in its possession information and documents on Kurt Waldheim," a bipartisan group of 59 congressmen and women wrote to President Clinton in 1998.

Rendered Safe

The letter, likely in reference to rumors that Waldheim had been blackmailed by the Russian KGB to hide his Nazi past, went on to state, "There is no more onerous example of the harm these hidden files can cause than the fact that Kurt Waldheim was elected Secretary-General of the United Nations."

An example of the harm Waldheim fairly was alleged to have caused arose from his lack of even-handedness when dealing with Middle East players and events. Waldheim did make efforts toward achieving a settlement of the long-standing Arab-Israeli dispute. After the Yom Kippur War in October 1973, at the request of the Security Council, he organized the U.N. Emergency Force as a buffer between the armies of Egypt and Israel. But Waldheim also endorsed Palestinian statehood without mentioning Israel's right to exist. In 1973, Waldheim refused, despite entreaties, to wear a *kippah* (Jewish skullcap) when entering the Holocaust memorial at Yad Vashem, professing to consider the covering of his head incompatible with his position as Secretary-General. In July 1976, after an Israeli commando unit staged a dramatic rescue of Israeli hostages at Entebbe airport in Uganda, headed by the ruthless dictator Idi Amin, Waldheim immediately labelled the action "a serious violation of the national sovereignty of a United Nations member state." Yet in 1979, he was slow to condemn the Soviet invasion of Afghanistan. When Syria invaded Lebanon in 1976, the U.N. did nothing, but when Israel also moved into Lebanon two years later in response to a PLO attack, Waldheim was quick to organize a resolution condemning the Israeli intervention. Waldheim's seeming anti-Israel bias helped to set a precedent that exists to this day.

[24] Prominent examples were Ted Donald, who was shot in the head and chest while responding to a burglary in a Bronx housing project, Michael Russell, who was shot in the stomach while off-duty as he attempted to arrest a man who had killed a civilian, and Melvin Hopkins, who was shot while stopping the robbery of a store in Bedford-Stuyvesant owned by his uncle.

Endnotes

[25] Since 2014, the Police Academy has been housed in three adjoining state-of-the-art buildings in College Point, Queens, that include a mock subway station, courthouse, and precinct house.

[26] Zigo was a great storyteller. One recounted the time he dressed up as an old lady to help find robbers preying on elderly women. Upon being robbed, Zigo realized his Smith and Wesson had slipped out of his dress in the police car, so "I had to swing my handbag at the bad guys." After Zigo retired, he began a second career as a technical consultant on TV and film projects plus bit parts in movies. Martin Sheen played Zigo in a 2011 movie—*Out of the Darkness*—about the hunt for Son of Sam.

[27] The Satmar Hasidim and the Betz Hasidim dress in similar black gabardine coats and felt hats. They shun the modern world and immerse themselves in the practice of Jewish law and custom. Political and religious differences, including sharply contrasting views on Israel, had divided the two groups.

[28] On December 2, 1978, shortly before noon, hundreds of angry Hasidic Jews, outraged over the fatal stabbing of an elderly Jewish man in a predawn street robbery and demanding greater police protection, besieged and briefly took over the 66th Precinct police station in Brooklyn. They were ejected after a bloody, 30-minute melee of screams, punches, swinging clubs, and hurtling rocks. The clash left at least 70 people injured, 62 of them police officers. About 100 police reinforcements and a dozen ambulances and other emergency vehicles rushed to the scene, where around 2,000 protesters milled around outside. 150 to 200 more were inside the station. Cops being cops, the 66th Precinct earned the nickname "Fort Surrender."

[29] Historically, NYPD police used two types of batons, depending on the time of day. The one for night use was longer to provide extra protection, leading to its name.

Rendered Safe

[30] In spite of the boredom that inevitably accompanied manning a fixer, Donald was ever vigilant, mindful it was dangerous work. In June 1977, three armed Croatian nationalists invaded the Yugoslav Mission to the United Nations, wounding one person. Two years later, a bomb planted by the anti-Castro terrorist group "Omega 7" detonated at the side entrance of the Cuban mission to the United Nations at 38th Street and Lexington Avenue. Two civilians and a patrolman were injured by flying debris. That was followed by Omega 7 exploding a bomb at the Soviet embassy on East 67th Street between Lexington and Third Avenues, across from the 19th Precinct station house, sending bricks flying, shattering windows throughout much of the block, and injuring four police officers as well as several mission employees.

[31] In 1983, Dennis Tueller, a Utah police officer and firearms instructor, published an article discussing the need to defend against an attacker armed with a knife or edged weapon. Through his tests and studies, he determined that a person would be in danger if the attacker came at him from 21 feet or less. In short, the attacker could get to his victim before the victim was able to draw and accurately fire his handgun.

[32] The SCU, which made a much larger number of arrests than did uniformed patrol officers, particularly those firearms-related, was disbanded following the controversial killing of Amadou Diallo in February 1999. Diallo, a 23-year-old immigrant from Guinea, was shot by four SCU plain-clothed officers who were charged with second-degree murder but acquitted at trial.

[33] A case in point occurred on September 20, 1989, when USAir Flight 5050 crashed on takeoff from LaGuardia Airport and plunged into Bowery Bay. Due in large part to the swift, expert response by the ESU, 61 of the 63 passengers and crew members survived.

[34] In the 1960s and 1970s, the Tactical Police Force had a six-foot height requirement, which would have immediately disqualified Don.

Endnotes

[35] Benjamin Ward had a groundbreaking career with the Department. When he joined in 1951, black patrolmen were assigned only to black districts, and none had climbed far up the chain of command. While remaining in the NYPD, Ward earned his law degree and prosecuted other cops in Departmental trials.

[36] Bomb Squad headquarters now is scheduled to move to a six-story building on West 26th Street.

[37] Metesky's answer to an open letter published in that newspaper provided a key clue to his identity—he held a grudge against Consolidated Edison, which had dismissed him many years before.

[38] The hijackers ultimately would fly the plane to Paris and surrender there, without harming any of the passengers. The two were extradited back to the U.S. and each convicted of aircraft piracy.

[39] Kathleen Murray would go on to lobby the city on behalf of all widows and children of fallen police officers and help create the "Survivors of the Shield" organization that supports the families of slain NYPD officers. In October 2014, Charles Street in lower Manhattan was renamed Police Officer Brian Murray Way in his honor.

[40] As noted by J.E. Fishman in his book *Dynamite: A Concise History of the NYPD Bomb Squad*, during the 1980s, the Squad's yearly average of jobs was: 1,600 calls, 300 suspicious packages, 16 detonated IEDs, 500 security searches, and 90 calls for removal of dangerous chemicals.

[41] Those trucks were distinctive because they were painted red and had "Danger" printed in large letters on each side.

[42] At the end of his Bomb Squad service, Murphy was severely injured during a training exercise, when he was rappelling from an NYPD helicopter and a gear malfunction caused him to fall to the ground.

[43] The Bomb Squad's facilities were heavily damaged in October 2012 during Superstorm Sandy and are scheduled to be replaced by a state-of-the-art building.

[44] In the 1990s, the school added a training program for weapons of mass destruction.

[45] The Port Authority, a bi-state agency, oversees much of the regional transportation infrastructure, including bridges, tunnels, airports, and seaports, within the New York City-Newark port area.

[46] Northern Ireland at that time was engorged in violent conflict. The key issue was its constitutional status, with unionists/loyalists, who were mostly Protestants, wanting Northern Ireland to remain within the United Kingdom, and nationalists/republicans, who were mostly Catholics, wanting Northern Ireland to leave the United Kingdom and join a united Ireland.

[47] After an explosion, the leading shock front of compressed gases expands at fast speed outward, followed by a blast wind of negative pressure that sucks items back in toward the center as would a vacuum cleaner.

[48] Cops and detectives are roughly the same rank, although detectives assume dominance in the jobs that require their expertise. Detectives also generally enjoy higher salary and status. Becoming a detective provides an alternative career path to move up in rank. While Bomb Squad members technically hold the rank of detective, they consider themselves more as technicians, whose primary job is to render safe IEDs.

[49] The jury forewoman told a reporter that Davis was a "young and innocent kid who got recruited by a few corrupt policemen . . . they came in to wipe him out . . . they wanted him dead so he couldn't

squeal on them . . . they would have killed him." She said the jury believed the defense assertion that the police fired first and that Davis was defending himself.

[50] There is a product-identification system for packaged explosive products manufactured in the United States. Malvasi had removed the code that would have indicated the date, work shift, and plant manufacture for his dynamite.

[51] Mulcahy was remarkable in yet another way. In 1975, during the height of "The Troubles" in Northern Ireland, when the region was rife with killing zones and a boiling pot of political struggle between Catholics and Protestants, Denis, along with his wife Miriam and brother, Pat, founded Project Children. Over four decades, that organization provided six-week summer vacations in the United States with host families for more than 22,000 Protestant and Catholic children from Belfast, Derry, and other areas of Northern Ireland, giving them a break from the violence and an opportunity to live and play together. For his work, Denis was twice nominated for the Nobel Peace Prize.

One of the first children to be helped by Project Children, a Protestant boy from Belfast who came to the United States in the summer of 1975, said in his adulthood, "As were most of the children growing up in Belfast at the time, I was a ticking time bomb. Denis Mulcahy cut my wire."

[52] D'Atri had a remarkable career with the ATF, including being shot five times while working undercover in 1982 for the South Florida Task Force. According to John Miller, "D'Atri would have caught Malvasi eventually. He was the world's most dogged law-enforcement agent."

[53] Kopp was also wanted by Canadian authorities for allegedly wounding an abortion doctor in Ontario in 1995.

54 France detained Kopp for 14 months, turning him over to the United States only after receiving assurances he would not face the death penalty.

55 There were, in fact, protests near the U.N. by separate groups of Afghans, Armenians, Estonians, Jews, Latvians, and Ukrainians asking for more of their landsmen to be allowed to emigrate.

56 In his famous speech at the U.N., which presaged the end of the Cold War, Gorbachev outlined his vision for a new, more united international system, declared that the threat of force should not be an instrument of foreign policy, and announced that he would unilaterally withdraw 50,000 Soviet troops from Eastern Bloc nations.

57 With a magnificent view of lower Manhattan, Governor's Island experienced its first media invasion in 1986, when Reagan arrived and, with the flick of a switch, lit a new torch on the nearby Statue of Liberty to honor its one-hundredth anniversary.

58 On November 30, 1989, Alfred Herrhausen, the head of Deutsche Bank, West Germany's largest commercial bank, was killed when terrorists detonated via light beam a remote-controlled bomb, demolishing the automobile in which he was being driven to work.

59 Hurst eventually created an assortment of tools, such as cutters, spreaders, and rams that were powered by a hydraulic pump. A Hurst spreader, for example, has two arms that come together in a narrow tip, using hydraulic fluid conveyed in a hose under pressure to spread the arms. They were faster, stronger, and more versatile tools, allowing rescue workers to cut, open, and even lift a vehicle to remove the occupant.

60 The camp, ironically, had been set up with the support of the Central Intelligence Agency.

Endnotes

[61] An interesting aspect of the Ajaj case was the government's contention that the writings in one of his documents contemplating attacks in Israel were evidence of his violation of the little-used Neutrality Act, which prohibits the knowing participation in, preparation for, or financing of a "hostile expedition from within the United States against a nation with which the United States is at peace."

[62] Several intelligence analysts have suggested Yousef was an agent of the Iraqi government.

[63] Jersey City, situated directly across from lower Manhattan, with a close view of the World Trade Center, has for decades been one of the most ethnically diverse cities in the country. By the early 1990s, the revitalization of its waterfront district, previously occupied largely by rail yards and factories, led it to become a financial and banking center known as "Wall Street West."

[64] Yousef later admitted to investigators that, had he had more money, among other things he would have added to the bomb was sodium cyanide, which when mixed with nitric acid forms hydrogen cyanide, an extremely toxic gas.

[65] In 1986, a prescient Port Authority report had warned that the World Trade Center was "an inviting target for terrorism" and that "parking for 2,000 vehicles in the underground garage" presented a danger because terrorists could "park explosive-filled vehicles."

[66] Opened in 1981, the Vista Hotel was the first hotel built in Lower Manhattan since 1836.

[67] Emergency-power generators were also damaged by the blast and shut down.

[68] On 9/11, attempts to be rescued from the roofs of the towers failed because of locked doors and due to dense smoke, intense heat, and swirling matter that wouldn't allow choppers to fly in.

Rendered Safe

⁶⁹ Investigators concluded it fortunate that Yousef and Ismoil did not park their van next to one of the 36-inch steel columns anchoring the North Tower. Rather, the blast's epicenter was under the northeast corner of the Vista Hotel, and the most serious damage was to the parking garage itself. But, as noted by Denis Mulcahy, "that bomb alone would not have taken the tower down."

⁷⁰ Kelly, yet another ex-Marine and Vietnam vet, was at the beginning of the first of his two stints as Police Commissioner. He would later pronounce the bombing "the first dramatic demonstration that terrorism is theater and New York is the biggest stage."

⁷¹ As noted by Malcolm Brady, the ATF lead in the investigation, "An explosion doesn't destroy the evidence—it just makes it smaller. Eventually, if we sift long enough, we'll find what we're looking for."

⁷² In 2009, after the ATF was transferred to the Justice Department, in which the FBI is housed, to help quell the hostility, a report issued by the Department's Inspector General found that the conflict "can delay investigations, undermine federal and local relationships, and may project to local agency responders a disjointed federal response to explosives incidents in their area."

⁷³ The group included a photographer, evidence technician, schematic artist, forensic chemist, and explosives technician.

⁷⁴ Initially, a plumb line was dropped from the plaza level down the hole to the bottom, which was the temporary marker for the blast origin.

⁷⁵ Gotthold had an interesting lineage. Her mother, who was her lifelong hero, was the founder in the mid-1970s of *Working Women's* magazine and an icon in the publishing field, having been the first female vice president of the New York Times Corporation. Her father, who escaped Nazi Germany when he was fifteen and

Endnotes

fought in the U.S. Army during WWII, was a noted innovator and entrepreneur. He founded Tec-Cast, Inc., a solid-mold investment casting company whose products were used, among others, by NASA for the Apollo missions and space shuttles. And Gotthold's uncle, Justus Buchler, was a well-known American philosopher.

[76] Merrill's head of security was Patrick Murphy, a renowned NYPD Commissioner during the 1970s.

[77] Supporters in Egypt had purchased for Salameh a plane ticket out of the country, but it was for an infant. Salameh, short on cash, needed his deposit back to upgrade the ticket. Certain intelligence experts surmise that Yousef intended for Salameh to be desperate for cash and, thus, to be caught, to fool authorities into thinking they had apprehended the main perpetrator.

[78] More than a dozen organizations claimed responsibility for the bombing.

[79] In December 2007, Bhutto was assassinated by a member of the Pakistani Taliban.

[80] Dalton would later be commended by Malcolm Brady, the head of the ATF's National Response Team, for being "instrumental in defusing sensitive situations between other agencies, contractors, and others that had an interest in this tragic event." And Brady would praise Dodge for being "the consummate tactician and logistician."

[81] Many of the ATF agents from the National Response Team were housed in apartments in nearby Battery Park City.

[82] The FBI at the time did not have its own evidence-collection team.

[83] The hotel underwent a 20-month renovation.

Rendered Safe

[84] On February 28, 1993, two days after the bombing, ATF agents were assigned to execute federal warrants at the Branch Davidian compound in Waco, Texas. The heavily armed cult members were waiting in ambush as the agents unloaded from their vehicles. During a two-and-a-half-hour gunfight, four ATF agents were killed and twenty wounded. On the following day, the ATF agents working at the World Trade Center reported for work with black bands over their badges, and a minute of silence was observed.

[85] As all the London and New York letters bore Alexandria, Egypt, postmarks, the top suspect quickly became the Blind Sheikh, who was serving a life sentence in federal prison.

[86] The South Lebanon conflict, which lasted from 1985 to 2000, was between the Lebanese Christian proxy militias with military and logistic support of Israel Defense Forces against Lebanese Muslim guerrillas led by the Iranian-backed Hezbollah.

[87] Two stairways (Stairways A&C) ended at the mezzanine level, where there were doors to exit the tower. The third stairway (Stairway B) ran down to the Concourse level and all six basement levels.

[88] In July 2008, during the FBI's 100th anniversary commemoration, Miller was lauded by FBI Director Robert Mueller for his extraordinary bravery.

[89] In the well-known documentary *9/11* by the French brothers Jules and Gédéon Naudet, Donald can be briefly seen with his jacket off and tie loosened sitting and recuperating behind the information desk.

[90] With Richards at the time was Steve Berberich, who was wounded when a piece of rebar flew through his knee, leading to six operations and a permanent limp.

Endnotes

[91] Kim pled guilty to several U.S. felony charges and received a three-year prison sentence.

[92] Stewart was granted a "compassionate release" from prison in January 2014 because of terminal breast cancer and died in May 2017, less than three weeks after the Sheikh's death.

ABOUT THE AUTHOR

Jeff is a financial-industry consultant with extensive senior-management experience in both government service and the private sector.

Aside from his work in the financial industry, Jeff is the author of books, short stories, and screenplays, for which he has won numerous awards. His first screenplay was the basis for a film, entitled *Crypto,* starring Kurt Russell and Alexis Bledel, that was released by Lionsgate in April 2019. One of his novels, entitled *Shattered Lives,* is being made into a documentary film by Mactavish Pictures.

A graduate of Queens College and NYU Law School, Jeff lives with his wife in Jersey City.

INDEX

Numbers

9/11: Day That Changed the World, 302

62 Green Street, restaurant at. *see* John's Bar and Grille (62 Green Street)

A

Abdel-Rahman, Omar (the "Blind Sheikh"), 171, 175–176, 232–234, 320
Abortion Bomber, 137–146, 147–150
Abouhalima, Mahmud, 175–176, 179, 230
Abrams, Sergeant, 76
Ahearn, Joe, 107, 285–287
Ajaj, Ahmed Mohammed, 173–174, 229–230
Al-Farouk Mosque, 175
al-Gama'at al-Islamiyya, 258
Ali, Mohammed, 44
Al-Jama'a al'Islamiyya, 175
al-Qaeda, 174
Anastasia, Albert, 3
Anticev, John, 227, 232, 233, 258

Arafat, Yasser, 44, 282
"Army of God," 152–153
Astor, Brooke, 159
Automotive High School ("Brooklyn Automotive"), 12–15, 17
Ayyad, Nidal, 178, 229–230

B

Barak, Ehud, 281–283
Bee Gees, 44
Begin, Menachem, 48
Beirut bombing, 208
Benedict of Nursia, Saint, 141
Benedict XVI, Pope, 142
Berberich, Steve "Ziggy," 157–159, 191, 197, 254, *319*
Berkowitz, David, 55
Bernadotte, Folke, 48
Bernstein, Steve, 274
Bhutto, Benazir, 231
Bhutto, Zulfikar Ali, 29
bin Laden, Osama, 172, 231, 255
Black Hand, 83–84
Black Liberation Army, 87
Boeh, Dan, *223*

371

Rendered Safe

Bomb Data Center, US, 272
Bomb Squad, NYPD
   1993 World Trade Center Bombing, 178–179, 191–199, 202–203, 205–218, 248–249
   1997 attempted UN letter bombing, 268–270
   anti-Israel terrorism and, 273–279
   car bomb cases, 163–165
   Donald Sadowy's application to, 75–81
   Donald Sadowy's early service on, 93–99
   Donald Sadowy's training for, 107–111
   ESU and, 72
   fireworks incidents, 120
   Gorbachev visit and, 155–162
   grenade incidents, 115–116
   hazardous materials incidents, 118–119
   history of, 83–92
   IED incidents, 117–118
   James Kopp case and, 152–154
   Linne Gunther case, 165–166
   navigated robots and, 116–117
   pipe bomb incidents, 114–115
   relationship with State Department, 273
   TWA Flight 800, 258–259
   United Nations and, 121–125
bomb suits, 127–128
bomb-sniffing dogs, 98–99
Bomilie, Sammy, *76*
Borelli, Joe, 150, 192, 251
Boser, Walter, 150, 166, 192, 194, 196, 201, 205, 248, 249, 271, 275
Brady, Malcolm, 205
Brower, Chris, 139
Burkart, David, 247, 305
Burkart, Pat, 305–306
Burmeister, Steven, 218, 228
Bush, Barbara, 159
Bush, George H.W., 155, 169

C

Caliendo, John, 62, 316
Carter, Paul, *319*
Caruso, Enrico, 84
Castellano, Paul, 163
Castro, Fidel, 45–46
Chamberlain, Owen, 165
Chiarini, Steve, 122–123, 268, 274
Clinton, Bill, 170, 231, 254–255, 282
Clinton, Hillary, 254–255
Coccaro, Richard, *223*
Connelly, Tom, 118
Connor, Joe, 183, 235
Cousteau, Jacques, 44
Cuomo, Mario, 202

Index

D

Dalton, Pete, 108, 129, 202, *223*, 236, 241, 243–244, 249, 254, 265
D'Atri, Alex, 145
Davidson, Bill, 22
Davis, Larry, 133–136
Dayan, Moshe, 47
DeCicco, Frank, 163
Dergham, Raghida, 267–268
DiGiovanni, John, 189
Dodge, Steve, 141, 178, 195, 202, 228, 236, 243, 245–246, 249–250, 251, 290
Doherty, Kevin, *76*
Dolinich, Pauline, 1–2, 5
Dudonis, Kenneth, 89
Duffy, Kevin, 230, 233
Duffy, William, 186

E

el-Gawli, Sultan, 176
Emergency Services Unit, NYPD, 72–73, 94, 128, 133–135, 141, 148–149, 157, 167, 186, 198, 216, 241, 247, 305–306, 312, 315

F

Fallon, Ed, *76*
Fallon, John, 33–34
Farrell, Timothy, 186
Fasullo, Gene, 186
Fernald, Michael, 325–326, 329–330, *332*

Fighters for a Free Croatia, 87
fireworks incidents, 120
Flegenheimer, Arthur Simon ("Dutch" Schultz), 3–5
Flynn, Chuck, *66*
Fonda, Henry, 44
Forensic Investigative Division, NYPD Detective Bureau's, 93–99
Fox, James, 207, 248
Frank, Anne, 44
Frost, David, 44
Fuerzas Armadas de Liberación Nacional (FALN), 87, 90–91

G

Gallagher, Peter, 232
Gallatin, Larry, *262*
Gaze, Donald Sadowy's visit to, 285–287
Ghana, Donald Sadowy's visit to, 325–332
Giuliani, Rudy, 269, 275
Goetz, John, 207, 211, *223*, 236, 242
Gorbachev, Mikhail, 155–162
Gorbachev, Raisa, 156, 159
Gotthold, Jessica, 210–211, 225, 244
Gotti, John, 163–164, 322–323
Greenpoint, Brooklyn neighborhood, 1–15
grenade incidents, 115–116
Guccione, Joseph, 319

373

Guedes, Mike, 76
Gunther, Linne, 165

H
Hackford, Richie, 120–121, 129, 140, 166–168, 193, 217, 268–269, 311
Hahn, Rick, 183, 197, 207, 209, 225, 236–239
Haldeman, Donald, 202, 228
Hanlin, Joe, 212–213, 215–216, 248, 254, 290
Harden, Marcia Gay, 232
Hazardous Devices School at Redstone Arsenal, 101–105
"Hell's Kitchen," 2
Herman, Neil, 207
Hezbollah, 282
Hub Social Club, 2–3
Hurley, Don, 109–110, *119*, 128
Hurst, George, 167–169
Hussein, Saddam, 174, 229

I
IED incidents, 117–118
intelligence coordinator position, Sadowy's, 271–272, 275
Ismoil, Eyad, 179, 182, 232–233
Israel, Donald Sadowy's relationship with, 273–279, 281–283, 285–287
"Italian Squad," 84

J
John Paul II, Pope, 45, 231
John's Bar and Grille (62 Green Street), 3–7
Johnson, Bernard, 162, 273, 276, 287, 333
Jones, Kevin, 76
Judge, Father Mychal, 296

K
Kahane, Meir, 175–176, 230, 233
Katulak, Arthur, 6–7
Katulak, Cecelia Ann "Cissy," 7, *12*, 18, 25
Katulak, John, 2–3, 5–7, *12*
Katulak, John Jr., 6
Katulak, Victoria, 11
Kelleher, Pat, 269
Kelley, Paul X., 97
Kelly, Jack, 107–108, 129, 206
Kelly, Ray, 192, 201, 207, 249–250
Kennedy, Brian, 76
Kim, Steven, 316
Kim Jong-Il, 316
Kirkpatrick, Bob, 189
Kissinger, Henry, 53
Kittel, Ed, 259–261, *262*, 264–265
Knapp, Steven, 189
Koch, Ed, 73–74, 91–92, 117
Koetl, Judge, 322
Kopp, James, 151
Koppel, Ted, 248
Kunstler, William, 136

L
Labrador Retrievers, 98–99
Lang, Timothy, 181, 187
Langone, Caitlin, 312
Langone, Peter, 312

Index

Langone, Thomas, 312
Leonard, Sergeant, 76
Littleton, Marshall, 223
Loehr, Alexander, 49–50
Lowe, Tommy, 76
Lueken, Veronica, 139
Lupack, Alex, 11, 13, 19, 25
Luxor Massacre, 1997, 175
Lynch, John, 86

M

Macko, Bill, 189
Malvasi, Dennis John, 137–146, 147–148, 151–153
Manhattan South Task Force, NYPD's, 74
Margie, Aunt, 10, 334
Marine Corps, Donald Sadowy's service in, 17–28
Marra, Loretta, 151–154
Marra, William, 151, 153
Martella, Joseph, 246
Masin, Edward, 226
Masjid al-Salaam, 176
Matlin, Jeff, 62, 66, 68
Mayaguez incident, 25
McAdoo, William, 84
McCann, Michael, 268–269
McCarthy, Bill, 107
McClain, Roy, 262
McCune, Larry, 223
McNally, Dan, 108
McTigue, Terence, 88
Mercado, Olga, 245–246
Mercado, William, 202–203, 217, 245–246
Merrill Lynch, Donald Sadowy at, 289–290, 314, 315

Metesky, George, 86–87
Michael Stapleton Associates, Donald Sadowy's position with, 315
Miller, John, 142–146, 147, 150, 254
Miller, Peter, 116
Miller, Rod, 292–294
"Minute by Minute" series, 290
Mohammed, Khalid Shaikh, 172, 178, 231
Molloy, Brenda, 223
Morgan, J.P., 32–37
Moro, Aldo, 39–40
Mossad, 287
Mubarak, Hosni, 234
Mulcahy, Denis, 115–116, 139–140, 202, 223, 243, 246–247, 250, 251
Murphy, Brian, 115–116
Murphy, George, 93, 94–96
Murray, Brian, 88, 111, 127
Murray, Kathleen, 88–89

N

navigated robots, 116–117
Netanyahu, Benjamin, 282
New York Fire Department, 1993 WTC bombing and, 184–185
New York Police Department
Donald Sadowy's early career with, 53–69
Emergency Services Unit, 72–73, 94, 128, 133–135, 141, 148–149, 157, 167, 186, 198, 216, 241, 247, 305–306, 312, 315

375

Street Crime Unit, 71–72
United Nations and,
    67–69, 121–125
Newton-John, Olivia, 44
Noe, Joey, 3
Nosair, El Sayyid, 175–176
Nowicki, Ed, 143–145

O

O'Connor, James, 89
O'Connor, John, 145
O'Hagan, Ray, 303–304
O'Leary, Larry, 76
Omega 7, 87
Onassis, Jackie, 44
Operation Pressure Point,
    NYPD's, 74
Orminski, Donna, 22–23, 28
Our Lady of the Roses group,
    138–139

P

Palace Chop House and
    Tavern, 5
Palmice, Mikey, 254
Pan Am Flight 103 disaster
    (Lockerbie bombing), 208
Panzarino, Nick, 39, 42
Pastorella, Richard, 90–91,
    111–112, 117
*Path to 9/11: The Untold Story
    of the World Trade Center
    Bombing*, 254
Paul VI, Pope, 39
Petrosino, Giuseppe (Joseph),
    84
pipe bomb incidents, 114–115
Polignani, Emilio, 84

Pyke, James, 86

R

Radner, Gilda, 44
Reagan, Nancy, 159
Reagan, Ronald, 155, 158
"Red Guerrilla Defense," 96
Reeves, Lee, 76
Reid, Richard Colvin, 317
remote mechanical vehicle
    entry research, 167–169
Resolution 3379, 50
Riccio, Larry, 214
Richards, Claude "Danny," 312
Ritschel, Elisabeth, 40–41
Rockefeller, Nelson, 9
Rodman's Neck, 97, 120
Ruggirello, Tony, 148–150,
    197–198
Ruland, Mr., 17
Russo, Jimmy, 56–57

S

Sadowy (Burkart), Kathy Ann,
    17, 25, 31, 79–80, 96, 130,
    250, 254, 289, 302, 305, 307,
    309–310, 315, 334, 336
Sadowy, Donald John
    9/11 Tribute Center and
        9/11 Museum docent
        jobs, 334–336
    1993 World Trade Center
        Bombing, 191–199,
        201–203, 205–218, *223*,
        225, 235–239, 241–255
    1997 attempted UN letter
        bombing, 267–270

Index

2002 Steven Kim shooting, 315–318
Abortion Bomber case, 147–150, 151
application to the Bomb Squad, 75–81
Bomb Squad service to UN and, 123–125
car bomb cases, 163–165
childhood, 10–15
early NYPD career, 53–69
early service on Bomb Squad, 93–99
fireworks incidents, 120
first "long walk," 128–131
Gaza visit, 285–287
Ghana visit, 325–332
Gorbachev visit, 155–162
Hazardous Devices School and, 101–105
hazardous materials incidents, 118–119
IED incidents, 117–118
intelligence coordinator position, 271–272, 275
Israel visit, 275–279, 281–283, 285–287
Larry Davis incident and, 134–136
Linne Gunther case, 165–166
Merrill Lynch position, 289–290, 314, 315
military service, 17–28
New York Police Department career, 28
NYPD Emergency Service Unit and, 72–73
NYPD Street Crime Unit and, 71–72
NYPD Tactical Police Force Unit and, 73–75
pipe bomb incidents, 114–115
promotion Detective Third Grade, 131
relationship with Israeli security, 273–279, 287
relationship with State Department, 272–273
research on remote mechanical vehicle entry, 166–169
retirement, 333–337
September 11th attacks, 289–297, 299–307, 309–314
trainer for other bomb techs, 169
training for Bomb Squad, 107–111
TWA Flight 800, 257–258, 261–265
UN security staff job, 28–29, 32–37, 39–51, 53–54
US Marshall's office, 319–323, 333–334
wedding of, 31–32, 36
Sadowy, Donald Jr., 169, 250, 257, 336–337
Sadowy, John Anthony, 7–10, 31–32
Sadowy, Kaitlin, 250, 309–310
Safir, Howard, 269

Salameh, Mohammad, 176–179, 181–183, 226–228, 230
Salem, Emad, 232–233
Sampson, Teddy, 76
Santos, John, 109, 134–136
Sapienza, Al, 254
Sardone, John, 225–226, 250
Sattar, Ahmed, 321
Selinger, Carl, 185–186
Senft, Anthony, 90–91, 111–112, 117
September 11th attacks, 289–297, 299–307, 309–314
Shah of Iran, 44
Sharpton, Al, 75
Shea, Kevin, 187–188
Sheehan, Susan, 9–10
Shin Bet, 273–279, 282–283, 287
Slepian, Barnett, 152–153
Sliwa, Curtis, 322
Smith, Monica Rodriguez, 188, 189, 236
Smolanick, Dan, 122–124, 155, 159
Socha, Ferdinand, 86
Solis, Greg, 61
St. Helena, 279
St. Paul's Episcopal Chapel, 312–313
Stahl, Leslie, 229
Stewart, Lynne, 136, 320–321
Stewart, Rod, 44
"Subway Slasher," 65–67
"Sunday Bomber," 87

T
Teitelbaum, Donald, 325–326
Teymour, Aly, 156, 158, 161
Tocci, Emil, 311
Torre, Mark, 118, 121, 193–194, 196, 257
Trimble, Harold, 36, 54
TWA Flight 800, 257–265

U
Uliano, Maria, 143
United Nations
    1997 attempted bombing, 267–270
    conflict with NYPD, 67–69
    Donald Sadowy at, 28–29, 32–37, 39–51, 53–54
    Donald Sadowy's position with Michael Stapleton Associates, 315
    Gorbachev visit and, 156, 165
    NYPD Bomb Squad and, 121–125
US Marshall's office, Donald Sadowy and, 319–323, 333–334

V
Valentine, Bill, 160
Veyera, Steve, 174, 202, 208–209, 242
von Braun, Werner, 101–102

W
Waldheim, Kurt, 29, 32–34, 39–50, 53–54
Walters, Barbara, 159
Ward, Ben, 73–75, 135
Washington, Kevin, *223*

Index

Waskon, Tom, *223*
Weather Underground, 87
Webster, William H., *97*
Welch, Glenn, 140, 147–150
Welding, Delta, 28
Wells, Charles, 76, 78–79, 95–96, 107, 110–111, 127–128
White, Michael, 152, 269, 275
Whitehead, Curtis, 65, *67*
Williams, David, 208–210, 215, 217, 236–237, 248, 254
Williams, Kendrick, 202
Williams, Ted, 95–96
Winkler, Henry, 44
Wong, Jimmy, 296
World Trade Center Bombing, 1993, 171–180, 181–189, 191–199, 201–203, 205–223, 225–234, 235–239, 241–255

Y

Yasin, Abdul Rahman, 177–178, 228–229
Yeltsin, Boris, 44, 169
Yousef, Ramzi Ahmed (Abdul Basit Mahmoud Abdul Karim), 171–180, 181–182, 228, 230–233
Yousry, Mohammad, 321

Z

Zigo, Edward, 55

379

www.ingramcontent.com/pod-product-compliance
Lightning Source LLC
Chambersburg PA
CBHW020637300426
44112CB00007B/146